Reading ARABIA

Contemporary Issues in the Middle East

Mehran Kamrava *and* Carol Fadda-Conrey, *Series Advisers*

Reading
ARABIA

British Orientalism in the Age of
Mass Publication, 1880–1930

Andrew C. Long

Syracuse University Press

First Edition 2014
14 15 16 17 18 19   6 5 4 3 2 1

∞ The paper used in this publication meets the minimum requirements of the American National Standard for Information Sciences—Permanence of Paper for Printed Library Materials, ANSI Z39.48-1992.

For a listing of books published and distributed by Syracuse University Press, visit our website at www.SyracuseUniversityPress.syr.edu.

ISBN: 978-0-8156-3323-5 (cloth)   978-0-8156-5232-8 (e-book)

Library of Congress Cataloging-in-Publication Data
Long, Andrew C.
    Reading Arabia : British Orientalism in the age of mass publication, 1880–1930 / Andrew C. Long.
        pages cm. — (Contemporary issues in the Middle East)
    Includes bibliographical references and index.
    ISBN 978-0-8156-3323-5 (cloth : alkaline paper) — ISBN 978-0-8156-5232-8 (ebook) 1. Great Britain—Relations—Arab countries.   2. Arab countries—Relations—Great Britain.   3. Arab countries—Foreign public opinion, British.   4. Orientalism—Great Britain—History.   5. Arabs in popular culture—Great Britain—History.   6. Arabs in mass media.   7. British literature—History and criticism.   8. Arabs in literature.   9. Fantasy in literature.   10. Stereotypes (Social psychology) in literature.   I. Title.
    DS63.2.G7L66 2014
    303.48'24105309041—dc23   2013049871

Manufactured in the United States of America

For Lounes and Tassadit

Andrew C. Long currently teaches in the Department of Cultural Studies at the Claremont Graduate University. He taught at the City University of New York and the American University of Beirut before moving to southern California. He has published essays on topics including modern writers and texts, conspiracy and informing, the pamphleteer, and politics and culture in the modern Middle East.

Contents

Illustrations

Acknowledgments

THIS BOOK WAS WRITTEN over the course of a rough period in my life, in both a personal and professional sense, though it was always a resource of hope. I especially enjoyed the research process, which admittedly was a kind of escape as I was lost in thought in various libraries and archives, working with compelling documents and manuscripts. Still, writing this book also involved that special pleasure of sharing something new and offering what I believe are original insights about an important feature of modern and contemporary world culture: the place of the fantasy of the Orient in everyday life and mass culture, especially in mass-produced print culture.

I would never have completed the manuscript without support from many people who read the initial book proposal or helped me publish early versions of two of the book chapters. This group includes Eric Hooglund, Tony Crowley, Saree Makdisi, Robert Myers, and my copy editor and friend Steve Holtje. From the beginning to the end of this process Granville Ganter read drafts and offered his insights, a special effort that was crucial for completion of the book, and for which I am forever grateful. Others who always offered support and patiently listened to my complaints include my friend and colleague, Henry Krips, and my family, Sarah Ann Long, James Long, and Allen Long. My colleagues and friends from Lebanon provided support and critical insight, a group that includes Nisrine Chahine, Asma en Nasser, Romy Lynn Attieh, Huda Fakhreddine, Tamer Amin, Lina Choueiri, Nisrine Sfeir, Gillian Piggott, and John Wall. In the early stages I was assisted by two most intelligent and engaged graduate assistants at the

American University of Beirut, Rania el Turk and Katia Aranji, and I am very grateful for their assistance and friendship. Of course the support of Syracuse University Press and especially Mary Selden Evans and Deanna McCay was critical, while Kay Steinmetz gave me the all-necessary final editorial push. I am also grateful to the Huntington Library for a 2007 summer fellowship and to the Ahmanson Reading Room staff, as well as to Alan Jutzi, who helped me with rare source material about and by Hall Caine, Leonard Smithers, Richard Burton, and T. E. Lawrence. Of course, no part of this project would have been possible without the Aïtels: Fazia, Tassadit, and Lounes.

Reading A R A B I A

Introduction

Britain at the Fin de Siècle
and the Orientalist Unconscious

> Indeed, my real argument is that Orientalism is—and
> does not simply represent—a considerable dimension of
> modern political-intellectual culture, and as such has less
> to do with the Orient than it does with "our" world.
> —Edward Said, *Orientalism*

THIS BOOK IS A STUDY of the Middle East—specifically, the portrayal of the Arab world in the British cultural imaginary during the period 1880–1930. I focus on the depictions of this time and place through close readings of work by Captain Richard Francis Burton, Charles Montagu Doughty, Robert Cunninghame Graham, Marmaduke Pickthall, and T. E. Lawrence. All of these writers were writer-adventurers who built their popular reputations in good part through writing about the Near East and North Africa. Even today many of these texts are still widely read and revered as objective reportage, despite Edward Said's influential critique of Orientalism and the subsequent work of countless postcolonial critics. *Reading Arabia* addresses the resilience of Orientalism and asks a key question: Why must we still read about the Near East and North Africa—the Arab Muslim world—in certain ways? To answer this query, I examine these ways of reading and finally point to what I identify and refer to as the "constitutive fantasy of the Orient."

Most important is the constitutive function of the Oriental fantasy for the formation and function of British society in modern times, that is, the late nineteenth century through the present. As I will elaborate shortly, the Oriental fantasy is intertwined with the commodity culture—the consumer economy—of the late Empire. This commodity culture includes packaged goods, mass entertainment, new forms of everyday life, and packaged words—texts ready for mass consumption by both young people and adults. The Orient, then, is a subject of discourse and also a driving force for fantasies of the fin de siècle period. These fantasies (representations of Sultans and harems, for example) are to an extent a key component in the desire structure that provides the impetus and basis upon which commodities/consumables are both exchanged and consumed. The function of this desire structure served to make these fantasies integral to daily life in modern Britain in the late nineteenth and early twentieth centuries—and indeed, even continuing into the present.

While some of the preceding discussion may seem contentious, I maintain these are points worth pursuing. However, in this book I have chosen to concentrate for the most part on literary texts and print culture. I have focused on a select group of writers and texts to exemplify the form and function of the fantasy in a literary context, and then I will show how the fantasy warped and mediated the life struggle of each writer. Yet there is more, as these writers were working within a context of great political and cultural change, specifically within a literary tradition that had hitherto been the purview of an informed elite. Though some of these writers were part of the same elite and some were not, all nonetheless found themselves in the midst of a cultural sea change that affected their literary idiom, Orientalism, and their métier, that of the professional writer. This shift also swept each of them into a new life and set of life experiences as cultural icons.

Their respective struggles with the fantasy of the Orient became all the more poignant and important as their work, which involved the word as commodity and fundamental form of the fantasy of the Orient in mass culture, gained a new priority with regard to the marketing of the British Empire and its colonies. Simply put, while these texts are commodities—popular fiction and textuality as a commodity form—they are also linked to a new market of more traditional commodity forms. These commodities, which we now know as the material forms of mass culture, include packaged food and sweets, household goods, tobacco products, entertainment (such as songs and films), and travel. I will revisit the Oriental archive to locate the place and formative function of these texts in the consumerist milieu of the 1880–1930 period.

The importance of this effort can be viewed in the context of how the fantasy of the Orient is still with us, albeit in various guises, and is now part of everyday life in the West. And so, with recourse to the work of Jacques Lacan and his contemporary interpreter (and theorist in his own right) Slavoj Žižek, I will trace and then analyze the fantasy of the Orient as part of the Western political unconscious and also as a feature of everyday life. This effort mediates each of the following chapters in different ways, but it is the primary objective that theoretically binds the book as a whole.

Postcolonialism and the Critique of Everyday Life

Clearly this project sits squarely within postcolonial studies, at least as a critical genealogy of the colonial imaginary, though there is an important difference. I will return to the relationship between *Reading Arabia* and postcolonial studies in the conclusion. But for now we should simply consider that while Orientalism certainly overlaps with this area of study, and Edward Said's work is a part of the canon of postcolonial studies, the new wrinkle is that the "truth" of the people and cultures of North Africa and the Near East is not the stake, contrary to some iterations of this area of critical scholarship. Moreover, perhaps this "truth" might be so shrouded or blocked out by fantasy as to make it unknowable, even necessarily unknowable, to the extent that this truth has a constitutive function in tandem with a kind of political unconscious that decisively mediates the way we have formed our respective societies in Britain and the United States. So, with regard to Said's statement in the epigraph that opens this chapter, the study of British Orientalism has as much to do with British cultural studies and literary modernism, "our" world, as with Middle Eastern and postcolonial studies.

The everydayness of interest here is just that, the culture of everyday life in modern times. This includes the routines of mass-produced culture (e.g., commuting, eating, and working) that make the "known" trajectory of middle- and working-class life itself seem to be a set of natural expectations—indeed, the trajectory of life as such.[1] This culture, a commodity culture, made its full appearance in the 1880s and in new forms that have persisted to this day. These forms are a key component of globalization as an economic and political system and a homogenous (and homogenizing) form of culture.

Still, and staying with Said and his emphasis on literature, everyday life entails a crucial textual hinge: literally, the printed word that makes the attendant material culture possible and "knowable." This last point cannot be emphasized too much, and it is just what this book is about—popular texts that demonstrate and articulate the form and function of the Oriental fantasy and its relationship to the modern world in Britain and the West.

A Perambulation Full of Eastern Promise

The period I focus on here, the 1880s through the 1930s, was the moment in Britain when commodity culture blossomed, bringing a new world of mass-produced consumables of every size, shape, and form, as well as new functions such as the typewriter. Moreover, the role of literature as a mass-produced commodity is critical to the discussion here, while the place of the fantasy of the Orient, as a fantasy within the printed word, is paramount.

In many ways, however, this moment or epoch was felt, or intuited, and not ostensibly connected to intellectual processes such as those of the conscious mind, not to mention language and the printed word. If language is an unreliable mediator, then it seems that commodity culture has made an end run around it with a direct appeal to the consuming subject. It is as though this culture entered the bloodstream of the unconscious through the body, coupled with forbidden ideas and fantasies of sensual indulgence and wrapped in packaging that allows these fantasies to slip past the gates of repression or, rather, the dominant conceptions of Victorian and Edwardian propriety and culture. A good deal of this new commodity culture was related to the Near East and North Africa. Examples of these types of commodities include Egyptian cotton; perhaps, in later decades, petroleum; political association, such as the Arabi uprising of 1879–1882, led by Colonel Ahmed Arabi in opposition to European influence; or the place of the fantasy of the Orient in British (and American) consumer culture.

It is then odd to shift from the text to the street—from the material word to the imaginary and ineffable. But we might best grasp the fantasy of the Orient with a fictitious walking tour of London, the capital of the Empire, the metropole of metropoles, as well as other English cities of the period.[2] I have examined photographs, largely street scenes, in major collections accessible online, such as those of the London Transport Museum and the W H Smith newsagent kiosk chain. This tour will be an apt way to start looking for the truth of British Orientalism precisely because its legacy in scholarship and discourse about the Arab world today is not rooted in the streets of Cairo and Damascus. Indeed, whatever truth we might discover in a similar exercise, looking at photographs from the Bonfils studios, for example, is irrelevant. The fantasy that underpins British Orientalism, which is still operative today, was born in the cities of Great Britain as a mass-cultural phenomenon. The truth of the Middle East does not matter; it is the fantasy of the Orient that rules the day, even now.

If we crossed Trafalgar Square in 1900, we could not help but notice a statue of General Charles Gordon (or "Chinese Gordon" as he was popularly known after his success as a commander in China in the 1860s), a recently fallen and much-revered hero of the Empire.[3] Gordon was a British consul to the Sudan during the Mahdist uprising of the 1880s. He was martyred when the fortifications of Khartoum were breached and the Mahdi Army entered the city and slaughtered its citizenry. According to legend, Gordon was killed on the stairs of the Consul's Palace and promptly beheaded. His death caused great consternation across the Empire, and Queen Victoria herself expressed outrage and upset at his death. Boys clubs, such as the newly formed Boy Scouts, advertised in boys' magazines in order to raise funds for memorials in Gordon's honor. When Khartoum was eventually retaken, nearly twenty years later, a boys' college was founded in his honor, the Gordon College of Khartoum.

Near this somber, sentimental monument to a martyr of the Empire in Trafalgar Square, we might notice billboards and signs painted on the sides of buildings. Or perhaps we might also see advertisements attached to the sides of buses (then powered by steam) or similar placards affixed to newsstands in the railway and underground stations. These advertisement boards would champion a range of commodities, such as soap, especially Pears soap; Eno's Fruit Salts (with a slogan proclaiming "How Kandahar was won"); and, most of all, packaged food, edibles, and prepared drinks.[4] We might see an ad for Bovril, a most British "beverage," or perhaps for Horlicks, and a whole range of milk-based offerings from Nestlé. The latter would hawk their goods with plain block signs featuring mainly text and few images. Others would use images, though usually graphics rather than photographs. In *Imperial Leather* Anne McClintock makes much of these ads and their connection to the Empire, and she points to Pears soap ads in particular. Janice Boddy takes the case further with a trenchant analysis of these Pears soap ads and their connection to the Anglo-Egyptian War in the Sudan, also known as "General Gordon's War."[5] Both scholars are right insofar as they show the relationship between an emergent commodity culture—a new world of packaged goods and mass consumption—and Empire. But they do not pursue the point further to explore the relationship between the commodity—packaged goods produced, distributed, and consumed under the aegis of imperial and global finance capitalism-and the attendant fantasy of Africa and the Near East.

In his book *London 1900: The Imperial Metropolis,* Jonathan Schneer writes about a truly imperial city where all the politics of the Empire were active, whether as a matter of administration or even resistance. Regarding the latter, he devotes chapters to resistance movements in

India and Africa. He also comments on the commercial aspect of the Empire and speculates:

> Workers in Eno's Fruit Salts perhaps took pride in manufacturing "The antiseptics of Empire," as a typical advertisement put it. The employees of Bovril, a company which produced beef extract thought to contain health promoting qualities and which was given therefore to soldiers wounded in South Africa, might preen themselves on "upholding the British flag and contributing to the success of British valour."[6]

He continues with a similar comment about Monkey Soap and its advertising slogan's reference to "scouring Boers from Africa." But he does not note that a good deal of these advertisements made reference to the Near East in some manner or to the Arab world in general. What is remarkable but unremarked on is just how central the Arab world is to this new commodity culture, which marks a new shift in global capitalism and its imperial guise.

Fry's Cocoa was a company located in the city of Bristol to the south and west of London, based near the docks that were the former eighteenth-century port of departure for British slave ships headed to the Americas—a legacy that survives in street names such as Blackboy Hill and White Ladies Road. The ships also brought back rum and tobacco (the Wills family and their cigarette brand were Bristol-based) as part of what Paul Gilroy identifies as a triangle of exchange, that is the Black Atlantic slave trade. Indeed, even in the late nineteenth century Fry's was advertising its cocoa products across the country with ads that featured a young African boy holding a cup of hot chocolate out to an unseen colonial master, announcing, "Cocoa Sah!"

The use of the Empire in Fry's ad campaign is obvious. But even more striking (though less horrifying) are the advertisements used to market of one of its other sweet consumables, first marketed in 1914: "Fry's Turkish Delight." This confection entails a chocolate coating around rose-colored Lokum, which came packaged in a purple foil wrapper bearing the sales slogan "Full of Eastern Promise." What we should note here is that the exotic references in many of these advertisements, whether on ad boards or packaging, are connected to goods relating to the body. The ads refer to smelling nice, health and cleanliness, or an intense sugar burst. Here, then, is something radical and new, and most combustible in all senses. A simple combination of text and a catchy slogan invoke an idea suggesting something exotic and sensual in a far-off land, yet available here and now in a shiny purple wrapper.

If we stay in Bristol and travel to the working-class industrial outskirts of Eastville, we might see the stadium where the newly formed football team plays (though they moved nearby to a new stadium later in the twentieth century): the (Bristol) Black Arabs, founded in 1883. The team was formed in the year of the Anglo-Egyptian War and so is connected by inference to Gordon's martyrdom. The team name was taken from a nearby rugby team, while "black" referred to the jersey color (another rugby team, the Saracens, still plays under this team name today). The Bristol Rovers, as they are now known, remain an active club, though they are now nicknamed the "Pirates"—also an oblique reference to the Bristol docks, and the setting for the opening of Robert Louis Stevenson's *Treasure Island* in a pub that is still functioning, Llandoger Trow—and plays in the English Football Association's League Two. Though the club is not particularly successful on the pitch, it has a loyal fan base, of which one influential group is known as the "Black Arabs." On the 125th anniversary of the club in 2008, and for one game, the Bristol Rovers wore the Black Arabs' kit, which is still available for purchase. It is not particularly lavish, despite the exotic promise of the name, and amounts to a black jersey with a yellow diagonal stripe or sash.

If we move to the south and the east, to the city of Portsmouth, we might see emblazoned on storefronts and in public places the insignia of the football club of that city, a multipointed gold star above a horizontal crescent moon reminiscent of a slightly turned Turkish or Algerian flag. The imagery is clearly Islamic in reference, and it is associated with the charter for the city. The football club can be traced to Richard I (the crusader king known as the "Coeur de Leon"), though it is not surprising that, like the Bristol Rovers, the club was founded in

1898, the year Kitchener annihilated the Mahdi Army of the Sudanese Caliphate at Omdurman, a "battle" that was over in a matter of hours and featured heavy use of Gatling and Maxim guns against men armed with spears.

Araby, or the Fantasy in Print

> The unity of the large ensemble of texts I analyze is due in part to the fact that they frequently refer to each other: Orientalism is after all a system for citing works and authors.
> —Edward Said, *Orientalism*

The typewriter has a place in the Oriental fantasy. It might seem odd to tie this mechanical, nineteenth-century object, a proper (analog) writing machine, to something so ineffable and antimodern as a fantasy of the desert and Eastern antiquity, but thinking through the paradoxes reveals a good deal about how the Oriental fantasy functions. To this end Friedrich Kittler's *Gramophone, Film, Typewriter* is loaded with details and insights. We can start by noting that Alan Turing referred to one of his six-foot-tall Enigma machines (the famous code-cracking machines of World War II, part typewriter and part computer) as a "large copper-coloured cupboard . . . which on first glance looked like an oriental goddess."[7]

Perhaps, however, the relationship between the typewriter and the fantasy of the Orient is not so odd. The Anglo-Sudanese War was documented by daily reports from professional reporters who used typewriters and related machines, such as the telegraph system and its keyboard, to bring details of the campaign to the British public. But in so many ways, as Kittler notes, the typewriter was most analogous with that other late-nineteenth-century machine, the machine gun, in its Gatling and Maxim variants. As the latter spat out bullets, so the typewriter, a machine pioneered by the gunmaker Remington, spat out words at a rapid rate in even sequences. The sequences or time intervals of bullets fired are analogous to the evenly spaced words on the page, as the typewriter was a kind of personal and portable printing press. Indeed, and here Kittler summons Heidegger, Derrida, and eventually Foucault, the typewriter replaces the hand, supplanting authorial authority and the type of author and even the kind of work that marked an earlier epoch.[8] The pen was replaced by the machine as though, again, there was a short circuit, a direct route to the brain and the production of text. Kittler documents the use of the typewriter by Nietzsche, who in turn noted that the machine changed the way he thought and wrote. Using a typewriter he could move from elaborated ideas to shorter elliptical texts, the aphorisms that made his style, or use the fragment, a feature of modernist, and postmodernist, theory.[9]

Nietzsche eventually gave up typing for himself and hired women to type for him. One of them was Lou Andreas-Salomé, with whom Nietzsche was romantically entangled.[10] This last point is not mere scholarly gossip but is notable in that the process of writing for Nietzsche, and for writing as such in the age of the typist, was marked as a feminine activity, if only because it was women in the nineteenth century and into the present who were most associated (in the West) with the typewriter and its digital legacy and remain so due to sexism in the job market. Kittler also associates the typewriter with the symbolic in Lacan's schema or, simply put, with the Law insofar as the typewriter renders the chaos of expression, the spoken word, into evenly spaced printed text in regular blocks and formations. There is not much to argue with here, and it is obvious that the typewriter has had a tremendous influence on poetry, in particular, but there is more. Because women are so strongly associated with the typed page its regular spaces, which differentiates and produces meaning, there is something here that exceeds the authority of the symbolic.

Consider then the new kind of romance that accompanied the rise of middle-class life in the period, with regular commutes and regulated social space, the suburbs and bedroom communities of London. This form of illicit romance offered something sleazy and exciting, something forbidden that was carried out in the spaces of everyday life—train platforms, alleyways, cheap hotels—just as in the desert, truly a page across which a romance novelist might write.

Kittler references T. S. Eliot and his typewritten poem *The Wasteland*, and also notes the connection between Joyce's Leopold Bloom and his thoughts at Paddy Dignam's funeral in *Ulysses*, but does not make much more of the latter writer and his most famous novel.[11] Indeed, *Ulysses* is the best and most trenchant commentary and working-through of every point Kittler has made about the typewriter and the consequences for the unconscious. Consider that en route to the funeral every step taken by the jingle-besotten adman Bloom is mediated by the printed word, which he in turn sees around him on biscuit tins and packaged meat, while his fantasies are intertwined with fragmentary and illicit missives, such as postcards and brief letters sent to other women. Even his toilet paper is cheap literature, *Matcham's Masterstroke.*

I will return to Joyce momentarily, but for now also consider the connection between the typewriter and the printed word of modernity to the fantasy of the Orient. There is a vintage photograph in W H Smith's photographic archive of the Euston Station newsstand. This image struck me from the first because it is, in some ways, so familiar, yet was taken in the 1920s. It is familiar because the stand looks like contemporary newsstands in the underground and railway system in Britain, as well as in American cities, especially New York City. The kiosk is not very large, with just enough space to enclose various consumable goods such as tobacco, cigarettes, and sweets. The exterior of the kiosk is covered in newspapers of all sorts, with various headlines, some concerning local events, others not. It is a striking image in part because of its familiarity (that is, we have seen it before), but it is also striking because of the mundane cultural breakthrough and phenomenon it represents: commuters reading en route to work, possibly smoking, or eating and drinking. W H Smith even operated a lending library and published their own line of "railway novels," the kind that "shopgirls" might have read. It is mundane, perhaps, but this image ties the everyday, the routine of the daily commute, to the kind of Orientalist popular-consumer culture noted above. The image is from the 1920s, but W H Smith held the concession in Euston Station for several decades prior, stretching back to the years of the Anglo-Egyptian war in the Sudan, and surely then the ads and newspapers would have proclaimed all sorts of Oriental travesty and delight.

My point here is that the Orientalist unconscious is rooted in a textual unconscious; indeed the whole period from 1880 to 1930 is a period marked by this culture and its slow shift from text and textuality to the image and the movie screen. Malek Alloula's brilliant book, *The Colonial Harem*, was a breakthrough effort in its time, bringing to the fore of academic research a form of popular culture of the nineteenth- and twentieth-century colonial period that few noticed otherwise. The book is about postcards of course, French postcards, mainly from North Africa, and primarily "about" North African women, and most of them would be considered pornographic by contemporary standards. In *Governing Pleasures*, Lisa Sigel has also written about these kinds of cards, the British variant, and she rightly emphasizes that they represent a popularization in popular culture of a hitherto elite cultural "form," photography of the Orient and especially Oriental women. The postcard images do not stand alone, however, for they are "explained" by a range of texts on Arab and Muslim sexuality and domestic life and other pseudo-anthropological or ethnographic discourse, along with strange comments by the card senders. Some say nothing about the image, which is, perhaps, most odd.

James Joyce was probably the exemplary writer who recognized this period for what it was about—that is, mass-produced texts and Oriental promise—in a series of scenes and references in *Ulysses* and especially in his short story "Araby." Consider from *Ulysses* Bloom's references to the scent of Jaffa oranges crossed with thoughts of various women. Another example is the entire Nighttown scene, the walk through the redlight district with the drunken Stephen near the end of the novel, suggesting a passage through an Oriental souk of licentious wares.[12]

"Araby" is, from the Orientalist title, a bit more obvious. The short story was written in 1905, nearly a decade before the author began work in 1914 on *Ulysses* proper, and probably referenced the Grand Oriental Fete that visited Dublin in May 1894, which was marketed with a song with the following lines:

I'll sing thee songs of Araby,
And tales of fair Cashmere,

Wild tales to cheat thee of a sign,
Or charm thee to a tear.[13]

The "hero" of the story, a young boy, is fired by the romance of Orientalist knight-errantry akin to Don Quixote, intertwined with references to another Oriental narrative, the Passion of Christ. Mangan's sister, the love object (who is named after an Irish Orientalist poet, James Clarence Mangan) is both sexual and ideal for the boy, but by the time he arrives at the fair, or rather bazaar, his desire has been definitely converted into pence. As he stands before a young English woman, flanked by round vases, he realizes he does not have enough money to purchase a trophy for his love, and the story ends: "I saw myself as a creature driven and derided by vanity."[14] Critics make much of the references to Ireland, religion, and sexual awareness, and rightly so, but all of these aspects of the story find form under the aegis of "Araby," an Orientalist frame. Moreover, this is about the unsettling intertwining of money and desire, coin and love, as the boy counts the change in his pocket attempting to convert it into something palpable if not ineffable, as in a tale in Burton's translation of *The Arabian Nights*.

The Break

Joyce's "Araby" references a mass-cultural phenomenon of at least the two previous decades, stretching back into the 1880s, a period marking a break in British culture and history, especially that of the "masses" (the working class and the rising middle class). The 1880s, for example, saw a number of technological and social factors that contributed to the development of a market for cheap entertainment literature of the sort Joyce mocks throughout his work. These factors include the Education Act of 1870, the lifting of stamp and paper taxes, new and faster linotype printing presses, cheaper pulp formulas, the improvement of mass transit systems, and, importantly, as noted above, the W H Smith news kiosk franchise, which placed reading material in every train station and on every platform. The result was that a huge market opened up for adventure literature such as H. Rider Haggard's stories set in Africa and North Africa (*She* and *King Solomon's Mines*) and John

MacGregor's *Rob Roy* series set in the Near East (especially *The Rob Roy on the Jordan, Nile, Red Sea, & Gennesareth*).

Two points mediate the way we should consider Orientalist texts from this period. First, after the 1880s the established elitist literary tradition of Orientalist writing, sponsored by the Royal Geographic Society and other private entities, became alloyed with popular culture and mass publication. The second point is that the writers and texts addressed here fall into a tradition of British travel narrative about the Arab and Muslim world, with roots in the eighteenth century and probably earlier, but that in the early nineteenth century fully coheres as a way of seeing and writing about this region and its peoples. As Brian Street and, of course, Edward Said have noted, this tradition is so powerful and prevalent that anyone writing about the region is invariably caught up in the established narrative paradigms, formulas, and received observations. This literary tradition is a simple example of an Orientalist "always-already"—explorers find exactly what their literary predecessors told them they would find and perpetuate the figures and imagery of the tradition as well as its pleasures. From Palgrave to Lane and Burton, through to Blunt, Doughty, Bell, and Lawrence, the narratives are, after all, compelling as these writer-adventurers bring together a number of discourses that range from "low" to "high" in respectability and credibility. In Burton's *Personal Narrative* we find an adventure story that also includes some archaeology, ethnography, political commentary, comparative religion, and sexual titillation (albeit not as pronounced as in his later work with the Kama Shastra Society). Clearly these writer-adventurers became pop figures, celebrated as much as anyone else in their time. Indeed, while Said comments on Burton's dressing in Arabic clothing, and how he had "become" Arab in his mind, he fails to note how this feature of the narrative appealed to (excited!) a wide audience. By the 1880s the adventurer/archaeologist/ethnologist could add sexologist to his list of successful personae, for, notably, with publication of *The Arabian Nights,* he and his wife no longer needed the income he derived from his consular duties.[15]

Consider also that during the 1880s with the Sudan Campaign there was an explosion of popular writing in cheap booklets, novels, and newspapers about General Gordon, the Sudanese Mahdi, and the fall of Khartoum.[16] These new forms of mass print culture were available for a newly expanded British reading public, on trains and platforms, in pubs and cafes, and in the city streets. Also, following the fall of Khartoum there were stage productions about the Sudanese war, some of which, strangely, reworked history with a British victory, albeit retaining the martyrdom of Gordon.[17] Some of this literature is popular, with little traditional "literary" merit, and most of it is openly supportive of empire. We should note that by the 1880s Arabia, the Dar el Islam, is no longer confined to the Arabian peninsula or Palestine but, at least in the popular mind, where it counts most, takes in North Africa and the Near East and stretches all the way through Persia. Drawing upon this tradition, the key themes of the adventure narrative about the Arab and Muslim world usually include Oriental despotism (e.g., the 1820s pornographic "classic" *The Lustful Turk*); doing the hajj (as a Christian Westerner and traveling as an "Arab," e.g., Burton's *Personal Narrative*); captivity (e.g., texts about the Sudanese Campaign of the 1880s); ethnography and archaeology (e.g., Lane's *Manners*, much of Burton's work, and texts by Gertrude Bell and many Egyptologists); Islam (e.g., Blunt's *The Future of Islam* and Pickthall's *The Meaning of the Glorious Koran*); and Arab women and sexuality (again *The Lustful Turk* is one example, though Burton is truly the key figure here with his Kama Shastra Society publications of the 1880s). Other contemporary popular literature set in the region includes Robert Hichens's turn-of-the-century bestseller *The Garden of Allah*, E. M. Hull's *The Sheik* (the novel on which the silent film classic starring Rudolph Valentino was based), Edith Wharton's travelogue *In Morocco*, and Walter Harris's series of books about his adventures in Morocco in the second half of the nineteenth century, especially his *Morocco That Was*.

In *The Savage in Literature,* Brian Street offered an introduction and broad analysis of the appeal of such Orientalist discourses in popular texts, and argued for their importance with respect to colonialist ideology.[18] Patrick Brantlinger took this project further in *Rule of Darkness*, in which he pairs popular writers with distinguished anthropologists.[19] He focuses on late Victorian and Edwardian examples, demonstrating the pervasiveness of some ideas or tropes of colonialist discourses, despite the apparent divides of class and education, showing how these ideas and discourses crossed over into the twentieth century. Joseph Bristow's *Empire Boys* is another groundbreaking work on print culture, which, except for a single well-known essay by George Orwell, was largely neglected by scholars. With boys' magazines such as *Boy's Own Paper* and *Union Jack,* we see the merger of print capitalism and imperialism as a new market of readers is at once discovered and formed under the directorship of writers such as G. A. Henty. These three scholars opened the way for this kind of broad literary (print culture) analysis of colonialist ideology in the 1970s and 1980s, though unfortunately their project has not been adequately developed in recent years as it has been split between a documentarian tendency on the one hand and a theoretical tendency on the other, at the expense of a kind of Saidian political engagement.

The cultural residue of this convergence of popular and elite culture requires a much more flexible and synthetic mode of analysis. After all, this residue, which we find in novels, newspapers, postcards, and ephemera, is the stuff of the stereotype, but identifying it as such is insufficient. To that end, in his chapter "The Other Question: Stereotype, discrimination and the discourse of colonialism" in *The Location of Culture,* Homi Bhabha offers some useful insights into the discursive pleasures, or persistence of Orientalism, in its most vulgar form: the stereotype.[20] For Bhabha this term refers to the epithets and common "knowledge" (what "they do" and what "they want") by which individual colonial subjects, or anyone from formerly colonized, immigrant, or oppressed groups, are referred to or known by mainstream society in the West. His concern is for the way that the stereotype functions in the "subjectification" of the colonial subject. Bhabha starts from Said's proposal for a semiotics of Orientalism, which he notes is grounded in the latter's nod to Freud and then the power/knowledge paradigm of Foucault. But for Bhabha the explanatory power of Said's theory is finally "underdeveloped" with regard to the "question of power and desire."[21] To that end he proposes a supplementary theory, and returning to Freud argues that the latter's theory of fetishism offers some insight into the way the stereotype functions and persists. Bhabha links the persistence, and then the pleasure of fetishism, to castration anxiety and the necessary disavowals that comprise the formation of the subject. And so, he writes:

> [T]he scene of fetishism is also the scene of the reactivation and repetition of primal fantasy—the subject's desire for a pure origin that is always threatened by its division, for the subject must be gendered to be engendered, to be spoken.[22]

As he goes on to explain, the colonial subject of the stereotype is an "impossible object" that is "imbricated" with a desire for a "pure, undifferentiated origin."[23] The everyday consequence is that even the most well-meaning and legitimate discourse—"official knowledges"—on the colonial subject is grounded in a fantasy of origin and typology that precludes difference or, for Bhabha, the hybrid subject.

Though Bhabha's text is useful for this project, it too falls short in some respects. First, his object of scrutiny, the stereotype, is at least etymologically grounded in print culture. After all, the word "stereotype" is derived from print technology, notably mass-publication techniques. Moreover, the very discursive prevalence or distribution that lends power and the authority of knowledge to Bhabha's stereotype is finally the result of mass publication, such as the publications of legitimate entities such as the Royal Geographic Society, as well as the reports read in the cheap illustrated news journals of the nineteenth and twentieth centuries.

Reading Arabia

I attempt to capture, here, this moment of cultural and ideological transition and rearticulation, the period from 1880 to 1930, and demonstrate what this means for British Orientalism as an area of study but also, most of all, as a geopolitical idea. The first two chapters present the historical break in two respects. The first is literary and historical: I focus on two writers who redefined the Orient in this period, in very different ways and at least initially for different audiences. The first figure is Richard Francis Burton, the adventurer and "scholar" of the Arab and Muslim world, who achieved popular fame and notoriety with his unexpurgated translations of *The Arabian Nights* and other Orientalist erotica, including *The Kama Sutra* and *The Perfumed Garden of Sheikh Nefzaoui*. Given the public condemnation of Burton's rendering of the *Nights*, especially the famous "Terminal Essay" and his pseudo-scholarship on homosexuality in the Orient, surprisingly this version served as the basis for many reprints, including editions for children. For the popular mind of the period, then, Burton was an action figure of sorts and also a scholar, albeit one with predilections.

Burton's antithesis, the prophet to his dandy, was Charles Montagu Doughty, the ascetic and morally upright author of *Travels in Arabia Deserta*. This book was not widely known until the 1920s, but it was read by and influenced a range of important writers, including T. S. Eliot and T. E. Lawrence. It was influential for the content but, I argue, even more so for the pose Doughty assumed, that of the ascetic "Khalil" following the hajj to the holy cities as a Christian and Western scholar documenting the geology and pre-Islamic Nabatean ruins. Together Burton and Doughty form the two tangents of British Orientalism and make up the tendencies that mark Middle East studies, as well as the personae of regional experts even today. However, I have documented the way these two tendencies work in examples taken from popular literature in the early twentieth century: Hall Caine's *The White Prophet*, Robert Hichens's bestseller *The Garden of Allah*, and Edith Hull's *The Sheik*, the latter marking the transition from popular text to screen, from one form of mass culture to another.

The historical context for this break in British Orientalism was determined, for the most part, by the long and disastrous Anglo-Egyptian War in the Sudan (1883 to 1898), the so-called river war where Winston Churchill, Lord Kitchener, and General Gordon all served. With a series of quick defeats, and the repeated destruction of the famous British square (a defensive infantry formation), the Islamic nationalist army of the Sudanese Mahdi seized—or rather terrified—the imagination of the British reading public. Newspapers, journals, and popular presses struggled to catch up with interest in the area and the issues, and W. T. Stead's *Pall Mall Gazette* distinguished itself for both its daily coverage and the type of coverage it offered. Stead and his editors seem to have manipulated British foreign policy single-handedly with sensational coverage and headlines—"Smash the Mahdi!"—and the use of interviews, including a last-minute interview with Gordon before he left for the Khartoum rescue mission. The public interest only increased when Khartoum fell and Gordon was martyred, and never really abated until World War I offered a replacement focus for this public obsession. In chapter 2 I document the coverage of the war and demonstrate what it meant for the advent of a new kind of mass culture–based thinking about the Arab and Muslim world. In the second part of the chapter I link this legacy to the late-twentieth-century Sudanese writer Tayeb Salih and his acclaimed novel *Season of Migration to the North*. In this novel Salih shows how the cultural legacy of this period—and it is clearly a mass-cultural legacy—dominated the consciousness of the British public then (the 1960s). The novel portrays the consciousness of a Sudanese intellectual who is a professor of economics, Mustapha Said, and his double, a poet and English professor also of Sudanese descent. Both are trapped in an Orientalist fantasy they can neither manipulate nor escape, which finally kills Mustapha Said.

Many of the British Orientalists also tried to slip the net of the fantasy, knowing full well what it meant as a matter of imperial domination and culture. A striking example is Robert Cunninghame Graham and his late-nineteenth-century Morocco travelogue, *Mogreb-el-Acksa*. Cunninghame Graham is especially interesting because he was a close friend and correspondent of Joseph Conrad, and also because he worked very hard to challenge the discursive, or at least rhetorical, hegemony of British imperialism as he found it in stereotypes and epithets. His travelogue is the best example of this attempt to traverse the Orientalist fantasy, though finally, as with Mustapha Said, one has to wonder if this is possible. The fantasy is too deep, too constitutive, while a traversal is more akin to the ironic pose of so many modernist writers and their attempt to escape the routine and vagaries of everyday life in the modern world. Indeed, in the last move in this chapter I link Cunninghame Graham to both the modernists and their twentieth-century champions, the New York intellectuals, in an attempt to explore more connections and tangents within the modern Arabist discourse.

If the fantasy could not be beaten, then some chose to cross over completely and convert to Islam. Like Cunninghame Graham, the fin de siècle writer Marmaduke Pickthall was successful in making a name and income selling his short fiction and nonfiction to successful and prestigious journals such as *Cornhill Magazine* and the edgier *New Age*. In some ways—and this is another link to the mid-twentieth-century intellectual scene in the United States and Great Britain—both writers were forerunners of the left intellectuals who founded or made their careers with left-oriented monthlies and journals such as *The Nation*. What makes Pickthall interesting are his autobiographical writings about Syria and Lebanon in the late nineteenth century, and especially his novel, *Said the Fisherman*, which "produces" the period, framed by sectarian riots and upheaval in Damascus and the Mount Lebanon area and the bombardment of Alexandria in 1882 with the subsequent sectarian violence. Clearly he was interested in sectarian conflict; unable to analyze it fully, he did the best he could and represented it in a narrative about a ne'er-do-well who makes a fortune in Damascus, loses it during the sectarian problems, and dies in Alexandria, with a brief sojourn in London. Pickthall's subsequent conversion and open support for the crumbling Ottoman Empire, espoused during World War I, were part of a process of self-marginalization as he effectively gave up his career as a traditional writer and wrote largely about Islamic issues, notably his commentary on the *Koran*.

It is hard to describe T. E. Lawrence's dalliance with the Arab world as a traversal, though he certainly claimed to have entered fully the "Arab" mindset and found a place in Arab society. On the other hand he never claimed to have converted. While he ostensibly adopted some of the ascetic aspects of Muslim culture, this might be the influence of the Christian moralist Doughty as much as anyone or anything else; Lawrence remained essentially British. When he returned to England he quickly picked up where he left off with his love for motorcycles and fine press books. *Seven Pillars of Wisdom*, his war book and the basis for his literary fame, is the result of this last interest in so many ways, though it is mediated by two other factors new to Lawrence's life. The first was his fame: as "Lawrence of Arabia," he was the basis of a highly successful international stage show/spectacle, making him a pop icon of the first order at a time when such were new. The second factor was apparently due to his war experience, the Deraa incident where he was raped by a Turkish commander. Until his death, Lawrence of Arabia would arrange for secret beatings—birchings, as they are known—while his close company was that of a very few men. This conjunction of mass culture—Lawrence of Arabia—and his sexual trauma and compulsion are not entirely separate nor entirely distinct to Lawrence and his biography. In chapter 5 I explore this connection between mass culture; mass publication and its antithesis, fine press books; and sexual trauma.

The Scholarly Context of *Reading Arabia*

Reading Arabia is unique insofar as it brings to bear the interpretive techniques of cultural studies on areas decidedly non-Western, the Near East and North Africa.

There are several eminent scholars and estimable books that inform our knowledge about Orientalism, commodity culture, and other issues addressed here. Holding the work of Edward Said in abeyance momentarily, Timothy Mitchell's *Colonizing Egypt* is a most prominent example that should be acknowledged. Mitchell's book, published in 1988, addresses Egyptian engagement with both the French and British colonial presence in the nineteenth century, insofar as Egyptians incorporated or rejected various features of Western life and culture—institutions, architecture, and planning—in the period of the 1880s, which slightly overlaps with that of *Reading Arabia*. *Colonizing Egypt* is a tour de force of research and interpretation and is rightly viewed as a most significant contribution to what we now know as the critique of Orientalism—following Said's lead, of course—and, in a certain way, to postcolonial critique and Middle East studies. Moreover, insofar as *Colonizing Egypt* addresses ways of thinking (that is, the ideas, structures, and institutions that accompanied the French and then British colonization of Egypt), there appear to be other commonalities with this project. Mitchell's book addresses an array of colonialist spectacles and institutions, among them the Eighth International Congress of Orientalists held in 1889 in Stockholm; contemporary travel accounts from Egyptian visitors to Europe and Britain—and some are quite humorous; various housing schemes; conscription declarations; and *Eight Words*, an Egyptian nationalist text from the period of the Arabi uprising. The range of material is certainly compelling, especially to any reader with a cultural studies bent, and at least here this book has much in common with *Reading Arabia*.

Consider, however, that from the outset and at the beginning of almost every chapter, Mitchell declares his allegiance to Michel Foucault and his microcritique of social space, institutions, and the function of power therein. Indeed, even as Mitchell ties his project to Foucault, he declares that he has exceeded the project and scope of the master's work and has brought a Foucauldian critique to bear on colonial power in a new way. Thus, he writes,

> Foucault's analyses are focused on France and northern Europe, yet forms of power based on the re-ordering of space and surveillance and control of its occupants were by nature colonising in method. Moreover examples of the Panopticon and similar disciplinary institutions were developed and introduced in many cases not in France or England but on the colonial frontiers of Europe, in places like Russia, India, North and South America, and Egypt.[24]

While we must honor Mitchell's command of the colonial archive, as well as a book replete with reference to texts in English, Arabic, and French—and by a range of writers, many of whom are, notably, Egyptian or Arabophone—there is an obvious difference around content and the significance thereof. To be clear, this initial difference concerns what material is of interest or relevant, and why, and then why the project as a whole has any contemporary meaning and worthiness beyond a limited scholarly justification.

The decisive distinction between Mitchell's book and this project, however, is rooted in the difference between the theoretical positions of Foucault and Lacan. To simplify this point, consider that the former's work is a vast critique of the psychoanalytic subject, indeed perhaps the subject and agency altogether, as some read Foucault. Here, however, one word, "ideology," is most important as a matter of emphasis, content, and analysis—the constitutive function of Orientalist ideas in British politics and everyday life. As for subject matter and content, *Reading Arabia* is almost entirely based on texts, as here we find the best examples of ideology, the imaginary realized in both material and abstract form.

Other than *Colonizing Egypt*, there are books that are very close in many respects to *Reading Arabia*. One example that functions as a complementary text is Geoffrey P. Nash's *From Empire to Orient: Travellers to the Middle East 1830–1926*. Nash's book is a rigorously researched political and intellectual history that covers many of the same figures addressed here and within the same time frame, though *Reading Arabia* hinges on a historic break in the 1880s that is ideological, social, economic, and political and as such is a British concern. Hence my emphasis on the fantasy as a British phenomenon and concern, mediating British politics and everyday life, as much as that of the colonies (and like Mitchell, Nash is attentive to intellectual and political life in the colonies, the other half of this larger project). Indeed, Nash's introduction and his chapter on Marmaduke Pickthall were very useful, though here we also see the difference between the two books. Where Nash dissects Pickthall's Turcophilia, largely with reference to the articles published in *New Age*, the emphasis here is on the imaginary—the discursive features of the fantasy as found in Pickthall's fiction—which drives and gives these same ideas both form and popular appeal and, most of all, accounts for an explicit discursive aspect of Pickthall's work and cultural politics (what I call his "standpoint").

In his important book *Belated Travelers: Orientalism in the Age of Colonial Dissolution*, Ali Behdad also covers an area shared with this project, the British and European travelers to the "Orient" in the period after 1850. These were belated travelers in the sense that they followed the greats who preceded them, such as Palgrave and Lane, but they were also belated in the sense that they visited during a time when so much was already known about the region, and there was so little to discover in the sense that Stanley "discovered" the African interior. These late-nineteenth-century traveler-writers were also belated insofar as their writing was clearly written with their predecessors in mind, within a tradition of writing about the Arab and Muslim world. I maintain, contrary to Behdad's argument, that Burton, Blunt, Doughty, and Bell all felt strongly that they were improving, if not trumping, the earlier texts with their own books. Moreover, far from taking a melancholy and "belated" turn, the relationship of these authors to the tradition is affirmative, even when competitive. And this affirmation is key, for what is finally confirmed is the core of how Arabia is known, thus, the new Orientalist discourses. With this last point in mind, we should note that Behdad's group of travelers are all canonical literary figures, such as Nerval and Flaubert, and with Isabelle Eberhart they are mostly Francophone. The national aspect of the tradition is a critical aspect of the politics of these texts, while the popular, noncanonical mediations are also central, as noted above. Lastly, missing is some account of the influence of Doughty's *Travels in Arabia Deserta*, which was decisive in its influence on these turn-of-the-century travelers, especially Gertrude Bell and T. E. Lawrence. Indeed, Lawrence notes in his introduction to Edward Garnett's abridged edition that only at the end of the century did Doughty achieve the audience he deserved, largely due to the cheaper edition of Garnett (and that Garnett, the most influential editor of the period, was involved is an important detail).

The point we must bear in mind is that these Arabists claimed a new audience, an audience of new readers engaged in a new print-culture context, one of mass publication and mass readership. Indeed, in her pithy chapter on British travel literature about the Middle East in *The Cambridge Companion to Travel Literature*, Billie Melman offers a useful historicization of the notion of the Arabist. Specifically, and with reference to Ali Behdad, Lisa Lowe, and others, she argues against what she perceives as the binarism and seamless continuity of Said's rendering of Orientalism.[25] Moreover, Melman maintains that the later writers in Behdad's "belated" group are what we now know as Arabists, military and government specialists on the region with a colonialist agenda of native rule (she does not mention Lugard, but this is the model). While this point is true of Burton and Gordon, and then Bell, Lawrence, and Philby in the twentieth century, it is definitely not true of the Blunts and Doughty nor of Robert Cunninghame Graham. The Arabism of Blunt and Cunninghame Graham—which Philby espoused as Ibn Saud's adviser—was grounded in an argument for political Islam, as Blunt lays out in *The Future of Islam*, and so is a rejection of the British Empire and imperialism as such.

Martin Green long ago established the link between Orientalism and popular literature, especially adventure narratives, in *Dreams of Adventure, Deeds of Empire.* Green argues that the impetus, the driving force for much of the imperial effort, is traceable to the sort of boys' literature noted above, and especially novels. Although Green does not address the Middle East/Orient in particular, it is commonplace to see his work either as a complement to that of Edward Said or as its popular antithesis. Whereas Said focuses on canonical or otherwise erudite texts and writers, Green's writers wrote for the common reader. While there is a valid point in this critique of Said, and I will address it shortly, with regard to Orientalism in particular such thinking misses the point. The point is that Orientalism, as Said described it in 1978, is a whole system of thought, largely textual, and is connected to the most intimate and instrumental aspects of Western culture and power. *Reading Arabia* is focused on the 1880s and the emergence of Orientalism as a defining feature of the new mass culture, especially that of mass publication, but the point is to show what this means within the broader culture. Texts produce ideas, true, but they do not make them (despite the hopes of some literary critics). These ideas—or a culture as a whole way of life, as the culturalist school might put it—are produced within a complex of mediations and production. And so, while T. E. Lawrence may definitely be part of the adventure literature tradition, this is not all he was within British Orientalism. He was indeed an important military figure and played a major role in the creation of the modern Middle East, where his handiwork is being undone or modified even today, and he was also a British man. The Lawrence legend is very important to any serious study of twentieth-century culture, gender, and sexuality. This is certainly also true for Richard Burton, as well as for so many of the sexual aspects of British Orientalism. To that extent this book is a study of British Orientalism as a kind of genealogy of identity in the modern world, that is, an analysis of Englishness, as well as that of "Arabness." In both respects British Orientalism provides a paradigm of identity, where one position requires the other, caught in a frozen dialectic of desire. Consider how often we love what we loathe, which is the best way to describe how some of these British Orientalists felt about the Arab and Muslim world and also best describes the entirety of Middle East relations today. In *Reading Arabia* I have attempted to engage all of these themes and problems as they make up the identity and profession of the Arabist and, just as important, mediate popular culture in the Middle East today. It is the extratextual and ideological scope of this book that finally distinguishes it from possibly more modest, wise, or simply limited efforts elsewhere.[26]

Another keyword and concept upon which *Reading Arabia* hinges is the commodity, as it is central to the thesis of this project and distinguishes it from other books, such as *Imperial Leather* and Arjun Appadurai's *The Social Life of Things*. The latter book, published in 1986, is an important collection of essays about the commodity and cultural critique. It is an important book in that Appadurai and his collaborators set out to reconsider the ideas and practices surrounding the commodity form, an idea that they also open up and thus counter more limited notions of materialist critique. Also, in that they consider premodern forms of exchange, which they identify as a commodity exchange, and they are interested in the context and ideas that make the exchange possible, they are clearly working against dogmatic, even simplistic conceptions of Marxist analysis.

Appadurai's introductory essay, "Introduction: Commodities and the Politics of Value," is most useful here, then, as a rigorous foil against which the contours and specificity of this project might be defined. Thus, in the collection, and through the work of fellow scholars—mostly anthropologists, which is notable—Appadurai sets out to argue for the importance of exchange with regard to the way we should understand the commodity, following the work of the early-twentieth-century German social theorist Georg Simmel. In the following essay,

"The Cultural Biography of Things," Igor Kopytoff argues for the life of the commodity, which is certainly a provocative idea when so much has been written about commodity fetishism and "false consciousness." This two-pronged project is clearly an attempt to move away from a certain kind of political and materialist anthropology toward, at least here, an understanding of the commodity that is transhistorical, even as it is grounded in cultural specificity.

In a sense Appadurai and his cowriters have set out to counter a Marxist conception of history with their own, what we might call "historicism," or what he calls the "situation" of the commodity. The important difference here is the relationship between situations, for where one group might see a continuum and elegant narrative of connected "situations," the other group, that of the Marxist tradition, sees only a series of breaks and ruptures. Instead *Reading Arabia* is deliberately built on what I argue are ideological fault lines, the ruptures in Orientalist thought in the 1880–1930 period. With regard to the commodity form, this book also differs in that the commodity here is a feature of modernity and the capitalist world system, and then discusses what this historic specificity means for everyday life in Britain and the fantasy of the Orient. Though this conception of the commodity and its social significance is carried elsewhere with the global market, it is nonetheless limited in time and space and is far from transhistorical in character.

As with scholarship on advertising and Empire, there are excellent books on the rise of the department store and the shopgirl and the commodity market in the period, such as Lise Shapiro Sanders's *Consuming Fantasies*, among many others. Sanders's work is especially interesting in that she focuses on the theme of the shopgirl in texts and popular culture in conjunction with contemporary discourse concerning prostitution and women's health issues. For her the text and culture are active and meaningful, though the same point is even more powerful with regard to the kind of commodities that were sold with an Oriental imprint. Cooks Tours on the Nile, chocolates and sweets, hot drinks, packaged medicines, soap, and other such items all concern the body to some extent, and herein lies the difference. The Orientalist commodity is more than a part of a larger culture or society of the spectacle, for it hinges on selling something that brings immediate and "felt" satisfaction. Or it promises a change in the everyday life of a new middle-class subject, and the middle class was the rising class in this period. Indeed, here are commodities that reference sensuality and the mystical (in this case, the mysterious Orient), and then yield satisfaction, albeit in other and new ways. There is a kind of short-circuiting of the conscious mind at work here, as the reference and the pleasure of the body take a direct route toward the consummation of Desire, or so the commercial narrative suggests. What we have here, finally, is an Oriental unconscious, a convergence of material and psychological phenomena constitutive of modern society and modern subjectivity in the West and, today, increasingly in the Middle East and elsewhere around the world.

The Legacy of Edward Said

This book is clearly indebted to the work of Edward Said, particularly his monumental *Orientalism*. In some ways perhaps *Reading Arabia* is derivative, though I firmly believe it marks a departure from the work of the master. The critics of Said have been many, and their points are well known, yet the book and its legacy have survived and today seem as vibrant and relevant as ever. Indeed the Middle East and North African studies of Bernard Lewis (*What Went Wrong: Western Impact and Middle Eastern Response*), Clifford Geertz (that is, his fieldwork with the Berbers of Morocco), and Ernest Gellner (author of the most estimable *Saints of the Atlas*) all seem passé now, at least after the Arab revolutions of 2010–2011, and with renewed and more up-to-date scholarship on the two regions.

Gellner and Geertz are, of course, established names in anthropology, have contributed studies of North Africa, and are hardly as partisan in their reputations as Lewis. But nonetheless, since both wrote about the Berbers of North Africa, I am not sure that their research and analysis should be the theoretical basis of any contemporary work on the Amazigh peoples (Berbers), especially as neither was actively engaged in scholarship concerning North Africa or the Middle East during the *Orientalism* debates. Moreover, even in the late 1970s, and especially now, the respective Berber identity movements were deeply influenced by the diaspora and modernity (popular music on cassette, radio shows, university study groups in Paris, Twitter, Facebook, the Internet as such, etc.)— all of which have reshaped the substance and style of the communal movements concerned.

Finally, and with regard to Lewis and his political work on Islam and Islamist movements, and setting aside his partisanship and public disagreements with Edward Said, it is quite obvious that a new mode of analysis is needed to understand the rise and appeal of various Salafi movements across the Arab world. This nuanced mode of analysis would take into account mass culture and representation in the context of globalization. Manfred Steger's analysis of the well-known image of Osama bin Laden—in the introduction to his primer, *Globalization: A Very Short Introduction*—dressed in a Russian military coat and traditional garb, and holding an AK 47 while sporting a Timex watch on his wrist—is much more apt and insightful.[27]

Billie Melman and others who have subsequently focused on the same tradition of texts and figures of Orientalism are misguided in their criticism of Said's so-called binarism—the Orient and the West— at least here with regard to the importance of the unconscious level at which Orientalist print culture works. So, in answer to the purported Orientalist binary, it is critical to note that Said engages the discursive field as he encounters it. Thus his work is the result of an immanent reading of Orientalist texts and discourse, which it was his project to deconstruct. The binary opposition of East and West is, in other words, the organizing principle of Orientalist discourse, not something Said imposes or otherwise introduces. For our purposes the binary of the "Occident" and the "Orient" is the very framework within which Burton, Cunninghame Graham, and others worked and against which they struggled to one extent or another. These forms of Orientalist discourse fully blossom with the advent of mass politics and mass culture, and it is no surprise that they are particularly evident in popular literature and other forms of popular entertainment.[28]

James Clifford is a friendly critic of *Orientalism* who recognizes the faults of Said's book, such as its problematic adaptation of Foucauldian analytic modes, especially discourse as a critical term, as well as the hopelessly wide scope of *Orientalism* and its regional specificity. He is right, though I would emphasize Clifford's point that Said was putting Foucault to work in an engaged project, in the pioneering intellectual spirit of the time, while the historical sweep was intended to reinforce a long-standing relationship—and place in the shifting cultural imaginary—of the Near East for the Christian West. The Near East is a special place for the West, and has been for thousands of years, and this is hardly a controversial point. Clifford's main point concerns the book as a kind of political existential gesture, and to that extent his praise is for Edward Said the engaged intellectual. In this regard I both agree and, in a modest way, I emulate.

What I have added to Said's critique are really sharpened or differently tuned versions of ideas and figures central to his formation and analysis. For example, while Said gives Raymond Williams, the figure most associated with a study of the discursive implications of "masses" and "mass culture," a nod of approval, at a deeper and more substantial level he simply does not fully account for the pleasures of Orientalism and the way in which they have infiltrated and overwhelmed the imagination of middle-class and working-class citizens of the West for over a century. So class and desire are emphasized here in new ways. There is also a different account of Freud's work here, one decisively influenced by the work of Jacques Lacan and more recently that of Slavoj Žižek. Practically this means a good deal in that the emphasis here is on fantasy and pleasure, pain, and of course sexuality, in respects that Said did not investigate. Perhaps this was due to the implications of this different Freud, one who reemerges in the 1950s in the United States as a kind of Cold War intellectual, where agency and collective forms of activism are linked to left authoritarianism and worse. Of course Said is not an anti-Communist, far from it, but underlying a good deal of his work on Orientalism and modern literature (such as his comments on the work of Joseph Conrad) are some of the attendant Cold War values and an aesthetic of irony and individuality, which run counter to the form and function of the Oriental fantasy as it is understood here, again following Lacan and Žižek.

1

The Two Tangents of British Orientalism

Burton and Doughty, Dandy and Prophet in the 1880s

Of Orientalist Text and Sex

IN THE INTRODUCTION I showed how the 1880s were a significant period in British history and culture. In Orientalist letters, two figures emerged from this period to popular acclaim, albeit not entirely in the moment: Richard Francis Burton and Charles Montagu Doughty. Though one could not find two more different writers, they and their work comprise the two strains of British Orientalism in the twentieth century. Burton and Doughty write their respective texts and emerge as figures important to popular literature and culture, marking a decisive break with the tradition of the past.

The first tangent of British Orientalism in the period covered here is best represented by the work of Richard Burton, particularly the series of erotic publications he published under the imprint of, and on subscription through, the Kama Shastra Society. This entity was ostensibly composed of subscribers who funded various translations of Orientalist erotica, particularly manuals about lovemaking such as the *Kama Sutra* (1883), the *Ananga Ranga* (1885), and *The Perfumed Garden* (1886). (The latter text was also known as *The Scented Garden* and was famously burned by Isabel Burton after her husband's death.)[1] In fact the Kama Shastra Society was a front for the pornographic publishing schemes of Burton and Foster Fitzgerald Arbuthnot, his friend, collaborator, and business partner. They met in India in 1854, as Arbuthnot was a former civil servant in Bombay; their publishing plans came to fruition some thirty years later. The Kama Shastra Society claimed to be based in both London and Benares, India's publishing center, while the city of publication was the obviously fictitious "Cosmopoli."[2] Their reasons for publishing in this way, on a subscription basis and through a front group, were mostly due to the Obscene Publications Act of 1857, as Dane Kennedy notes.[3] Burton, however, was also obsessed with Victorian moralism, which he dubbed "Mrs. Grundy," and seemed determined to poke "her" in the eye.

As for his rationale for publishing pornographic material, there were Burton's stated reasons, as well as those of his contemporaries and of scholars today. Burton claimed science and nature as his primary motivation, suggesting that these texts were about the human condition and that they argued against a narrow notion of existence propagated in the industrial West. In this line of argument we see that he has opposed culture—the human condition and especially sexuality and sexual practices—against the repressive mores of civilization, Victoria's England. The assumption is that since culture is separate from civilization it must also precede it, making so-called primitive and ancient cultures somehow purer or at least of great interest.[4] Of course there was no way that Burton would trade his British identity and affiliation for a non-Western and colonized identity, but the prospect certainly appealed to him and served as the basis for his meteoric rise as a public persona in Victoria's Empire. He was, after all, a master of disguise, language, and culture who could move freely in almost any circumstance, whether with Mormons or with pilgrims, the Hajjis, en route to the holy cities of Mecca and Medina.

In her brief account of the Kama Shastra Society, Lisa Sigel notes Burton's involvement with the Cannibal Club, an informal group derived from the membership of the newly founded Anthropological Society.[5] The Cannibals included well-known members of Victorian society and the arts, such as the politician Richard Monckton Milnes (Lord Houghton), the renowned poet Algernon Charles Swinburne, and even the radical politician and atheist Charles Bradlaugh.[6] Indeed, all were enthusiasts for exotic pornography. Sigel emphasizes the link between this group's interest in shocking pornographic images and erotica and Empire, while deemphasizing the admittedly putative scholarly aspect of their activities.[7] Indeed, it is hard to determine the seriousness with which the Cannibals framed their activities or that Burton realized in the Kama Shastra Society. But it is too easy to condemn the group and this sort of pornography as the worst sort of colonial oppression and thus to overlook the complicated—and no less objectionable—link between knowledge, power, and desire.[8] Indeed, in the last part of his life Burton worked with the lawyer and pornographic publisher Leonard Smithers, particularly with his translations of erotic Latin poetry and the infamous *Priapiae*. However, this relationship was brief and probably motivated as much by possible profit as by desire, perverse or otherwise. Smithers in fact worked more with Isabel Burton on publication of her own version of the *Nights*, as well as new editions of Burton's *Nights*. So to some extent, despite the titillating possibilities, the reality of Smithers's connection to Richard Burton was brief. Indeed, for years following Burton's death Smithers attempted to pry texts from Isabel, which she duly loaned to him (in her opinion, for an unduly long time).[9]

Among these texts, the most important is Burton's translation of *The Arabian Nights* or, as he named it, *A Plain and Literal Translation of the Arabian Nights' Entertainments, Now Entituled The Book of the Thousand Nights and a Night*. This is a major version of the singularly most important text of nineteenth-century British literature. Much of the commentary and scholarship on *The Arabian Nights* and its various translations have identified the modern or, alternately, nonmodern features of the text. In truth there is little anyone finds modern about the text itself, but much is found in the commentary, while the circumstances surrounding the text(s) and their editorial history is certainly modern. Perhaps the need to find the Orient and a mystical past in the tales points to another need for a narrative counterpoint to industrial Britain. The story of the text and the translations, however, makes *The Arabian Nights* a most modern, if not postmodern, cultural phenomenon.

In his famous "Terminal Essay," Burton makes some interesting comments about the origin of *The Arabian Nights*. He claims that it is derived from stories told by communal storytellers, that is, orally transmitted narratives. Thus, much like the oral roots of the Homeric epics, the tales are not clearly traceable to a single tale or author but are based in murky antiquity:

> We may, I believe, safely compare the history of The Nights with the so-called Homeric poems, the Iliad and the Odyssey, a collection of immortal ballads and old Epic formulae and verses traditionally handed down from rhapsode to rhapsode, incorporated in a slowly-increasing body of poetry and finally welded together about the age of Pericles.[10]

In this passage Burton has alluded to his own theories as to how the tales gained their unity and "mutual resemblance." As he reads the various manuscripts, it was due to the "editors" and "translators" of recent times rather than their origin in antiquity. It is an interesting remark, and typical of Burton for its irony, though he himself was surely taken in by at least one manuscript, the Wortley-Montague manuscript of the Bodleian, which some believe to be the work of a well-known forger and charlatan.

In *The Arabian Nights: A Companion*, Robert Irwin, a scholar of *The Arabian Nights*, claims that Burton's translation was largely derived from what is known as the Calcutta II text, with liberal recourse to the recent translation by Payne.[11] The story of the manuscripts is of some interest and relevance here. As Irwin explains, the four main printed source texts are known as Calcutta I, Calcutta II, the Bulaq text, and the Breslau text.[12]

The Bulaq text was printed in Egypt in 1835 under the supervision, as Irwin notes, of a "certain Sheikh Abd al-Rahman al-Safti al-Sharqawi," who used unidentified sources now presumably lost.[13] This text was the basis for Lane's translation as well as the Calcutta II text noted below.

Calcutta I, also known as the Shirwanee text, and was printed earlier in 1814–1818. It was translated from lost sources by a local teacher, Sheikh Shirwanee, who used it for Arabic instruction. The Calcutta II text, also known as the Macnaghten text, contained the stories of 200 nights and was printed in 1839–42. It was Burton's primary source for his translation and had been the basis for Payne's meticulous translation preceding Burton's effort. Calcutta II was compiled by W. H. Macnaghten using other manuscripts, including the Bulaq text. As Irwin notes, since this text drew on other recognized sources it was used as the basis for several major translations.

The Breslau text was not as important a source as the other texts, though it has a colorful provenance and itinerary that is worth noting. It was "discovered" by a German Arabist, Maximillian Habicht, who claimed to have received a manuscript from Tunisia that was sent from a certain Mordecai ibn Najjar. Irwin states that the source manuscript probably never existed and the Habicht translation is a collage of translations from existing and accessible manuscripts in Europe. As with all of the figures associated with the *Nights* in the nineteenth century, money was probably the motivation, hence the story of the source manuscript.

Irwin also offers a scholarly and insightful overview of the various English translations and translators of the *Nights*, though he leaves out the kind of prejudice and detail that makes Richard Burton's work so compelling in his inimitable manner. For example, in Part II of his "Terminal Essay," Burton describes each of the translations with some biography and, of course, edgy commentary about the translators. Antoine Galland, he declares, "was the first to discover the marvellous fund of material for the story-teller buried in the Oriental mine."[14] Burton argues that without the high standard and popularity of Galland's translation, Edward Lane's translation would never have found a readership:

> Without the name and fame won for the work by the brilliant paraphrase of the learned and single-minded Frenchman, Lane's curious hash and Latinized English, at once turgid and emasculated, would have found few readers.[15]

I will return to Lane and the other translator shortly, but for now we should simply note the place of Galland's work in the mind of a significant nineteenth-century man of letters. Burton offers several pages of biography, with details that give greater insight into the *Nights* as a modern cultural phenomenon.

Burton also begins his translation with a story of the text. He writes that Antoine Galland was born in 1646 into a peasant family, though he "was born for letters" and so ran off to Paris to live with an elderly female relative. She introduced him to various religious figures and educators who helped him. Galland pursued Oriental studies at the Collège du Plessis and the Collège Mazarin, and also worked with a certain Professor Goduin who was experimenting with what we would now characterize as an intensive, or speed-learning, Latin course that included conversation as well as reading and writing.[16] In 1660, still a young teenager, Galland was hired as the attaché-secretary for M. de Nointel, the French ambassador to Constantinople. As Burton relates the story, he was to help collect information on the Greek Church, and in doing so he spent a good deal of time in the city's cafes, listening to the tale-tellers and learning Romaic. Galland returned to the Levant (as it was known then), traveling further and further afield and for different employers. By this time Galland was also known as a numismatist, a detail Burton includes, and which is certainly curious, for it suggests both the fetish of the nineteenth-century collector as well as a form of economic determinism—a whole culture and history can be read on a coin. Galland also worked with one of the most famous of Orientalists, Barthélemy d'Herbelot, and even worked on the latter's *Bibliothèque orientale* after his death.

According to Irwin, Galland "published [his translations of] the Sinbad stories in 1701" and, encouraged by their reception, he obtained a copy of the *Nights* manuscript from Syria—though Burton claims otherwise—and started his famous translation. The first and second volumes were published in 1704, and the twelfth and last volume appeared in 1717. There are three source manuscripts for Galland's translation, dated from the fourteenth or fifteenth centuries, which are held in the Bibliothèque nationale de France. Irwin notes that there is undoubtedly a missing fourth-volume source, while Galland also used "native informants" to provide colorful detail and to explicate some cultural aspects of the stories.[17]

Before the distinguished and well-known translations noted above, as well as those which followed, including one version by Robert Louis Stevenson, there were bad translations and adaptations of Galland's edition of the *Nights*. These appeared in the eighteenth century and certainly influenced the Romantic poets as well as most other writers of the period through the nineteenth century. Indeed, most of the major novelists of the nineteenth century, including Thackeray, Dickens, and the Bronte sisters, were profoundly influenced by Galland's *Nights*, whether in French or a bad English translation.[18] Yet, it was Dickens who clearly tied the *Nights* to children's literature, which, perhaps, gives us more insight into the hybrid readership—children and adults—he reached with his own writing.[19] And so, it is to children's literature that we should look first, to understand better the impact of Burton's *Nights* and the direction taken with this tangent of popular Orientalism.[20] In one of the kinder and supportive reviews of Burton's *Nights*, the reviewer in *The Bat* (September 29, 1885) comments:

> *The Arabian Nights Entertainments* has been the playbook of gen-erations, the delight of the nursery and the school-room for nearly two hundred years. Now it is high time that scholars and students should be allowed to know what *The Arabian Nights Entertainments* really is.[21]

In his essay on the place of the *Nights* in children's literature, Brian Alderson concludes:

> For in all the long registers of editions of the *Nights* that are to be found in the major libraries of the English-speaking world, only a small proportion of the entries relate to editions intended for adults, and it may be hazarded that almost everyone today who "knows" the *Nights* does so, or began to do so, through the medium of chil-dren's books.[22]

Yet if the *Nights* was promoted in English as children's literature, it was also important as children's literature for a number of reasons. First, as noted by Mary Thwaite, a scholar of children's literature who traces the trajectory of children's literature from early and medieval examples, it was a genre that was first given a boost by a key figure in Anglophone publishing and book history, William Caxton, and thus became more common in the eighteenth century and burgeoned in the nineteenth century. The difference between the two last periods has a good deal to do with content, and though Thwaite does not refer to the *Nights* at all, surprisingly, the point she makes is that while eighteenth-century children's literature was popular, it was didactic for the most part as well as moralistic. She mocks these works as featuring good little boys and girls who show up bad children and especially mentions the tremendously popular Peter Parley stories.

With the Romantic period at the turn of the century, a new interest in literature of the fantastic and supernatural developed, and even the religious-based publishers had to adapt to a new market.[23] Indeed, there were eighteenth-century renditions of the "Persian tale," adapted as didactic children's literature, while others appeared that turned the *Nights* into tales with a moral message.[24] One volume is titled *The Oriental Moralist; or, the Beauties of the Arabian Nights Entertainments. Translated from the Original and Accompanied with Suitable Reflection Adapted to Each Story*, which certainly suggests a willful if not ideological manipulation of the *Nights*. Indeed this is so, and Alderson reveals that though the text was "prepared by 'the Rev'd Mr Cooper,'" the author was a known hack writer, one Richard Johnson. As Alderson documents, Johnson admitted that he "abridged" the text, in this case Galland's translation, turning a "wild garden" into something suitable for young readers.[25] What he actually cut was the frame tale structure, and this is notable for two reasons. First, it obviates any mention of sexual betrayal; and second, it leaves out any reference to the most extreme form of domestic violence, wife murder.

The market for children's literature marked the advent of a new market for popular literature that reached a peak in the 1880s, and is best represented by the appearance of a publication of the Religious Tract Society, the *Boy's Own Paper*. The turn from literature of the fantastic and adventure stories to these full-blown commercial appeals to a children's market also coincided with the recognition of different kinds of child readers, as well as different groups (or classes) of parents who actually purchased the books and magazines. The *Boy's Own Paper*, for example, was clearly published for boys of a certain age—from, say, 8 to 16—and from the earliest numbers also included advertisements for various goods, whether toys or other commodities a boy might ask his parents to buy.

Returning to Richard Johnson's abridgement of the *Nights*, specifically his cutting the frame tale, I argue that Burton's translation was dead-on in its marketing and appeal. For as the text became a commodity, so it turned on a scene that is about the love, or desire, of/for the commodity. Consider the basis of the frame tale, and I will cite Burton's text to underline this point. Briefly put, the frame entails two kings who separately, then together, watch their wives having sex with slaves (or, as Burton emphasizes, black men). This scenting of the reader with a form of narrative voyeurism, a perverse pleasure, is followed in the same tale by the account of two brothers' encounter with a genie and their "forced" sexual union with the woman of the chest. All of this sets up Scheherazade's tales. Without the voyeurism and the shocking violence the frame does not work, for our tale-teller does not have to narrate for her life, and the tales are not mediated in so many ways by sexuality in licit and illicit forms.

In its strong and contrary review of Burton's *Nights*, the *Edinburgh Review* proclaimed "Galland for the nursery, Lane for the library, Payne for the study, and Burton for the sewers." Another journal, *Echo*, simply condemned Burton and his volumes as "moral filth," and there were similar denunciations elsewhere, notably from W. T. Stead's *Pall Mall Gazette*, which prominently featured its review, titled "Pantagruelism or Pornography," written by one "Sigma," a pseudonym for the associate editor.[26] The *Edinburgh Review* was right at least in one respect, for they recognized that with Burton's *Nights* the text had broken away from a staid tradition that was rooted in children's literature and now openly appealed to the male and scholarly readership Burton named in his introduction. Indeed, perhaps only now had the *Nights* truly emerged from the "darkness" of the upper-class study and gentlemen's club to be ready for mass publication and a whole new group of readers around the Anglophone world.

Most modern scholars of the *Nights* believe that the moralistic denunciations and hyperbolic commentary were due to the infamous "Terminal Essay" that accompanied the first ten volumes of 1885–1886. In this supplementary text Burton unleashed the scholarship and ideas that had marked his life from his early days in Lahore and his review of the boys' brothels of that city. In the "Terminal Essay" Burton offers scholarship on the text and his own editorial and interpretive practice while working with the various manuscripts, but most of all he includes a section on what he identifies as the "sotadic zone," a region around the equator where men are variously bisexual or pederasts. Most Mediterranean men, for example, are bisexual, while Arabs, according to Burton's best research, are pederasts. Of course this is laughable today, and though his *Nights* was published on a subscriber-only basis, it was clear that the potential for a mass market was there. This was a frightening possibility for those whom Burton dubbed "Mrs. Grundy," that is, the prurient and moralistic censors of the British establishment.

For all the comment on the "Terminal Essay" and Burton's commentary on pederasty, the more shocking moment in his *Nights* appears very early in the text, on the sixth page of the first volume of his subscriber edition; it is the seventh footnote and the longest to that point. Indeed, this footnote is linked to the frame tale, containing Burton's "scholarly" commentary on the spectacle the two kings observed in the bedroom and palace garden: bluntly put, a black man penetrating their wives. Burton went out of his way, as Irwin notes, to emphasize this part of the tale, and scent the reader with racist language, changing the Arabic "black slave" of the source manuscripts to "a big slobbering blackamoor with rolling eyes which showed the whites, a truly hideous sight."[27] Yet this is not only racism, as the seventh footnote makes clear, but part of Burton's colonialist "scholarship" and, I argue, a critical component of both Orientalist and modern thought. Consider the footnote then, despite its objectionable content and language:

> Debauched women prefer negroes on account of the size of their parts. I measured one man in Somali-land who, when quiescent,

numbered nearly six inches. This is a characteristic of the negro race and of African animals: e.g. the horse; whereas the pure Arab, man and beast, is below the average of Europe; one of the best proofs, by the by, that the Egyptian is not an Asiatic, but a negro partially white washed. Moreover, these imposing parts do not increase proportionally during erection; consequently the "deed of kind" takes a much longer time and adds greatly to the woman's enjoyment. In my time no honest Hindi Moslem would take his womenfolk to Zanzibar on account of the huge attractions and enormous temptations there and thereby offered to them. Upon the subject of Imshak = rentention of semen and "prolongation of pleasure," I shall find it necessary to say more.[28]

One might be inclined to laugh, for this sort of racist sexual fantasy is so common and trite today. Yet several points need to be made with regard to Burton's project, British Orientalism, and the relationship between culture, sexuality, race, and Empire.

The first point is that this is not simply another example of knowledge as power, that is, power over the bodies of nonwhite men and women or overcolonized bodies as a whole. Of course it is such, as it is a one-sided fantasy about power, which is articulated here, at least, as a discourse of knowledge—actually two discourses, ethnography and sexuality. It may seem obvious, but it needs to be stated clearly that this description of sexual intercourse between black men and white women is also an end in itself, a textual desire formation—that is, pornography. Stephen Marcus, in his landmark chapter in *The Other Victorians* on *The Lustful Turk*, makes the point that from the first-person narrative form—as well as the epistolary form—to the emphasis on the penis (porn is created by men for men) to the machine references, this text is not really about anything but itself as a text that produces pleasure (it has been in print without break since the early nineteenth century). As he states, the "governing tendency of pornography in fact is towards the elimination of external or social reality."[29]

Marcus's astute reading of *The Lustful Turk* and how the anonymous text employs textual borrowings and interpolations, as well as its yoking together of machines and human sexuality, brings us to another point about pornography and Burton's *Nights*. Pornography is a truly modern cultural form, a point Lynn Hunt makes succinctly in *The Invention of Pornography*:

> Early modern pornography reveals some of the most important nascent characteristics of modern culture. It was linked to free-thinking and heresy, to science and natural philosophy, and to attacks on absolutist political authority [thus the Algerian Dey of *The Lustful Turk*]. It was especially revealing about the gender differentiations being developed within the culture of modernity.[30]

The most obvious Burtonian example of Hunt's grounding pornography in the culture of the Enlightenment and modernity is the use of footnotes, as with this example and throughout his *Nights*. In the footnote in question, clearly it is used as a tool to demonstrate the writer-translator's scholarly expertise; as a footnote, this is visually realized. The expertise is not worked into the text but set off, spatially and intellectually. Moreover, though Burton presents his thoughts as scholarship, it is firsthand knowledge by his own admission. Indeed, as he claims in the footnote, he measured a man's penis in "Somali-land," which, like some of the other outrageous claims of his circle in the Royal Geographic Society, is a weird blend of ethnography and pornography with racialist discourse, all under the aegis of classification (measurement and firsthand observation).

Not all of the footnotes are serious, nor do they seem to be offered seriously by Burton. Irwin lists a few favorites, all examples of what he dubs "barmy erudition," such as Burton's claim that the prophet Abraham was the first person to part his hair and use a toothpick, as well as many digressions about farting.[31] There is, then, a claim to the modern and to science made through this textual form, the footnote, yet there is also an erotic or, rather, a pornographic pleasure dimension in play here. This is so not simply because the "information" is pornographic but because there is something perverse about knowledge as such, as a "for itself," leading us to think of literary characters such as Sartre's "self-taught man" of *Nausea*.

Doughty the Prophet

The second tangent of British Orientalism in the 1880–1930 period is that of Charles Montagu Doughty and his latter-day epic narrative *Travels in Arabia Deserta*. Doughty set out with the hajj from Damascus in 1877 intending to document Nabatean inscriptions and other ancient and pre-Islamic archaeology as well as the geography and geology of the interior of the Arabian peninsula. Like many English travelers before him he took on an Arab name, Khalil, and to anyone who asked proclaimed himself "Nasrany," a Christian. He did not expect to spend so long on his expedition, but after breaking away alone from the caravan and journeying south he had adventures, setbacks, and terrible bouts of sickness that slowed him down. At least two reversals of plan, if not fortune, took him back to places he had previously visited, and nearly two years later, and barely alive, he left Jidda for home. Along the way Doughty made friends and enemies, meeting peasants and nomads, emirs and sheiks. His narrative is just that, though it does not cohere with a clear beginning, middle, and end. It is best to read it as a text of episodes, with shifts between soaring, sometimes bizarre prose and prosaic descriptions, as well as worn-out stereotypes of the Arab people and Muslims.

Though *Travels* was written in 1879–1883, it was not published until 1888 due to the slow pace of the publication process at Cambridge University Press and the sheer length and density of the book. Stephen E. Tabachnik, the premier scholar of Doughty's work, notes that the author was rejected by several publishers before Cambridge agreed to take the text, but then caused great consternation with his laborious and expensive emendations.[32] Doughty's inflexible stance toward his editors slowed the project down, and it took four years to publish.[33]

From the opening paragraph of *Travels*, the contemporary reader understands one aspect of the difficult publication history of this book, as well as its appeal to an elite group of cognoscenti. Briefly put, the prose is awkward and sometimes hard to read at all, refusing ready interpretation. Consider:

> A new voice hailed me of an old friend when, first returned from the Peninsula, I paced again in that long street of Damascus which

is called Straight; and suddenly taking me wondering by the hand "Tell me (said he), since thou art here again in the peace and assurance of Ullah, and whilst we walk, as in former years, toward the new blossoming orchards, full of sweet spring as the garden of God, what moved thee, or how couldst though take such journeys into the fanatic Arabia?"[34]

This paragraph is actually a single sentence made more complicated by the use of archaized syntax and pronoun use. Some argue that this is due to Doughty's attempt to render Arabic syntax, and while this might be part of his intention, for the most part the difficulty of the prose heightens the persona of the writer, a man not of his time, and reporting from a most mystical and biblical location (key to Christianity), Straight Street in Damascus.

The first edition (both volumes together) in English was over one thousand pages in length, with plates and a map, a glossary of Arabic words and terminology, and a substantial index. The 1888 edition cost 3 guineas (3 pounds and 3 shillings), which as Stephen Tabichnick notes was a hefty price at the time. Only 500 copies were printed, but in 1905 many were still unsold and remaindered at the publishers.[35] However, at the urging of T. E. Lawrence the publisher Jonathan Cape reissued another 500 copies in 1921 (Warner Medici Society and Cape) and again in 1923 (Cape and Medici) with an introduction by the famous "Lawrence of Arabia." The cost of the 1921 edition was 9 guineas, which was still expensive for the time. Other editions appeared in 1926, 1930, 1936, and then in 1964, dates that mark British popular interest in the Lawrence of Arabia phenomenon as well as in British Orientalism as such. The first American edition appeared in 1934 (Boni & Liveright), with other editions in 1937 and more recently in 1979. Abridgements appeared in 1908, 1926, and 1949 under the title *Wanderings in Arabia*. The American versions under the same title appeared in 1908, 1924, and 1927. An excerpted version also first appeared under the title *Passages from Arabia Deserta* in 1931. A German translation was published in 1937, and a French translation appeared in 1949.[36] As Philip O'Brien notes, between 1907 and 1921 *Travels* was out of print except for the abridged versions. Of course this is not to underestimate the appeal of the abridgement, which would certainly have reached a larger audience due to accessibility and a lesser price.[37]

What we have to understand is that while Doughty's book was and remains influential, it was relatively unread until the 1920s when it was reissued in complete and abridged editions, with support and commentary from the most influential editor of the time, Edward Garnett, and one of the most famous writers of the period, T. E. Lawrence (a.k.a. T. E. Shaw). I will begin by contrasting two responses to *Travels* from two different times, the 1880s and the 1920s, so as to demonstrate the turns and historical differences between the two tangents of British Orientalism.

A good part of my interest in this book, and my claim that it represents a tangent in British Orientalism, lies with these two responses from two of Doughty's most famous readers, Richard Burton and T. E. Lawrence. Burton is the sharp critic of the 1880s, while Lawrence is the proponent of both book and author upon its reissue in the 1920s.

Burton reviewed *Travels in Arabia Deserta* in 1888 in *The Academy*, a reputable journal with a broad readership. He wasted little space in making his opinion of the book and author very clear, declaring:

> MEGA VIVLION MEGA KAKON will, I fear, be the verdict of the general reader and the public, after trial of these two bulky volumes, to which, however, the geographer, the epigraphist, the student of Arabic will attach the highest importance, admiring the while at the author's worldly unwisdom.[38]

Reference to "bulky volumes" and "worldly unwisdom" certainly prepare us for a frontal assault. Burton does not disappoint, going on to point out that Doughty's substantial contributions in archaeology and geography were outdated by the time the book was published, leaving little space for such an extensive and sizeable text. He mentions French and German specialists who published more up-to-date articles, one of which had appeared in *The Academy* several years earlier.

Still, he continues, we must "deal with a twice told tale writ large, [which] despite its affectations and eccentricities, its prejudices and misjudgments, is right well told."[39] Much has been made of Doughty's writing style, here in *Travels* and in his other work. T. S. Eliot, for example, admired his refusal of Latinisms and preference for the Anglo-Saxon in a 1916 review of another work, *Titans*. More recently critics have hailed Doughty's style as part of an aesthetic and worldview that set him apart from other writers in his time. Burton, however, ridicules Doughty, and offers passages to show what he views as a style "so archaic, so involved, and at times so enigmatical."[40]

Burton, the self-proclaimed linguist and specialist in Arab and Near Eastern culture, dedicated the last part of the review to Doughty's glossary and corrected his language errors, pointing out that the author's transliterations of common Arabic words were not only wrong but suggested a basic ignorance of the alphabet. The same goes for customs, as Burton points out that Doughty did not know of the differences between the various pilgrimages or related customs and traditions. All of this leads us back to the center of the review where Burton addresses the persona of *Travels*, Khalil Nasrany, a persona who would rival his own pilgrim identities and narrative. It is not surprising that Burton notes that Doughty did not read his "Pilgrimage" (as he refers to *Personal Narrative of a Voyage to Mecca and Medina*), nor the work of Edward Lane (presumably *Customs and Manners*), and he seems unaware of Burkhardt's work on Arabic, all to the detriment of the text and Doughty's interpretations. Early in *Orientalism* Said points out that Orientalism as a field and discourse has an internal coherence and self-justification insofar as it is self-referential: "The unity of the ensemble of texts I analyze is due in part to the fact that they frequently refer to each other: Orientalism is after all a system for citing works and authors."[41] With this point in mind, Doughty has clearly broken with a tradition in a radical way, which Burton finds intolerable.

I think the last comments by Burton are interesting in two ways, for here he clearly believes that Doughty bucked the Orientalist literary tradition in an archaic, regressive spirit, producing a bad book. Yet Burton does not stop there, but also criticizes Doughty for his travel persona, Khalil the Christian. In her essay "The True Nature of Doughty's Relationship with the Arabs," Janice Deledalle-Rhodes argues that Doughty chose a nonaggressive approach toward the Arabs he encountered, following his conscience as a Christian.[42] At the end of his review Burton addresses this point in particular and mocks Doughty's weapons, "a pen knife and a secret revolver," for as he understands the narrative it is this passive behavior combined with an identity—a Christian on the Hajj—that provoked anger and violence from devout Muslims, which makes for a questionable character and personal account. Of course, Burton is a man of his time and ends his review with an appropriate flourish, stating:

> [Y]et I cannot, for the life of me, see how the honored name of England can gain aught by the travel of an Englishman who at all times and in all places is compelled to stand the buffet from knaves that smell of sweat.[43]

In his introduction to the 1937 American edition, T. E. Lawrence writes that though Doughty refused to be the hero of his *Travels*, "he was very really the hero of his journey, and the Arabs knew how great he was."[44] Lawrence, always the self-promoter in bad faith, goes on to mention his own time in the Arabian peninsula, establishing his own Orientalist credentials, and follows with some interesting comments, especially by contrast with those of Burton. First, he claims that even forty years after Doughty's visit the tribes still talk of him, "a herald of the outside world."[45] Moreover, thanks to Doughty and later Wilfred Scawen Blunt and Gertrude Bell (Lawrence's mentor in important ways), "an Englishman finds a welcome in Arabia, and can travel, not indeed comfortably for it is a terrible land, but safely over the tracks which Doughty opened to them."[46] Lawrence continues pages later with his praise, proclaiming the "truth" of Doughty's text—that is, its descriptions and analysis. He writes, "Happily the beauty of the telling, its truth to life, the rich gallery of characters and landscapes in it, will remain for all time, and will keep it peerless, as the indispensible foundation of all true understanding of the desert."[47]

In between he makes a remarkable and, for our purposes, most interesting division among travelers to the Orient. Lawrence writes that travelers, Englishmen in "foreign parts," are of two classes:

Some feel deeply the influence of the native people, and try to adjust themselves to its atmosphere and spirit. To fit themselves modestly into the picture they suppress all in them that would be discordant with local habits and colours. They imitate the native as far as possible, and so avoid friction in their daily life. However, they cannot avoid the consequences of imitation, a hollow, worthless thing.[48]

The other group of Englishmen "assert their aloofness, their immunity . . . their complete loneliness and weakness." He continues that this second group gives "an ensample of the complete Englishman, the foreigner intact" and concludes that Doughty is of the second, "cleaner" class.[49] It is a remarkable statement if only as a disavowal of his own fame and persona, "Lawrence of Arabia," and an assertion of an aestheticized—"clean"—notion of "Englishness" that is unexpected from the writer. Yet, there is also the fear of loss of identity that is threatened when one "looks" and "acts" Arab. It is a fear that we can trace to other Orientalists and to Imperialist writers such as Kipling. Moreover, the fear of dalliance with the other is not only based on his being dirty but, in this instance, and referring back to Burton and his persona of the hajj, must surely concern the fear of conversion, of giving up Christianity as much as England. Though Doughty was tanned, was dressed in local garb, spoke Arabic, and was known as "Khalil the Nasrany," "his seeing is altogether English."[50]

Being of the "cleaner" second group also is also a matter of style:

The desert inhibits considered judgments; its bareness and openness make its inhabitants frank. Men in it speak out their minds suddenly and unreservedly. Words in the desert are clear-cut.[51]

I have quoted Lawrence at length because his comments are interesting with regard to his own persona and work, and otherwise striking in many respects. Most of all, though, there is a polemical quality, as though a manifesto of an alternative Orientalism is hereby proclaimed and defended.

As to the substance of this alternative Orientalism, we have to look back to Burton's objections to Doughty's book and persona. Again,

Burton's comments directly and indirectly tell us that he sees Doughty as an unorthodox traveler and, worse, as one who breaks with the Orientalist tradition with which he identifies, that of Lane and Palgrave. It is not just that Doughty does not make a pretense of "fitting in" and humoring the locals one way or another; it is that he defies their desires as well as the desire structure of the tradition to that point, the tradition of popular Orientalism in the 1880s. And then there is the spirit of Doughty's Orientalism, which is akin to a latter-day adoption of an ascetic biblical persona. With his humble, even dirty and bedraggled appearance, emaciated and sick, Doughty seems like a long-suffering prophet of the Old Testament, while the humiliations he endures from the women and children of Hayil, or the buffets from his near-captor, Abdullah of Kheybar, even suggest a Christlike figure.

This aspect of Doughty's "Khalil" jars with the excessive, bombastic, even pleasure-seeking and entertaining tradition associated with Burton's *Personal Narrative* and especially, and for obvious reasons, the books produced by the Kama Shastra Society. It also seems irreconcilable with the interpretation of recent Doughty scholarship, particularly the essay on *Travels* by Deledalle-Rhodes, "Doughty's Relationship with the Arabs." First, the title of her essay is troubling in this era, given the sweep of the Arab world then and now, and also because Doughty himself is careful to distinguish between various Bedouin tribes and city dwellers as well as the various racial, ethnic, and religious differences among them all. Yet the thrust of Deledalle-Rhodes's essay is to recuperate or vaunt Doughty as a writer who slipped the traps and pitfalls of the Arab stereotype. Doughty truly made friends with his hosts and saw them in an innocent and true fashion.[52] Deledalle-Rhodes insists that even when Doughty's encounters turned hostile, these were encounters "between equals" in Doughty's view.[53] Indeed, she concludes:

> Among nineteenth-century travelers to the Middle East Doughty alone, to my knowledge, made this conviction completely his own and treated the Arabs as men and equals. His views about them as expressed in *Arabia Deserta* reveal the exceptional nature of his relationship with them.[54]

That Doughty had good friends and was respected by some, perhaps even most, of those he met and spent time with is probably true. Yet I cannot accept this text as a groundbreaking event in ideology, for at the least Doughty is always a Christian in the face of Muslim people he knows will be antagonized by such an identity and proclamation. From this late modern perspective it does seem arrogant and provocative to act as he does, and I argue that this is one part of Burton's object, albeit couched in the language of masculinity and Empire. Still, how can we explain away typical characterizations of the Muslim population as "fanatic," with repeated use of this word as epithet and otherwise, and the needless provocations such as his blunt announcement, upon arriving in Kheybar, that he is there to visit the city of the Jews, presumably anticipating a strong response from the locals.

Much of Doughty's stance as an ascetic, lone, near-martyred traveler closely parallels the mission of Carlyle's prophet. In *Dandies and Desert Saints,* James Eli Adams outlines the two principal characters in Carlyle's thought, the dandy and the prophet, and elaborates the place and function of these figures in the larger Victorian intellectual culture. As Adams explains, Carlyle's dandy is a theatrical type who makes a spectacle of himself in appearance, affect, and language.[55] The dandy in this respect is akin to the popular notion of the dandy in the period, whether in Baudelaire's Paris or in Poe's city of "The Man of the Crowd."

Burton was certainly a dandy of sorts, suggested by any of the photographs of him as well as the spectacle he made of his life. On the other hand it is hard to read of Carlyle's prophet, in particular, and not think of Doughty's book persona, Khalil. Consider Adams's description of this prophet:

> Like the dandy and the gentleman, the prophet is a figure of masculine vocation defined in antagonism to the marketplace, or (more broadly) the influence of "circumstances"–whether those by physical constraints or the more subtle undermining of authority inherent in the pressures of respectability, that anxious middle-class decorum that Carlyle called "gigmanity." These models of manhood locate

authority not in action but in rich, charismatic subjectivity, which is intimated in, and in turn reinforced by, an individual's capacity for ascetic discipline.[56]

It is tempting to turn back to Burton and compare him to the dandy, or at least the "one" who is repudiated by the prophet, but for the moment we should stay with this figure with respect to Doughty/Khalil. As Adams reads Carlyle's prescription, the reader of his text, and the new prophet, must undergo a "Selbst-todtung," literally a destruction of self, in preparation for a "new birth."[57] We are aware of this idea in the popular culture of the United States, whether in "born-again" Christian discourse, the jargon of the American New Age movement, or renditions of non-Western religions. It is a death that destroys the exterior in favor of the interior life—the soul—and which clearly values pain over pleasure. Moreover, the mistrust of the exterior also entails a struggle with representation—the exterior, or body of the human subject—and with those of others. This mistrust even bleeds into language. As Adams tells us, "Language [following Carlyle] is not simply incapable of capturing the ineffable force that impels heroic selfhood: it actively enmeshes the hero [prophet] in a web of compromising social relations."[58] And so Carlyle vaunts inarticulate or rude religious-political figures ranging from Cromwell to Luther. Their blunt use of language both realizes this mistrust in the word itself and keeps the enmeshment of others at bay.[59] Indeed, Doughty's difficult style, with its convoluted structures and its deliberate archaisms, suggests a similar strategy.

Convergence

How do the two tangents of Burton and Doughty, the dandy and the prophet, converge? They do indeed converge, though in the early twentieth century and not in the same cultural and social context, as we shall see. In fact, Doughty's text is valuable not at the moment of publication in 1888 but nearly forty years later with the publication of the abridged editions and Lawrence's introduction. Moreover, given Lawrence's imprimatur, surely *Travels* was helped along in the publishing houses and with the reading public by a new and broader interest in things Oriental following the Lawrence-related stage show and pub-lication of *Seven Pillars of Wisdom* (discussed in chapter 5). Another famous literary reader and fan of *Travels* was T. S. Eliot, who by 1920 had established himself as an arbiter of significant literature and mod-ern culture with his journal, *Criterion*, and his position at the Faber publishing firm.[60] In two of his best-known poems, "The Love Song of J. Alfred Prufrock" and "The Waste Land," it is precisely this sort of ascetic persona and ravaged (and ravaging) landscape that Eliot valo-rizes, whether as the prophet-seer Tiresias or in the wasteland, the red rocky landscape described in the latter poem. The target is finally the same as well, for as Doughty opposes his faith and body, with word and deed—in a mortification of the flesh—so Eliot offers us hollow men, the modern man and woman who live yet are dead: modern subjects of routine and everyday language.

The 1920s was a period of new ideas, such as socialism, feminism, and anti-imperialism. All of these ideas and attendant social move-ments are contrary to the ethos and terms of Doughty and this revan-chist Orientalist tradition. Moreover, the mass cultural tendencies of the 1880s are intensified and develop into a global culture of the com-modity, bringing with it other social phenomena, such as a middle class, a middle-class culture, and attendant ways of "being." Doughty and then Eliot in a different way and idiom oppose this modern form of subjectivity, a culture of passivity, surface, and hollowness, with an ascetic notion of heroism founded in a putative return to premodern origins, whether of an essential conception of "Englishness" or the clas-sical tradition of Greece and Rome. The success or failure of Doughty's Chaucerian and Spencerian style is not really relevant, for as a stated gesture this is all we need to know.[61] He wanted to write a book that was not of his time, and to that extent the time and popularity of Doughty's *Travels* has to be later in the 1920s, when it functioned as a kind of popularized text of antimodernity.[62]

The dandy and the prophet, Doughty and Burton, thus share an antipathy to modern life, especially the routine and conformism of everyday life and the culture of the middle class, that is, Matthew Arnold's Philistines. Indeed, in European literature and criticism, a key figure in much nineteenth-century writing about modernity is the dandy, whether in Charles Baudelaire's hero of modern life as a kind of ironic avatar of modernity, a kind of modernist performance artist, or in the abject freedom of Walter Benjamin's flaneur.[63] In reaction to the literary avant-garde of the period, in many ways we might view the Arabs of Doughty's texts as dandies, as superficial and "exteriorized" individuals who are simply incapable of the kind of moral depth and substance of Carlyle's prophet or Doughty/Khalil. With regard to Lawrence, Doughty's champion, this is odd, for he was surely a dandy of sorts—as seen in the photo shoots with Lowell Thomas—and I will address this contradiction in a later chapter. For now Lawrence's union of these opposites, the dandy and the prophet, is notable, though as Adams points out, not surprising when understood dialectically. After all, these two opposites constitute the whole, the totality of a fantasy, and with respect to Burton and Doughty, an Orientalist fantasy.

Yet the convergence of the dandy and the prophet in the early twentieth century is different, at least as a matter of medium and audience. Again, the late 1880s saw a new, mass readership for Burton's *Nights* along with a broad set of consumers for mass-produced Orientalism, whether the pornographic or otherwise titillating postcards and images Sigel and Alloula write about or the stories and images in boys' magazines. But in the early twentieth century this interest expanded in exponential ways as bestselling novels about the Near East were adapted for the stage and then for a new media form, film of the silent era. Edith Hull's *The Sheik* is the most representative and best-known example of Orientalism in British and American mass culture and the best example of this shift. Unlike her male predecessors of the nineteenth century, Hull (a pseudonym for Edith Maude Winstanley)[64] was not of the aristocracy, nor from a wealthy family; rather, she was an otherwise ordinary wife of an English farmer.[65] Indeed, Hull did not even visit North Africa (*The Sheik* is set in Algeria) or the Near East until she and her family were able to do so with her earnings from the hugely popular novel. The novel was popular from the moment she published it in Britain in 1919 and the United States in 1921. As Susan Blake notes, "[I]t was the first novel to appear on the bestseller list two years in a row; by 1965, it had sold 1,194,000 hardback copies," and in the United States it ran through fifty printings in 1921.[66] The story remains familiar today, even for those who have never read the novel or seen the film, which fixed the place of Rudolph Valentino in Hollywood legend. The plot is about abduction and captivity, rape and humiliation, race (miscegenation) and religion (Islam), love, and class. This mix of plot elements might be found in part in other texts, but it is distinctly Orientalist as a group of collected features.

The adaptation of the novel to the screen is shrouded in Hollywood myth, with claims that the suggestion came from producer Jesse Lasky's secretary, and the cost to purchase the rights given variously as $7,500 on up to $50,000.[67] It is certain, however, that the film was a smash hit at the time, breaking attendance records at the two New York theaters where it was screened and bringing in 125,000 viewers in a matter of weeks.[68] Contemporary reviewers were not kind, however. It is significant that these were male reviewers, and that they largely denounced Valentino's effeminate robes and movements, with one dubbing him a "La La" and a kind of male copycat of Theda Bara's persona. Bara was the near originator of the role of the vamp, the consummate Oriental Woman and complement to the Sheik, a dark foreign lover.[69] (Interestingly, Bara's name, a pseudonym, was thought to be an anagram of "Arab Death.")[70] A male version was not acceptable, and as we shall address shortly, it is here that Gaylyn Studlar focuses her work with regard to the place of dance and masculinity in Orientalist mass culture.

The plot of *The Sheik* (the novel) follows the adventure/misadventure of Diana Mayo, an English aristocrat visiting Biskra, an oasis town in northeastern Algeria on the edge of the Sahara Desert. None of the scholars who have written about the novel seem to note that at that time Biskra was not an ordinary tourist destination, but it was infamous as the town of the Ouled Naïl dancing girls and prostitution for foreign visitors, Britons and Europeans.[71] Diana Mayo is very independent and is described as "very slender, standing erect with the easy, vigorous carriage of an athletic boy, her small head poised proudly."[72] She is comfortable shooting guns and fending off suitors of questionable masculinity, such as the wealthy American Arbuthnot (whose name recalls the Orientalist pornographer Foster Fitzgerald Arbuthnot, Burton's publishing partner in the Kama Shastra Society). Diana's brother and guardian, Sir Aubrey Mayo, is anxious to leave Algeria for America in order to search for a wife. As the narrator tells us, he does not care for the company of women and courting and so his sister's company and assistance are necessary, though he recognizes that the trouser-wearing Diana is at least a "Spartan" and hardly feminine in a traditional sense (we are told that in Aubrey's estimation Diana was "a girl by accident of birth only," and she had once "blacked" his eye). Instead Diana, who is clearly the flapper and New Woman of the 1920s, has planned an excursion out into the desert with a native guide, a local man named Mustapha Ali, and without any British male accompaniment—though they all try to dissuade her from leaving. The evening before she is set to leave on her excursion, she ventures out into Biskra alone and, disguised as a local woman (for she would be refused entry otherwise) sneaks into an Arab-"male only" auction of women for marriage. She is spotted by the most important man present, one Sheik Ahmed, who demonstrates that he is a man of wisdom and goodwill when he intervenes on behalf of a young slave girl and her poor lover. When confronted by Ahmed as a possible woman for auction, she is defiant. He immediately recognizes her as a Western woman whom he spied earlier in the day, and so he politely though firmly sends her out of the auction, though he visits her hotel that same evening and serenades her from the shadows, even as the weak Arbuthnot tries to woo her one last time.

The larger part of the novel has to do with the trip into the desert and Diana's abduction. Mustapha Ali, her guide, is apparently in the pay of Sheik Ahmed and he betrays her. On her horse, and though a good rider, she is pursued by Ahmed, and though she is a good rider she is melodramatically plucked from her saddle and placed in front of him, facing his body. The overwrought (and stylistically unremarkable) prose is that of the familiar romance novel, the bodice-ripper type:

> The hard muscular arm around her hurt her acutely, her ribs seemed
> to be almost breaking under its weight and strength, it was nearly

impossible to breathe with the close contact of his body. She was unusually strong for a girl, but against this steely strength that held her she was helpless. And for a time the sense of her helplessness and the pain that any resistance to the arm wrapped round her gave her made her lie quiet.[73]

First-time readers of this novel, certainly in the time of first publication, would have probably picked up on the foreshadowing of this moment, even as we do now, for this act of violence could only lead further to worse violence, sexual violence, which is described only pages later. Ahmed introduces himself to Diana; when she asks why he abducted her, he responds, "Are you not woman enough to know?"[74] After he had admired her beauty when he saw her in Biskra, he had plotted to abduct her, sneaking into her hotel room and exchanging the bullets in her gun for blanks, hence her failure to kill him during the initial chase. Ahmed forcibly kisses her, which we are told is her first kiss from a man, and leaves her for a bit before returning and raping her, as we are told when she reflects on these events the following morning:

> She had fought until the unequal struggle had left her exhausted and helpless in his arms, until her whole body was one agonized ache from the brutal hands that forced her to compliance, until her courageous spirit was crushed by the realization of her own power-lessness, and by the strange fear that the man himself had awakened in her, which had driven her at last moaning to her knees.[75]

Ahmed, she learns, is an odd Arab, for he keeps a French valet and reads French and English literature and journals. Still, despite her ambiguous feelings for Ahmed, she tries to escape but is quickly tracked down and brought back to the camp. Ahmed is not cruel to her, however, and within chapters Diana has been broken, like one of his horses. She loves him and is in fact covetous, fearing other lovers, such as Arab women:

> She knew that she was a fool to expect the abstinence of a monk in the strong, virile, desert man. And she was afraid for the future. She wanted him for herself alone, wanted his undivided love, and that he

was an Arab with Oriental instincts filled her with continual dread, dread of the real future about which she never dared to think, dread of the passing of his transient desire. She loved him so passionately, so completely, that beyond him was nothing.[76]

Even the arrival of Ahmed's closest friend, the writer and French aristocrat Raoul Saint Hubert—Diana has read his work—only shames her, for she does not try to use him to escape. Saint Hubert is horrified at what his friend has done and confronts him about it. While clearly falling in love with Diana as well, he tries to draw her out. They have an interesting discussion of gender relations during which, while Diana argues against inequality, at no point does she tell him about her situation or ask for assistance. The plot is resolved when Diana goes out for a ride with Gaston the valet as an escort, for Ahmed trusts her to not attempt another escape. Indeed she does not try, though they are ambushed by Ahmed's rival, Ibraheim Omair, the robber sheik. He is described in terms befitting the Oriental despot in the worst sense: a slovenly, dirty man, "lolling his great bulk on a pile of cushions" and dressed in once-rich robes now "stained and tumbled."[77] He too intends to rape Diana but, as with all adventure novels, Ahmed and a rescue party arrive at the last minute and save her, though Ahmed is seriously injured. His injury and possible death bring about the twists that made this plot so intriguing to readers of the novel and viewers of the film. Also, as Wintle points out, this moment brings about a series of reversals (and doublings) as Ahmed is now under the care of Diana. He is the lover, while she is now the loved one.[78]

The greatest reversal, however, involves Ahmed's true identity. As Ahmed lies in his sickbed, barely conscious, Raoul tells Diana his story. Ahmed is the son of a Spanish noblewoman "of Moorish blood" and an English father, Lord Glencaryll, a man known to Diana and her family. As his mother told the story, she deserted the father while pregnant and during a visit to Algeria, due to an unknown outrage and his frequent drunken and, we are to believe, violent outbursts. She was found by the older Sheik Ahmed's men and brought to his camp, where she lived for two years, bringing up young Ahmed as the son of the Sheik, though

refusing to marry the latter. When young Ahmed was 15 he was sent
to Paris to military school, under the care of Raoul's father, and after
a while also sent to England for further education with a tutor. At 18
he returned to Algeria and the desert and quickly resumed his previous
life, as Raoul describes him, as an "Arab of the Arabs."[79]

Again, Hull's *The Sheik* is not written in an innovative style, and
she is not an original artist or writer in the narrow sense in which
these designations are frequently used. Hull was a writer of popular
literature, and this novel is nothing more than such, with no pretense
otherwise. Many scholars have pointed this out, and Billie Melman's
strong defense of the novel and the genre, women's "desert romance"
novels, stands out in this respect.[80] After all, this novel and its writer,
Edith Hull, were and remain much more significant in a broader social
and cultural sense than almost all of her male contemporaries in the
British and American modernist canon. Of course, the reason why this
novel was significant in its time is not just that it is a prime example of
Orientalism, but rather that its plot turns on rape and race, which was
an explosive combination then as it is even now. Simply put, Ahmed
rapes Diana, an asexual, androgynous, and otherwise self-certain
young woman, and thereby breaks her spirit, reducing her to a love
slave. Indeed, she is the white love-slave of an Arab, or so the reader
and viewer must believe until late in the novel and film. At the time of
publication the novel was denounced for its salaciousness, and unfavor-
ably compared to de Sade's *Justine*, though compared to de Sade being
imprisoned by Napoleon, there was not the kind of outcry over Hull's
representation of rape and the role this violation plays in the plot, or
that it is perpetrated by an "Arab" at a time when the rape of a white
woman by a black man in D. W. Griffith's *Birth of a Nation* was linked
to deadly race riots.[81] Indeed, in her essay on Orientalist film—and I
will address the film shortly—Ella Shohat offers the denunciation of
the film, and by extension the novel, which we might expect today,
though her emphasis is on the colonialist aspects of the novel and film.
Shohat refers to the novel and film as a "projected Western female desire
for an 'exotic' lover, for a romantic, sensual, passionate, but nonlethal,
play with the *Liebestod*, a release of the id for the (segregated) upper

middle class occidental woman." She concludes that *The Sheik* and its ilk are part of a "disciplinary punishment of female desire for liberation" and demonstrate an "appreciation for the existing sexual, racial, and national order."[82] Clearly Empire and aberrant sex belong together as she reads these texts, and at least in this respect Shohat is correct, though with regard to female desire other critics disagree, and it is not clear that Hull's readers and the film's viewers were as outraged. In deference to Shohat, it is not self-evident that the readers of *The Sheik* were female, nor the viewers of the film, and indeed the idea of a rape sex fantasy is as much a male fantasy as it might be a female sex fantasy.

Sarah Wintle and Patricia Raub both acknowledge this troubling aspect of the novel, but then they turn the plot outrage upside down, arguing, in different ways and respects, that the novel is in fact about the transgressive potential of women's sexuality. Wintle in particular points to the tradition the novel draws upon, especially Hichens's desert romance *The Garden of Allah*, but a tradition also linked to Richard Burton's work of the 1880s as well as the nineteenth-century pornographic novel *A Night in a Moorish Harem* and, I should add, the earlier "hit" *The Lustful Turk*.[83] Possibly with tongue deep in her cheek, Wintle also links the novel to Edith Wharton's otherwise asexual travelogue, *In Morocco*.

In her chapter on *The Sheik*, Susan Blake argues that from the first the novel utilizes the traditional marriage plot of the British novel.[84] She is right, for after all, Diana is unmarried, and the narrative leads us to believe this is a problem, while Aubrey is searching for a wife. Both sister and brother seem to be drifting without their parents' guidance, even though they are both adults and otherwise independent. Ahmed is also the result of marriage problems, for his father was an alcoholic abuser, in contrast to the Algerian sheik who protected his mother when she left him with her young son. This last point is crucial, and I will return to it shortly. Elizabeth Gargano follows the same tack as Shohat, though without the denunciation, and draws upon the sexuality critique of Wintle and Raub and the work of the fin de siècle "sexologist" Havelock Ellis. She concludes that *The Sheik* is finally about the insecurities of "power and potency" of British imperial rule, a conflation of the personal and the political that positions it as a kind of text of displacement or an allegory of the unconscious of the British public.[85]

Sarah Wintle pursued the same point, identifying *The Sheik* as a kind of daydream, In doing so Wintle ironically inverts Q. D. Leavis's elitist dismissal of the novel as a "typist's daydream"; Wintle uses "daydream" in the same sense as Freud also used this word. And so, like in a daydream or just a dream, the text of the novel is a form drawn from the incongruities of everyday life, the residue of the previous day.[86] The daydream, in whatever Freudian sense, is inadequate to best understand the significance of *The Sheik* (in either novel or film form), and for that matter any of the primary examples of British and American Orientalism from this period insofar as these cultural phenomena bring together sexuality and Empire.

An important additional word that applies here is "consumerism." Following Gaylyn Studlar's work on *The Sheik* and the role of dance and mass culture that concerns dance and female desire in the early twentieth century, I substitute "fantasy" for "daydream." First, however, Studlar has struck upon the key to the text and the cultural problem at hand with her insistence on the place of the novel and film in consumer culture, a phenomenon and moment in the history of capitalism and capitalist social relations that was just emerging in the early decades of the twentieth century.[87] Walter Benjamin's work on Atget's photographs of late-nineteenth-century shop windows, as well as T. J. Clark's reading of Benjamin's commentary and the rise of consumer culture, points to a new form of desire, one that explicitly requires an endless process of expressed need and then disavowal, as one is either frustrated or "needs" something newer.[88] It is endless, this form of desire, and explicitly associated with women. Zola was also after this very same idea with his *Au bonheur des dames*. Of course what goes with this new economy of consumerism is the monotony of everyday life and new forms of work, whether the work of the typists dismissed as the readers of *The Sheik*, or the resentful male office clerks who felt their masculinity challenged by the "effeminate" Valentino and other

"Latin lovers" and "lounge lizards" of popular culture.[89] Indeed, the popularity of Valentino, himself the self-professed "slave" of his wife, Natacha Rambova, indicates how we should read mass-produced Orientalism of this period.

It is a mistake to expect coherent form from these texts, for coherence in turn brings us to expect intention. As Marx might have put it, culture is made by men and women, but not as they intend and not with a clear plan in mind. Instead, and now following Freud and Lacan, culture is bricolage and the producer is a bricoleur, putting together the "residue" in a functional, though not coherent, whole. That is *The Sheik* as both novel and film, and as the latter Studlar aptly notes that it brings together images and references to a range of earlier visual culture, whether as stage play, multimedia spectacle, or other silent films.[90] (The scene in the film when Diana first enters the auction of women, and encounters a dancing girl, is certainly one example, suggesting the censored Edison film *Fatima's Cootche Cootche Dance*—and this fact is notable—as well as scenes from Theda Bara's *Cleopatra* and D. W. Griffith's *Intolerance*. Also, Monte M. Katterjohn, the scriptwriter, suggested that the dancer should remain within the limits of the censors, though "rhythmic and undulating.")[91]

Moreover, the text is also a fantasy, and in that sense it is a protective screen. Blake's insistence on the role of race, presumably more so than rape—and rape is not explicit in the film—is correct, but without this sense of fantasy, and with the putative intention of the author in mind, she reads the novel as transgressive in ways it simply is not. With fantasy the reader/viewer can have it all! That Ahmed is really English is part of a tradition of Orientalist writing, and we need only turn to Burton's much-ballyhooed disguise as an Arab/Pathan and to Kipling's *Kim* for earlier examples. Yes, there is some titillation in being mistaken for the other, but the point is that only an Englishman can pretend to be an Arab or be mistaken for one. An Arab can never be an Englishman. As for why an Englishman might want to be mistaken for an Arab, with the place of race in the public discourse of the late nineteenth and early twentieth centuries, again, we turn to Burton who, in his "Terminal Essay," extols the way the Arab man understands the women in his life and is both a good lover and man. An Englishman can have the qualities of the Arab joined with his nobility of spirit and civilized soul, while the Arab is a static being, for as Said points out, for the Orientalist the Orient never changes and is stuck in antiquity, yet, we must presume, the Englishman can change.[92]

Indeed, if there is something that brings together all of the elements of the novel and film under the aegis of an Orientalist fantasy— a protective screen—it is masculinity. Blake hints at this but decides that the novel is about divorce. What she overlooks is that the bad father is not a real man, nor is Aubrey or his friend the limp Arbuthnot, and without a real man in her life Diana has wandered astray and does not feel herself to be a woman according to the novel's norm (and Ahmed's normative desire). What Ahmed has learned from the Father-Sheik is how to be a man and a lover—a "virile desert man," as Diana tells us—and so his masculinity is restored by the primitive and nonmodern, against the diminished men of the West, even the somewhat passive friend, Raoul. Indeed, the Father-Sheik and Ahmed are blends of the Burton and Doughty paradigms, at once capable and skilled with regard to carnal pleasure and women, and at the same time not venal or excessive. Ahmed is the perfect Englishman. In this sense, the novel and film might have outraged some men at the time, but in fact it is hardly a transgressive text, rather more akin to an ideological suture for an otherwise damaged and dysfunctional ideology of Western, or at least British and American, masculinity.

The balance of prophet and dandy in *The Sheik* tilts toward the former. Perhaps, for those who condemned the novel and film as well as its fans, without the fantasy of the lusty Sheik no notice would have been taken. To demonstrate this point we have only to consider a novel and play that entailed more of the prophet and not enough of the lusty sheik: Hall Caine's *The White Prophet*. Apart from his brief foray into melodrama set in the Near East, in this case Egypt, Caine was a successful novelist best known for his novel *The Manxman* (he was from the Isle of Man) and other bestsellers as well as for his "performance" as a late Victorian and Edwardian literary personality. Yet his two attempts to write about the "East" failed terribly. The first was a play, *The Mahdi, or Love and Race: A Drama in Story*, which he produced and staged in 1894, the same year *The Manxman* appeared. Despite the success of the novel, the play bombed. It was staged in Douglas on the Isle of Man, and then at the Haymarket Theatre in London on December 3, 1894. Though only intended as a reading for copyright purposes, it was very badly received in the press. The *Daily News* of December 4, 1894 (I found a copy of the review inserted into the copy of *The Mahdi* at the Huntington Library) reported that the cast included Israel Zangwill, the writer and British Jewish advocate of (first) Zionism and (later) the Jewish Territorial Movement. Oddly, Israel Zangwill himself read the part of the Jewish usurer, an ironic gesture on his part. Indeed the play was intended to represent to a British audience a different and more liberal version of Islam and also, as Caine himself writes, a Morocco for the "Moors, not Spanish, French, or English."

The *Daily News* noted that Caine himself was moving around the theater during the reading like an "unconcerned spectator" and was wearing an "ample cloak" and sombrero, while his face looked like "an unbaked pie crust." The writer's clear dislike for the author, who was known as a self-promoter with a carefully manicured image in all senses of this word, carried over to the 1909 publication of his other work related to the "Orient" and Islam, *The White Prophet*. Like *The Manxman*, this novel was published in Britain by Heinemann, a publisher that was to establish itself later, in our own time, for publishing novels by African writers—as well as an early edition of Joseph Conrad's *Heart of Darkness*—though the publisher's reputation, and that of the novel, did not help the sales. The novel did not sell well at all and only gained attention for the bad reviews in the press and for the objections raised by several Members of Parliament, particularly the comparisons between a Muslim leader and Jesus Christ and a failing senile governor, Lord Nuneham, with the revered Lord Cromer.

The novel is a melodrama concerning the rise of a new imam amongst the poor of Egypt, a man who while educated at the Al Azhar University is very much a man of the people and an Egyptian nationalist. His name is Ishmael Ameer, and the populace proclaims him a new

Mahdi, which in 1909 was certainly a tough topic for the British public. Indeed, the analogy with, first, the Mahdi Ahmed of the Sudan, the historical figure, and then with Jesus Christ, is obvious and rather strained. Ishmael's father was a Libyan carpenter and boat builder who moved to the Khartoum. His earliest memories are of a "white pasha" pacing the roof of the consular palace, looking for relief boats that never arrived. Again, for a British readership of the early twentieth century this is an obvious if not contrived reference to the siege of Khartoum and the eventual death of General Gordon and massacre of the Khartoum populace. Only slightly less obvious is a suggestion of the relationship between Jesus and Mary Magdalene when, while imprisoned for sedition, Ishmael is forced to marry a Coptic Christian woman, an insult that he instead embraced, loving this woman as his wife and inspiration.

The parallel narrative follows the rise of one Charles Gordon Lord, the son of the governor general, Lord Nuneham, and a rising star in the British army in Egypt. When the novel opens, we learn that he has had a longstanding love affair with Helen Graves, the daughter of his commanding officer, General Graves. Gordon, rather like the Orientalist heroes of the nineteenth century, grew up in Egypt, nursed by an Egyptian woman, Fatima, the mother of his closest friend and fellow soldier. Gordon also speaks Arabic and does not hide his love for the Arab world, in contrast to his lover and her father. At one point, echoing her father's sentiments, Helen proclaims that the British army must "Smash the Mahdi," a line lifted from the famous W. T. Stead interview with Gordon in the *Pall Mall Gazette*. It is not surprising then that Gordon defies his superior and argues with him about his plan to attack the new Mahdi's camp, angering the older man so that he assaults Gordon, and in the process falls to the ground and suffers a fatal heart attack.

The death is blamed on Ishmael, who had visited the general earlier in the day. Helen, believing this man killed her father, goes to his camp disguised as an Indian Muslim princess. She speaks Arabic and is familiar with Islam. Ishmael falls in love with her and marries her as his "Rani," though vowing it will never be a carnal marriage. As Helen plots to kill Ishmael, Gordon is also in disguise in the camp, determined to help Ishmael succeed given his support for the liberal and populist brand of Islamic nationalism. The story comes to a head when the Mahdi Ishmael and his people march on Cairo in a nonviolent tax protest and general demonstration against British rule, again suggesting Jesus and Roman rule. He is greeted in the streets, riding astride a donkey, and a military attack and disaster is narrowly averted. In the end Ishmael divorces Helen to help Gordon, and the latter is reinstated into the army and promoted.

The *New York Times* in a September 4, 1909 review was especially snide in its review, subtitling the piece "The Future of Islamism and British Rule in Egypt Presented in Melodramatic Form."[93] The title might have also been a jibe at Wilfrid Scawen Blunt and his *Future of Islam*, but the mention of melodrama certainly undercut the seriousness of Caine's novel. The reviewer points out that analogies between the novel's characters and living politicians (Lord Cromer, for example, Jesus Christ, and a hero named "Gordon" did little for the gravity of the novel, though American readers, the reviewer concedes, might not grasp some of the connotations. The novel is also too long, but mostly, however, the reviewer dismisses the love story. A look at typical passages bears out this criticism and explains the length of the text. Here is a passage from the moment when Ishmael considers sex, so we are to assume, with his Rani:

> "Why what is this, O my Rani? Have we not joined hands under the handkerchief? Are you not my wife? Am I not your husband? It is true that I pledged myself to renunciation. But renunciation is wrong. It is against religion, against God."
>
> He came nearer. She could feel his hot breath upon her face. It made her shiver with the race-feeling she had experienced before.[94]

In his passion Ishmael throws his arms around her and embraces her, only to be pushed away, and finally denounced as a "black man," while she is a "white woman."

Several chapters later Ishmael has visited Gordon and renounced his love for Helen and demanded that Gordon marry his Rani. A bit later he says the same to both of them, praising their true love and concluding by telling Helen three times, "I divorce thee," which the narrator tells us is "the Mohammedan form of divorce."[95]

Clearly *The White Prophet*—and we now know that Ishmael is actually "black" in the eyes of the British occupiers—is not *The Sheik*, for it does not titillate with miscegenation and violent sex. Rather to the contrary, it offers a steadfast refusal of such and substitutes forgiveness and fine sentiments for sentimentalism and sensation.

When the novel provoked a political outcry, George Bernard Shaw defended Caine, but this did little for the novel's sales. Indeed, Caine did not really understand the failure of his novel and instead rounded on his political critics in a self-published pamphlet, "Why I Wrote *The White Prophet*," responding with denunciation of the political dishonesty and incompetence of his critics and their objections to the "teaching" of his book.[96] As for those who criticized its literary qualities, he concedes these are legitimate. He mentions that some referred to *The White Prophet* as "Sunnyside Melodrama," which is possibly an American phrase derived from the location of the early silent film studios in Sunnyside in the Queens borough of New York City.[97] At least at this juncture, in the first two decades of the twentieth century, this sort of liberal-minded novel set in the Near East did not appeal to a broad readership and was not adapted for the stage or screen. But perhaps *The White Prophet* might sell today, albeit with some adjustment and sex scenes added.

The Garden of Allah is an interesting contrast to *The White Prophet*. As a "desert romance," as this subgenre of novels is known, it is a precursor to *The Sheik*.[98] *The Garden of Allah* was written by Robert Smythe Hichens, the author of the bestseller *The Green Carnation* of 1894. (This latter novel was a kind of roman à clef to the decadents of the period; Hichens was also embroiled in the prosecution of Oscar Wilde.) *The Garden of Allah* was also successful as a play and, like *Four Feathers*, was adapted for the film screen, three times: twice in the silent era (1916 and 1927), and in 1936 in a major production produced by Selznick International starring Marlene Dietrich, Charles Boyer, and Basil Rathbone, a major cast then and now.[99] The novel (and the three film adaptations) follows the love adventure of one aptly named Domini Enfilden, an English woman visitor to, again, the Algerian town of Biskra, where she encounters a mysterious and dark Eastern European traveler whose name she finally learns is Boris Androvsky. She is very devout, though sensual in her yearnings, while he rejects the church; he is not an atheist, but he is an ascetic, following the Carlyle/Doughty prophet model. Androvsky avoids Domini at first, and so encourages her interest; when they finally meet, they fall in love very quickly, but do not consummate it sexually. Their love blossoms in the exotic oasis garden of another European expatriate, Count Leoni, who acts as a kind of spiritual father. They eventually marry, but their bliss is abruptly shattered by the appearance of a priest, Father Roubier. They eventually have a sexual union, but it only leads Androvsky to confess his secret past, that he is a fallen monk, having abandoned his Trappist monastery and his vow of silence and celibacy after an encounter with a young woman visitor. At the end of the novel Androvsky returns to his monastery—famous for its wine!—and his vows, while Domini retires to the Count's garden to live a celibate life as well, though with the son she shares with Androvsky.[100]

Sarah Wintle links *The Garden of Allah* to *The Sheik*, though it is different in important ways. Domini Elfilden is worldly and openly desirous, contrary to the asexual Diana Mayo. Also, as Wintle points out, by contrast with Mayo, Elfilden is quite interested in the veiled women and prostitutes of Algeria: in Chapter 8 she watches the dancer Irena perform before Androvsky, who, caught between "his angel in fear" and "his devil," fumbles to place a coin on the dancer's forehead, as per custom. Yet *The Garden of Allah* does not entail even the slightest hint of miscegenation, and there is no violent or nonconsensual sex. Given this, one has to wonder why this novel was successful and was adapted for the stage and screen, and opened the market for *The Sheik*, whereas *The White Prophet* was a failure. Indeed, the latter novel at least included the possibility of miscegenation and sexual violence. I believe the answer lies with the character of Hichens's prose, and that the novel is about female desire, which is then mirrored by male desire. Consider the following passage from Chapter 15:

> She loved Androvsky. Everything in her loved him; all that she had been, all that she was, all that she could ever be loved him; that which was physical in her, that which was spiritual, the brain, the heart, the soul, body and flame burning within it—all that made her the wonder that is woman, loved him. She was love for Androvsky. It seemed to her that she was nothing else, had never been anything else. The past years were nothing, the pain by which she was stricken when her mother fled, by which she was tormented when her father died blaspheming, were nothing. There was no room in her for anything but love of Androvsky. At this moment even her love of God seemed to have been expelled from her. Afterwards she remembered that. She did not think of it now. For her there was a universe with but one figure in it—Androvsky. She was unconscious of herself except as love for him. She was unconscious of any Creative Power to whom she owed the fact that he was there to be loved by her. She was passion, and he was that to which passion flowed.[101]

There is something about this kind of prose, or the feeling it describes, which must have moved readers and then film viewers. Perhaps it is the belabored syntax, suggesting the pace and fever of her thought processes. Moreover, as Wintle has interpreted the narrative of *The Sheik*, the novels hinge on parallels or doublings of love, where Domini/Diana loves Androvsky/Ahmed, who at first do not require their love, though in the end the men finally love under dire and painful circumstances (Androvsky's guilty retreat to the monastery and Ahmed's near-mortal wounds). Love must hurt for all concerned, and all must suffer and renounce something. Indeed, the doubling and renunciation seem to lie at the heart of the attraction of the novel, though we should note that in Hichens's novel, love is expressed by a woman, then by a man, and then disavowed by both; while in Hull's novel, love metamorphoses from an illicit to a most acceptable feeling between a man and woman of the British aristocracy. Hichens, with this final destructive disavowal, even more than Hull seems to have synthesized the prophet and the sybarite, for there is no uneasy sense of reconciliation, redemption, or transcendence.

Today we look back on these novels and the film adaptations with some unease, as relics perhaps or as strange, disturbing, exotic dreams. The tendency is to assume that "that was then, this is now," as though these works are not part of our moment and we have shed this Orientalist legacy. And so much criticism of these novels and films stresses aspects that are important to contemporary liberal politics: race, women, and colonialism. This is understandable, and by no means a mistake, for we must make sense of our culture in meaningful terms. Yet these emphases rest on what, following Paul Gilroy, we might call absolutist discourses of gender, race, and imperialism. But not only is there more to these novels and films, their place in our culture is even more complicated. First, to interpret these novels and films as transgressive and as expressions of women's desire, as feminist texts, is to assume that desire is absolute and not dialectical in a pejorative sense. After all, it is not a theoretical stretch to claim that too often women, along with many oppressed groups, desire what they feel the dominant one or group wants. So desire is not so easily established, though by the same turn it is not absolutely a matter of abjection.

There is some play here that must be untangled, and the same point is relevant to any discussion of race. Race is, of course, entangled with desire, and whatever race might be as a matter of biological or forensic fact is irrelevant to what it means as fantasy, the form desire takes. Moreover, we should not forget that much of popular culture, even the novel in the British and American tradition, is not the place to look for transgression, never mind subversion. Indeed, it is to mass culture that we must look to understand how ideology functions—not as subversion but, in an effective sense, as affirmation of a given dominant ideology (using Marcuse's sense of affirmation). Popular culture, then, affirms dominant ideology, though not without contradiction. And this is where fantasy is important. As I noted earlier, these novels are like a bricolage of ideas and riffs popular in their moment. They are held together by fantasy, a kind of ideological glue. The point at which they do not work as entertainment, or when contradictions are simply too obvious, marks the moment when the fantasy has shifted in form and no longer coheres.

Addressing this interpretive conundrum, in *Colonial Desire* Robert J. C. Young brings together some points that are useful for interpreting the two tangents of British Orientalism represented here by the work of Richard Burton and Charles Doughty. Concerning colonialism and sexuality, and developing the ideas of DeQuincey about Asia, Young writes:

> Colonialism was a machine: a machine of war, of bureaucracy and administration, and above all, of power: "all sorts of engines and machinery . . . expressive of enormous power put forth, and resistance overcome." But as DeQuincey's dreams suggest, it was also a machine of fantasy, and of desire—desire that was constituted socially, collectively as the many examples of Western cultural representations of colonialism have shown us. Colonialism, in short, was not only a machine of war and administration, it was also a desiring machine.[102]

Young takes this idea in several interesting directions, notably the characterization of black men/Africans as sexual machines, capable of excessive, perhaps limitless desire and sensory expression.[103] He does not develop this idea, but it takes us back to *The Arabian Nights'* frame tale, for the partner in near-endless sexual activity is a woman, or women. Female sexuality here is also akin to the endless, the process of repetitive actions. A couple of points come to mind, the first of which is that the narrative is the result of this displaced sexuality, for every night, or at least for 1,001 nights—over three years!—Sheherazad weaves her narratives, which never really end but fold into others, suggesting an orgasm that simply leads to another, with no clear beginning, middle, or end. Only *jouissance*. Young seems to understand where this leads, for the repetitive act, an act without end, is like industrial productive processes and the production and proliferation of commodities, none unique, but "nestling in our hearts" as Walter Benjamin might put it. Young concludes his book with the following strong statement:

For it is clear that the forms of sexual exchange brought about by colonialism were themselves both mirrors and consequences of the modes of economic exchange that constituted the basis of colonial relations; the extended exchange of property which began with small trading-posts and the visiting slave ships originated, indeed, as much as an exchange of bodies as of goods, or rather of bodies as goods: as in that paradigm of respectability, marriage, economic and sexual exchange were intimately bound up, coupled with each other, from the very first.[104]

Young, like Adams, makes some good points here, but in this instance he is determined to avoid psychoanalysis in his interpretation of colonialist ideology, and so he eschews any mention of fantasy in a psychoanalytic sense.[105]

The mixture of race and sex also suggests miscegenation, which, in the United States at least, was a serious issue that provoked riots, lynchings, and civil disorder. D. W. Griffith's film *The Birth of a Nation* is a prime example. Another example is Charles Chesnutt's 1901 novel *The Marrow of Tradition*, about the deadly 1898 race riots in Wilmington, North Carolina. At the root of the riot, which led up to the event and stoked it, is a shared "white" father: a prominent Wilmington man shared between two young women, one "white" and prominent in the town, the other "black." Of course race and sex have a special place and history in the United States, but miscegenation was also a deliberate policy of colonial slaveholders in the Americas and elsewhere. In *Carnal Knowledge and Imperial Power* (2002), Ann Laura Stoler offers detailed research and analysis of such practices as a matter of colonial policy, in Java in particular in the nineteenth century and continuing into the twentieth. Still, I caution against some readings of this sort of work, for it leads to a critique of colonialism that has a rational and moral quality, discounting the level at which colonialism functions on the unconscious of the colonizer and the colonized. Simply put, though Adams and Young are not so instrumental in their analysis, the trajectory of their interpretations leads us to neat conclusions about colonialism and ideology. But if both Burton and Doughty are about

Desire, in affirmation or condemnation, and even share the Orientalist fantasy in many respects, again in affirmation and condemnation,
there has to be more beyond this ideological dead end.

In the introduction to Alain Grosrichard's monumental book *The
Sultan's Court*, Mladen Dolar offers a pithy definition of fantasy as
understood in psychoanalysis and with reference to the fantasy of the
Oriental despot. First, this fantasy, as Grosrichard argues, is widespread in the West and is the kernel of much Enlightenment thought,
particularly that of Montesquieu. Still, what interests both the commentator and writer is the enjoyment factor. The Sultan in question is
certainly a figure of arbitrary power, but most of all a despot of enjoyment who consumes and even wastes an endless flow of desirables,
whether women, food, art, or domains. The flow is one-way, for he is
strictly obeyed by his subjects, who cannot enjoy since he is the "one
who is supposed to enjoy." Yet there is something that exceeds a simple
economy of destruction here, which Dolar and Grosrichard, following Lacan, refer to as an economy of surplus enjoyment. That is, the
subjects who cannot enjoy nonetheless enjoy in another way, and this
surplus enjoyment accrues to the Sultan.[106] The enjoyment of despotic
subjection is grounded in belief, and it is a key feature of the fantasy,
for we need to believe in "their" belief, as Grosrichard recounts in his
readings of (historic examples of) Western attacks on the character
of the Prophet Mohammed and his Muslim followers.[107] Moreover, in
this sense—following the fantasy—Oriental despotism is not a system
of brute force after all, but in terms of the fantasy is all about sexuality
and obedience.[108]

If fantasy according to Dolar and Grosrichard is all about Desire
and the surplus of enjoyment, it also serves a masking or veiling function for something else that cannot find form in the conscious or
unconscious mind. Dolar writes:

> Here we touch upon the Real of the fantasy: the fantasy stands
> in the place of an impossible Real, a void which it disguises and
> discloses in one and the same gesture. This is why fantasy is never

simply a "hallucinatory satisfaction of desire," as it has frequently been described. It contains an evocation of the lack which organizes and supports desire. It does not simply procure a phantasmatic object to satisfy desire, it enables the subject to assume any desire at all. There is a strange loop, a circularity of fantasy: it itself fills the lack which it itself opens up and perpetuates. It opens it by filling it, and can fill it only by constantly evoking it. In a sense, one could say that the fantasy is its own constant "surpassing," "traversing," "going beyond."[109]

Contrary to expectation, at the center of the seraglio is a Sultan who is not an exemplar of fullness, of potency and virility, but rather of impotence. Moreover, the center is displaced to the harem garden, where there gapes the lack and abyss of fantasy.[110] The fantasy is a protective veil that mediates enjoyment and keeps us from the edge of this abyss and an annihilating fall into *jouissance.*

Insofar as I have emphasized material history here, with details about the production of texts and other material mediations in the development of what I have called the "two tangents" of British Orientalism, it seems strange to end in such an abstract, transhistorical place as the unconscious and so nowhere in particular. It is a mistake to think this way, for this Lacanian understanding of the Orientalist fantasy is decisively grounded in history: it is a fantasy and ideology that could only grow and finally blossom in a context of consumer culture. Moreover, in many obvious ways Dolar's description of the economy of the fantasy begs for this line of comparison. What we have outlined here is a crisis of masculinity, with two tangents or models emerging from the work of Burton and Doughty in the 1880s: the dandy and the prophet. By the early twentieth century this crisis of masculinity is clearly about more than "being a man." It is also about a crisis of power—that is, patriarchy and the forms of rule it might take in modern times. The sheik is clearly a kind of natural man, potent and active in a time of impotence, and a master of violence and good manners. What we have here, starting with the work of Burton and Doughty together, as an ensemble, and fully realized in the desert romances of the twentieth century, is a reconciliation of two extremes—the Tyrannical father with the Just Father—and the reinstatement of liberal order. So the fantasy of the virile desert man entails more than a veiling function here. Far from being subversive or an expression of some essential notion of feminine desire, this figure is a protofascist, a strong, potent Father with a pretty face and aristocratic blood lines.

2

Khartoum Nightmare

Popular Literature of the British Campaign in the Sudan

The sand of the desert is sodden red—
Red with the wreck of a square that broke
The gatling's jammed and the colonel dead,
And the regiment's blind with dust and smoke.
The river of death has brimmed its banks,
And England's far, and Honour a name,
But the voice of a schoolboy rallies the ranks—
"Play up! Play up! And play the game!"
—Sir Henry John Newbolt, "Vitai Lampada"

THE VERSE ABOVE was written in 1897, one year before Kitchener "avenged" Gordon—as the victory was then characterized—at Omdurman, where the Islamic nationalist Mahdi Army of the Sudanese Caliphate was systematically wiped out with the heavy use of Gatling guns and artillery and little loss of English life.[1] For several generations, and until recently—and I concede this is anecdotal—this poem was so well known that the reference to the Sudanese war, "The sand of the desert is sodden red," was simply passed over without notice. Indeed, it is possible that "playing up" and "playing the game" is still a part of colloquial speech in Britain, while the literary source of the phrases, this poem, is largely forgotten. The place of the poem and its reference in British popular culture is, then, my first point here. Second, consider the imagery of the poem: a tight cricket match at Clifton College, an elite public school in Bristol, is somehow compared to the horrific

75

British losses of the early 1880s in the Sudan. This analogy between the cricket pitch and the East African battlefield is so daft that it should not even need an explanation—but maybe that is just the point! Perhaps the analogy seems daft from a distant point in culture and time, while for earlier generations of British men, with different notions of masculinity, it was, indeed, all about the "organic" unity of cricket and colonial warfare. I start with this poem, then, to demonstrate just how deeply the Sudanese war and the commodity culture of sports and spectacle, with which it coincided, changed everyday life in Britain and influenced the form and character of culture, high and low, especially mass culture, in the twentieth century.

A massive burst of popular literature accompanied and followed the British war in the Sudan and continued unabated even when the war concluded fourteen years later when Kitchener's forces destroyed the Mahdi Army and regime at the Battle of Omdurman in 1898. This collection of popular literature is of special significance to any history and analysis of British Orientalism, more so than that of the Indian Mutiny, Crimea, or the later Boer War, and specifically marks a break in British Orientalist writing and thought as such. Of particular significance is that this new form of colonialist culture is actually Orientalism for the masses and therefore is found in various forms of mass culture. It is important to trace these various forms of Orientalist literary mass culture about the Sudanese campaign, for in the later stages the tone and reference shifts: the expression of Orientalism becomes more muted as it is absorbed and forms the basis for popular novels and then of films in the late nineteenth and early twentieth centuries.

To that end I will trace this movement with reference to two novels in particular, Arthur Conan Doyle's *The Tragedy of the Korosko* and A. E. W. Mason's oft-filmed but seldom read *The Four Feathers*. This legacy of popular literature would eventually take another turn and be the basis of a much later novel, *Season of Migration to the North*, by Sudanese novelist Tayeb Salih. Salih's novel demonstrates how this particular Orientalist legacy lies dormant yet remains virulent as it infects the consciousness of Mustafa Sa'eed, an otherwise strong-minded Sudanese intellectual of postindependence Sudan. More than many other novels, *Season of Migration to the North* produces, as it were, the subject matter mentioned in the first part of this chapter and makes a most powerful comment on how we must analyze colonial—and thus, post-colonial—culture and its legacy, even today.

Richard Altick writes in the introduction to *The Common Reader* that "the history of the mass reading audience is, in fact, the history of English democracy seen from a different angle."[2] That angle is apparent only a page later when he cites other common readers, such as unemployed and dispossessed workmen, a rheumatic street sweeper, and a working-class gathering in a London locksmith's shop. This aspect of his project relates to the work of Raymond Williams and his rich legacy of cultural studies. Yet, in their moment, both critics had to argue for popular culture—or alternative readings of elite culture—against narrow establishment notions of literature and art.[3] What they did not investigate, and have left to their critical legacy, is the pernicious role of mass culture as a constitutive basis and source of knowledge, which functions in a dialectic with its liberatory and populist potential, especially its grounding in Empire and the Near East.

When we turn to British Orientalism and literary production around the Sudan Campaign, we see some of the same issues and themes and, in a strange but familiar way, from the same angle, the point of view of the masses. Many argue that the rise of mass and commodity culture in Britain during the 1880s and 1890s coincided with the Sudan War to such an extent that the cultural epoch and the event cannot be separated. For the last decade or so, there has been renewed interest in the Sudan War and its connection to commodity culture, such as a recent article by Richard Fulton, "The Sudan Sensation of 1898." Fulton offers an interesting and very well researched essay on the "Sudan Sensation" of the post-Omdurman (1898) decade or so, when the British public reveled in "sensations" or multimedia spectacles. These events were, of course, examples of cultural triumphalism that also "educated" generations of schoolboys in military and colonial jargon—Gatlings, Maxims, and Henry Martinis. Though Fulton does not mention it, these spectacles certainly distracted public attention from the ongoing troubles in the African colonies, such as the disastrous Boer War.[4] There were also many plays about the Sudan that Edward Ziter documents in his book on British Orientalist drama at the fin de siècle, *The Orient on the Victorian Stage*. Most important here, Ziter emphasizes that these Sudan plays did not focus on the brutally efficient triumph of Kitchener, but on Gordon's martyrdom, either as replays of the Fall of Khartoum or in rewriting history so that Gordon prevailed. I will return to this later, for it suggests that the public interest was stronger in a perceived and "felt" defeat than in total victory.[5]

What both Fulton and Ziter document, however, is that the fourteen-year-long Sudan Campaign marked a central moment in the rise of British popular and commodity culture. Though Anne McClintock does not refer specifically to the Sudan Campaign in her groundbreaking book *Imperial Leather*, she identifies the mid-1880s as the moment when the commodity culture fully emerged in Britain and argues that it must necessarily be understood in tandem with colonial politics for the masses. With exceptional insight into popular culture, McClintock points to soap advertisements, especially for Pears soap, as they are marketed to the working and middle classes. These advertisements thus bring together internal domesticity and the bourgeois household with the "dirt" of the colonies, marking the advent of a particularly visceral blend of mass politics. In a related essay, Janice Boddy affirms McClintock's argument and, as with the argument here, points to a particular incident when British soldiers reproduced Pears soap and Eno Fruit Salts advertising slogans on opposing Sudanese hillsides, underlining the extent to which the war was about the spread of commercial signs and colonial semiotics as much as the commodities concerned.[6] Of course there is also the consciousness of British soldiers, colonized in a different way by these new wrapped and packaged commodities. What McClintock, Boddy, and Fulton do not address, however, is the extent to which these two decades of the colonial commodity and the Sudan Campaign were grounded first in texts, whether as advertising slogans, newsweeklies, or novels.

As for how we treat the Sudan Campaign, history, and British culture at the end of the nineteenth century, the war against the Mahdi was fought in two stages. In apparent contradiction to a history of rupture and break, I argue that it is in the first stage that we find the markers and ideas that will blossom and develop in the second. This is not to argue for continuity, as though the flower were the seed. There is a connection, but specificity and bracketing are crucial for any meaningful interpretation and understanding here. To that end, the following is a very brief narrative of the two stages and the role of mass culture in the first; the emphasis here is with the first stage of the campaign as I will explain.

The Mahdi emerged in the early 1880s and quickly gained a following of the devout and disaffected, as many were angry with Anglo-Egyptian taxes and the ban on the slave trade. By 1884 the Mahdi Army was large and growing, especially after the annihilation of the British Egyptian troops under Hicks Pasha. In early 1884 Gordon was sent to Khartoum to arrange the evacuation of Europeans, but once there he changed his mind, thinking he could beat a siege by the Mahdi Army. By February 1885, Khartoum had fallen and Gordon was dead. Gladstone did not respond immediately—he had no love for Gordon anyway—but appointed General Kitchener to take measures to defeat the Mahdi. The latter carefully built a railroad and supply system and nearly fourteen years later, at the Battle of Omdurman, decisively destroyed the Mahdi's Army, its leadership, and the Caliphate.[7]

In order to understand the rise of the later popular literature and novels of the 1890s, such as Conan Doyle's *Tragedy of the Korosko* and Mason's *Four Feathers*, we must look back to the prewar and wartime coverage in the *Illustrated London News* and the *Pall Mall Gazette*. The root of these novels in this early reportage is what I call "the condition of literary possibility," and it also demonstrates the shift and consolidation of thought around the war in the Sudan. For now, however, consider this: These two newspapers covered the events as reports and coverage were received. When the information ended, so did the published commentary, as these publications looked elsewhere for news to feed their readership. Indeed, and notably, the Fall of Khartoum was accompanied by controversy over Irish nationalist and anarchist "outrages," as terror events were known at the time, and English readers of the time were as obsessed with Irish nationalists as they were with

Sudanese Islamic nationalists.[8] After Gordon's death literary production shifted. There was a spate of books on the conflict, mostly about Gordon and the Mahdi, as well as various captivity narratives. The most famous of the latter is *Fire and Sword in the Sudan: A Personal Narrative of Fighting and Serving the Dervishes: 1879–1895*, a work by the Anglo-Austrian military man and diplomat, Pasha Rudolf Slatin.[9] Within a year of Gordon's death, writers were turning out biographies—really hagiographies—about the newfound martyr of the Empire. Gordon's posthumous fame was great, with fans in the royal court (including Victoria herself) and in the streets among the working and middle classes. Books about Gordon and the Mahdi continued to be published through the turn of the century. In some ways Strachey's inclusion of Gordon in *Eminent Victorians* marked the end of the martyr cult and public hysteria, due to the author's wry tone.

The third phase of literary production at the time of the Sudan Campaign lies with the novels mentioned above. These two novels are notable for the celebrity author of the *Tragedy* and the film history associated with *Four Feathers*. Yet there were other immensely popular—in all senses of this word—novels about the Sudan, such as George Alfred Henty's boys' novels *Dash for Khartoum* and *With Kitchener in the Sudan*. Late-nineteenth-century author Henty published numerous novels for boys—and a few for adults—where, by means of historically based narratives, he instilled the Christian values of the Empire as he knew and supported them. During a brief term as the editor of *Union Jack*, he pushed his cause even harder in that weekly boys' magazine, in addition to publishing some of his books in serial form. It is not surprising then that though I could not find any boys' magazine stories about the Sudan Campaign, especially from issues produced in the mid-1880s, Henty did write two related boys' novels, *Dash for Khartoum* and *With Kitchener in the Sudan*. *Dash* was written in 1891, six years after the Fall of Khartoum, while *Kitchener* was written in 1903, some five years after the destruction of the Caliphate at Omdurman. Given that both novels are for boys, and my concern here is with adult audiences, I will not address them at any length, only note that both involve lead characters who go native, in this case Arab and Dervish, by either staining their skin, as in *Dash;* or via a life decision, as in *Kitchener*, when the father of Gregory moves with his wife and baby boy, the hero of the story, to Cairo. The central idea here is that though a Briton of good birth grows up in Cairo, or looks like an Arab, his good birth, his blood, will see him through and cause him to stand out and up in key moments. This plot element is not new, and not specifically tied to Orientalism, except to the extent that the dangers of being mistaken for one of "them," the forced conversion to Islam, are existential, while the triumph of rising above the color of skin and upbringing is total. In this sense we see a trajectory of going "other" from Scott and Dickens to Kipling and numerous nineteenth- and early-twentieth-century popular travel narratives.

One might expect the boys' magazines of the period to include stories about the war in the Sudan or its heroes, Gordon and Kitchener. Surprisingly, a review of issues of *Magnet, Boy's Own Paper, Marvel, Gem,* and *Union Jack* from this first period yielded no stories specifically Sudan-based, only small news pieces and appeals for Gordon-related charities. This lacuna is notable given the place of Gordon's martyrdom in the greater adult mass culture of Britain in the time, and especially since Henty was the editor of *Union Jack*, which was unambiguously dedicated to promoting the Empire and colonialist values. Indeed, this boys' magazine even organized Boy Scout troops around Empire-related projects.

Yet none of these imaginative works were possible without a certain textual groundwork—again, what I call the condition of literary possibility. In particular, these other texts are two well-known newspapers, the *Illustrated London News* (*ILN*) and the *Pall Mall Gazette*. The *Illustrated London News* was founded in 1842 by Herbert Ingram with the popular market in mind. Ingram noticed that newspaper sales increased when accompanied by woodcuts, so news stories in the *ILN* were thereafter paired with drawings and related illustrations.[10] By 1862 the *ILN* weekly magazine had a circulation of 300,000, dwarfing the circulation of other dailies and weeklies. Also by the early 1880s the *ILN*, like other news-oriented publications, was covering the activity of the British army in Egypt; the suppression of the Arabi rebellion and bombardment of Alexandria; and the protection of the Suez Canal, Britain's best route to the colonial gem, India. A serialized story by William Black titled "Yolande," a melodrama about a young British woman, was featured in the *ILN* during the period. As the woman's romantic life progresses so do her travels, and she spends a good deal of time in the Mediterranean, especially in Egypt.[11]

The *ILN* also ran frequent articles about daily life in Egypt, a form of popular ethnography that was notably about the lives of poor people, informing the reading public and creating a kind of "knowable community."[12] One related series from the period is "Scenes from Cairo," which detailed the daily life of Cairenes, and of course these articles were accompanied by illustrations (this is "illustrated news," after all). For example, one tandem of article and illustration is about mat making and the dance of the stick in the streets of Cairo. Street Arabs indeed. By late 1883, however, the attention of the editors shifted to the Sudan and the Upper Nile, a region relatively unknown to most Britons. To that end the newspaper provided articles and drawings of notable sites on the Nile as well as other points of interest such as Asfouan, Jebel el Ain, and Jebel Abu Sinun. The latter two were near Kordofa where Colonel William Hicks (a.k.a. Hicks Pasha) and his dispirited and poorly supplied Egyptian troops—the remnants of Arabi's defeated army—were slaughtered, searing these names into the consciousness of many in the British reading public. When Hicks and his European officers were killed in action, the *ILN* offered portraits of the players, information on the battle, and more illustrations (December 4, 1883, front page). By December 1883 the illustrations about the Sudan were becoming more and more jingoistic and racist in their appeal. One illustration from December 1, 1883, titled "Exultation" (by S. Berkley), shows a Sudanese cavalryman throwing his sword in the air, clearly exulting—in the death of British soldiers, we are to assume. We still see this sort of image when, after some horror in the Middle East, Western photographers seek "exulting" Palestinians or Iraqis. Another notable illustration, featured in the December 24, 1883 *ILN*, is titled "The War in the Sudan: A Dervish Preaching the Holy War to Arab Chiefs." In this caption alone we have the identification of an enemy type, the dervish; his activity; and the nature of that activity. Here alone the audience learns how to read, how to know the Sudan and the British campaign in the region: it is a simple matter of British soldiers against Islamic madmen. In a similar vein, a December 15, 1884 illustration tells readers about another element in the Sudanese War, the Bashi Bazouks. It shows a group of Sudanese warriors kneeling in prayer in their head wraps and clothing—the famous jibbah—looking both fierce and devout.[13]

While the *ILN* continued to cover the campaign and the fall of Khartoum, it was not singular in its attention to the issues of the day. Under the editorship of W. T. Stead, the *Pall Mall Gazette* was immensely successful for a middlebrow daily newspaper, with a circulation of nearly 12,000 in the early 1880s, tapping into the new middle-class readership that subscribed to, say, *Nineteenth Century*.[14] In many ways the *Pall Mall Gazette (PMG)* was a historic text, for it not only set the tone of public response to the campaign but also, in a harbinger of recent war-related media tactics, set out to create consensus and even change official policy on behalf of Gordon. It was also innovative in content, particularly utilizing the interview and other types of coverage. From 1883 with the destruction of Stewart's units through the fall of Khartoum and the martyrdom of Gordon, *PMG* offered almost daily coverage of the conflict. A good deal of this coverage was on the front page of the newspaper, and if not there were always related articles inside. Again, the types of coverage are remarkable. Stead pioneered the use of the interview with the major players, gaining opinion and making news through direct contact with the source. In particular, Stead interviewed "Chinese Gordon" himself, just prior to his departure in 1884 for Khartoum.[15] In the interview, Gordon hinted at his disagreement with Gladstone's policy in the Sudan—the role of the Egyptian khedive, slavery, and how to handle the evacuation of the city. Stead went further and allowed Gordon to outline his assessment of the situation in the Sudan and propose alternative tactics. This was surely a confrontational and newspaper-savvy move by Stead, with the initial intent to cover news, and then make news and money, simultaneously.

Starting with Hicks's defeat and extending through 1885, the newspaper also provided expert information, which included June 3, 1884 background essays on the Mahdi and his origins, Mahdism and Islam, and the Sudan. (Mahdism is an Islamic belief in a prophesied redeemer; Muhammad Ahmad, a leader of the Samaniyya order, proclaimed himself the Mahdi in June 1881; his insurrectionist movement was called the Mahdiyya.[16]) *PMG* published British expert opinion as well as writers from the region, including both Egypt and the Sudan. Also, in a nod to the *ILN*, on March 3 and 10, 1884, the newspaper published images of battle diagrams showing the movement and formation of troops in both camps, as well as detailed analysis of the battle plans and results. An August 10, 1884 article was even centered on a drawing of a captured Mahdi flag, including a translation of the Arabic inscription.

As the siege of Khartoum continued, the front page was the place to look for the latest news. Like a good serial novelist, Stead and the *PMG* editors built up anticipation with headlines and coverage that satisfied readers but left them wanting more. Some headlines are memorable, either for their confrontational tone (e.g., "Gladstone as Destroying Angel," February 24, 1885, front page) or somber tone ("Too Late!" on February 5, 1885, p. 8, announcing the fall of Khartoum and the probable death of Gordon).

Also of note, Wilfrid Scawen Blunt, the well-known world traveler, poet, writer, and husband of Lady Anne Blunt, used *PMG*'s pages to advance his own solution to the siege of Khartoum. In a December 18, 1884 article in the newspaper and then later in a series of letters, he proposed to use his contacts within the Arab and Muslim world to arrange a meeting with the Mahdi and work out a lifting of the siege and safe passage for all foreigners in Khartoum. Blunt himself later authored a number of related books, including *The Future of Islam*, *The Secret History of the Occupation of Egypt*, and *Gordon at Khartoum*, where he detailed his meetings with Gordon as well as his attempt to land in Egypt. He was thwarted when threatened with immediate arrest if he left his steamer. Blunt represents the "respectable" aspect of popular writing. Though he was certainly someone who took advantage of what we might now identify as proto-middlebrow newspapers and journals, such as *PMG* and, again, *Nineteenth Century*, Blunt retained a certain aristocratic and intellectual reserve and remove.[17] He wrote for a mass audience but was definitely not of the masses.

All of this coverage laid out the structural and ideological characteristics that mark the subsequent production of mass culture, whether in text or packaged goods. With regard to textual examples, we move from boys' novels to adult adventure fiction: *The Tragedy of the Korosko* by Arthur Conan Doyle and a novel of Orientalist romance, *Four Feathers*.

Like Henty, Conan Doyle was a highly successful popular writer; also like Henty he followed his own successful formula with the Sherlock Holmes stories. The story turns on opposing scenes: The deck of the tourist steamer, the Korosko, is set up for tea, with elegant furniture and china, in contrast to the harsh heat and topography of the desert. Yet *The Tragedy of the Korosko* is little more than a cliffhanger type of adventure story set in the Sudan, where Doyle deployed all of the elements introduced in the press coverage of the Sudan Campaign in the early 1880s and in popular literature thereafter. Again, to that extent, and for lack of a better way of expressing this point, *Tragedy* is structured like a porn narrative, for the plot is simply a familiar, well-worn frame upon which scenes are threaded. Indeed even the scenes, the moments of the novel, are familiar, though grounded in the near twenty-year-long discourse of the conflict. The characters are not developed in depth nor with any complexity or interest as required for the players in popular stories. Indeed, there is no complexity of any sort in this novel, only stereotypes and well-trodden narrative ground. Consider, for example, the spinster auntie from Boston, Miss Adams, who—of course—is constantly concerned with cleanliness and complains about the dirty Sudanese, flies, and tries to clean one poor villager's house! And the Frenchman, Fardet, is whiny, duplicitous, arrogant, and disagrees with British foreign policy. When the group is initially surrounded by the Mahdists he shouts, "*Vive la Khalifate, Vive le Mahdi!*" Fardet's antagonist, Colonel Cochrane, recently retired from the British army, is similarly a known type. He is, it seems, the mouthpiece for Conan Doyle (who volunteered his services as a doctor during the Second Boer War, serving in the field for four months).[18] Consider the following passage where he describes British policy in the Near East:

> I am not a rich man . . . but I am prepared to lay all I am worth, that within three years of the British officers being withdrawn, the dervishes would be upon the Mediterranean. Where would the civilization of Egypt be? Where would the hundreds of millions [of British pounds] be which have been invested in this country? Where the monuments which all nations look upon as most precious memorials of the past?[19]

He and one of the Americans—Headingly, who is eventually killed by the Mahdists—agree that it is the "unpleasant" duty of the English-speaking nations to take care of "sick" countries, recently Greece and Spain, and now Egypt and the Sudan. As the American declares, "Each has his own mission."[20] But then the East never changes, as Cochrane makes clear.

We should not forget that these are tourists, on a packaged tour of the sort we now take for granted as part of middle-class life—Thomas Cook started tours to Egypt and the Near East in the 1860s.[21] Moreover, they follow a *Baedeker Guide* to the region, and they are for the most part interested in the ancient sites, not the present people. While touring one site, Abousir, they are attacked by the Mahdists, and as the coverage would have it, the latter appear as they should. They wear the patchwork tunic of the movement, the jibbah, a sign of Muslim piety and commitment, and are armed with spears and guns. They are a mix of Arabs and black Africans, known in the text as "negroes," and their leader is tall, thin, sports a long beard, and has a "piercing" gaze. Years later, and probably working with the same popular sources, Strachey described Mohammed Ahmad, the illiterate preacher from the Nile island of Dongala, as a tall, dark Sudanese man with a long black beard, big eyes, and a "piercing" gaze.

Of course, like Gordon before them the tourists are offered a deal where they can convert to Islam or die. They stall the process by debating with an elderly and befuddled imam. The tourists are eventually freed by the combination of bribes to former Egyptian soldiers in the Mahdist group and an attack from the Egyptian camel corps. As the Mahdists are surrounded and shot by the British forces they dismount from their camels, stand on their prayer rugs, and prepare to die, information that Colonel Cochrane relates to the women in the group—obviously derived from these same early 1880s press reports from the battlefield.

Two *PMG* articles are important when we turn to A. E. W. Mason's *Four Feathers*. In one 1883 article the design of the Maxim gun was challenged. By the end of the Sudan Campaign Kitchener had demonstrated its deadly and grotesque capabilities, wiping out the Caliphate's fighters in a matter of hours. Thousands of dead littered the battlefield near Omdurman. A contemporary photograph shows the leadership of the Caliphate lying dead on the ground, riddled with British bullets. Though effective warfare, this was clearly not the sort of victory image to be vaunted, for it really looked like the revenge scene so longed for after all those years, bloody and swift. To the contrary, with *Four Feathers*, written in 1902, we see the way the Sudan Campaign was supposed to be remembered, rooted firmly in the lead-up to the siege of Khartoum and then the martyrdom of Gordon. In fact, *Four Feathers* is really a love story, a kind of colonialist melodrama.

The story concerns Harry Faversham's apparent betrayal of his friends. When the story starts, he is at a ball with friends when word arrives that their regiment is to be called up for the relief of Gordon. Harry, due to marry Ethne, has already resigned his post, but he does not tell his comrades. When they find out they send him three feathers, which he receives in Ethne's presence. She asks him if he did act out of cowardice, and not for her. Harry is so honorable that he takes on the stigma of dishonor—cowardice—rather than have Ethne think he did this for her, for love. She hands him a fourth feather from her hat. The story centers around Harry's disappearance from society and then the country as he attempts to return the feathers to his comrades in the Sudan, even as his best friend Jack returns from the war, blinded—and intent on courting Ethne. The story starts, notably, with young Harry listening to his father and his Crimean War comrades recount their deeds at Redan, where British soldiers charged the Russian trenches in a very different kind of warfare. One of his father's friends, Sutch, extends himself to help Harry through his struggle, despite the stigma he bears. So, first, this is a novel about love lost and regained, as Harry eventually returns and Jack cedes his place in Ethne's life. And it is even more about friendship—not just friendship between soldiers, but soldiers as boys and men, young and old. Even in the Sudan Harry has a close friend, notably an Arab, named Abu Fatma who, following the stereotype of the loyal native, is honorable and brave beyond expectation and culture. Almost English!

Pushing further, two ideologies are at play here; first is the narrative of lost cause, and then the story of betrayal. So *Four Feathers*, though adapted as a film four times, is not really about the nitty gritty of the Sudan Campaign. The recent adaptation with Heath Ledger does great injustice to the novel, for a good deal is set in the Sudan, with dusty East African towns and scorching desert dunes. Again, this is what we want now, or so the producers seemed to believe. The better part of the novel takes place in drawing rooms in Britain and—notably—Ireland. The scenes from the Sudan are in fact often found in accounts told by various characters.

Just as the literature of the Sudan Campaign dwells on the early days of the war, and so evades its bloody resolution with Kitchener's victory, this emphasis also breathes life into the ideology of lost cause. By "lost cause" I refer to the defeat of an unquestionable and pure "good" and noble entity, whether a state, movement, or person representative of both. D. W. Griffith's *The Birth of a Nation* turns on this idea, romanticizing the antebellum Old South and its "pure" values against the injustice of the Northern occupation government. Gordon the outspoken and consummate Christian warrior of the Empire represented such a cause, and with his defeat launched a movement of lost cause. In some ways with his death, Gordon exceeded the Empire in fact and became its embodiment, producing a split where Gladstone, though prime minister, was somehow perceived as an alien agent. (Perhaps the public grief over Princess Diana's death is similar, where in the popular imagination she represented the royalty more than the queen herself.) Of course, a lost cause is even sweeter when mixed with betrayal. So the Old South was betrayed by poor leadership and Yankee conniving, and Gordon was betrayed by Gladstone and Cromer. There is abundant literature on this same point, and as already noted, Blunt himself wrote as much in his *Gordon at Khartoum*.

Four Feathers does not owe the same obvious debt to the literature of the Sudan Campaign as Henty's novels or *The Tragedy of the Korosko*, though its ideological and structural debt to the earlier writing is substantial. Also, *Four Feathers* is not written for boys or for the same popular audience that Conan Doyle usually reached. *Four Feathers* is literary in the usual ways, with carefully drawn and complex characters, and though it turns on a melodramatic and predictable plot, it does not seem a common story. In a nod to the popular imagination, Harry does deliver his feathers in disguise, taking us back to Burton's journey in "Arab" drag in *Pilgrimage to Mecca and Medina*, but he is disguised as a Greek musician, a zither player, who plays badly at that. Harry does not go all the way, as it were. Instead the novel's debt to our tradition is ideological and lies in the narrative, with its tale of lost cause and betrayal, rather than in details and words.[22] There are no bashi bazouks, dervishes, or long explanations of Mahdist custom. I suggest then that the novel is finally critical of the war and Empire, but that this opposition is implicit. If the values that emerge in *Four Feathers* are on the one hand embattled—the lost cause—and on the other hand fundamental and exclusive from the government or community as the state, then the novel is against the war. The war is about bad ends that upset decent people and cost human lives. Ironically, it is in the midst of mass society and through a mass cultural form that such humanist values are conveyed.

Mass Culture and the Consciousness of the Postcolonial Subject

When Mahmoud Wad Ahmed was brought in shackles to Kitchener after his defeat at the Battle of Atbara, Kitchener said to him, "Why have you come to my country to lay waste and plunder?" It was the intruder who said this to the person whose land it was, and the owner of the land bowed his head and said nothing. So let it be with me. In that court I hear the rattle of swords in Carthage and the clatter of the hooves of Allenby's horses desecrating the ground of Jerusalem. The ships at first sailed down the Nile carrying guns not bread, and the railways were originally set up to transport troops; the schools were started so as to teach us how to say "Yes" in their language.[23]

The memory and cultural forms that developed from and were associated with the Sudan Campaign persisted through the twentieth century, as I argued at the opening with reference to "Vitai Lampada." In *Season of Migration to the North*, Sudanese novelist Tayeb Salih makes this point and others in a dramatic and memorable way, through relating the life stories of two Sudanese intellectuals who try to "return" to village life along the Nile in the Sudan. In this respect Salih's novel produces the material culture and history I have documented here, and demonstrates the astonishing extent to which it influenced British and postcolonial Sudanese culture well through the mid-twentieth century.

Season of Migration to the North was originally published by Salih in Beirut in Arabic in 1967. When the novel was translated into English (1969), Salih gained a larger Anglophone readership, which has remained strong to the present day. As a kind of Sudanese retort to Conrad he uses a double narrator format, with the story of Mustafa Sa'eed and his voyage into the metropole as an academic inside the nameless narrator's tale of return to "his" village on the Nile. Some argue that the double narrator format can also be traced to the *hakawati* narrative forms of Arabic literature.[24] While I do not doubt this as one aspect of the novel's form, its debt to Conrad's *Heart of Darkness* is obvious and overdetermines how we can read it. The use of the river (the Nile for the Congo) and the opposition of the colonial metropole to the colony limit how we read the double narrator and narrative. There are even common phrases and allusions, such as to a "bend in the river," which, while common in another sense, lead the English reader back to Conrad's text. Even the opening lines remind informed readers more of Marlow, the narrator of *Heart of Darkness*, sitting cross-legged, palms out like an Eastern mystic, as he weaves his tale and addresses his listeners—gentlemen—than of a *hakawati* telling a story in an "authentic" coffeehouse of the past.

Indeed, *Season* is a complex of interwoven Western and Arabic literary forms, the novel and, again, *hakawati* traditions, combining poetry and prose with shifts in narrative voice and time, all as clever, ironically perhaps, as any high modernist text. Apart from textual links we should also note that the publisher of the English translation, Heinemann, also published the first separate edition of *Heart of Darkness* as well as other colonialist and Orientalist fiction of in the early twentieth century. By the 1960s Heinemann had shifted its ideological stance and established itself as the premier publisher of African literature in English, which it is today.

The use of the double narrator/narrative, the parallel stories of Mustafa Sa'eed and the unnamed narrator, both British-educated academics who have "returned" to a village on the Nile in the Sudan, invites extended comparisons to *Heart of Darkness* and Conrad's doubles, as well as to doubles and mimesis and Freud's uncanny. All of these responses to the text are profitable in one way or another, though in so many ways these two narrators and their stories are not really the same. Simply put, the narrator is prudish, cautious, judgmental, sentimental, and passive, whereas Mustafa Sa'eed is the opposite in every respect; when there is overlap, the life of Mustafa Sa'eed quite exceeds that of the narrator. Indeed, if this is the narrator's story as well, then it should be decidedly boring, hence the focus here. No, this is Mustafa Sa'eed's story, a fatherless child of Omdurman, born in 1898 (the year of Kitchener's victory and the demise of the Caliphate). He was educated at the college named after the martyr of Khartoum, Gordon College, and then at Victoria College in Cairo—now post-Nasser, known as Victory College; and finally in the metropole of the Empire in Bloomsbury at the University of London.[25] He disappears the year of Sudanese independence, 1956. As with the period—historical, cultural, and political—Mustafa is from nowhere in Sudan but he is Sudanese, and "from" there, as much as the villagers or the resentful narrator. In all of these senses, we must take the Sudanese War into account for any meaningful interpretation of the novel.

On the other hand, and for the most part, the scant scholarly criticism of the novel (in English) has focused on its debt to Shakespeare's *Othello* and on the cultural and literary aspects of the novel with respect to its relationship to Arab and British literature. In particular, Mona Takieddine-Amyuni's volume of essays on the novel develops along these thematic links, while more recently Saree Makdisi and Benita Parry have complicated the place of the novel in postcolonial fiction.[26] By place I refer to the same Arab and British literary roots, and in particular the idea of an "East" set against a dominating "West." Makdisi in particular sets out to undo previous work and reassert what he argues is the unique feature of the novel, its resolute refusal of this East–West binary. The novel in this sense is not simply about a "modern" West and a "primitive" East, as much literary and cultural criticism might have it, but rather synthesizes the dialectic through its two British-educated Sudanese narrators. In fact, as he writes, the space of the novel offers a middle ground, a third area:

> The novel lies between the traditional categories of East and West—that confusing zone in which the culture of an imperial power clashes with that of its victims—the antithetical relationship between which provides much of its driving force.[27]

Following Edward Said's work on the postcolonial intellectual, Makdisi goes on to note that Mustafa Sa'eed (and the narrator by extension) is the consummate native (or postcolonial) intellectual who is caught between the two binaries—colonizer–colonized and East–West—and so attempts to subvert or otherwise bring about some form of revolutionary synthesis. To this end the figure of the postcolonial intellectual—a writer, professor, or professional intellectual—might affirm some notion of traditional culture against the taint of the West, only to find this an empty and futile gesture. This is exactly as Frantz Fanon warned in *The Wretched of the Earth*. Makdisi's reading of the novel is one of the subtlest and most sophisticated to date. But he does not emphasize one major feature of the novel, which is that both Mustafa Sa'eed and the narrator never really belonged in any meaningful sense—or, to echo *Heart of Darkness*, like the cannibals on the deck of Marlow's steamer, they are out of "place." While he even refers to the passage where the narrator asserts that he is "from here just like the palm tree in the courtyard of our house," Makdisi does not point out that the villagers never really accept either the narrator or Mustafa Sa'eed. They are accepted with limits and conditions, but fundamentally remain outsiders. Perhaps this point is best found in the exchanges between the narrator and his childhood friend, Mahjoub, about the fate of Hosna, Mustafa Sa'eed's wife. His refusal to accept the customs of the village and larger culture concerning women mark the narrator as an outsider both in the eyes of the village and his own self-perception. He might be "from" and "in" the village, but the narrator is not "of" the village.

Benita Parry takes us in another direction, as she dismisses Makdisi's spatial analysis—incorrectly, I maintain—and emphasizes the complexity of the narrative, with its interwoven though diverse set of literary and cultural traditions and references along with the frank and disturbing sexual content of the novel. She comments at the outset that the novel's "singular unfolding of theme and meaning makes it at once legible and opaque."[28] As might be expected, she elaborates this point, as did Makdisi before her, pointing out that *Season* draws on multiple narrative and literary traditions and what she calls "disparate discourses" with "contradictory registers."[29] Parry is right in her reading at this juncture, but then it follows that *Season* is a modernist, if not a "high" modernist, novel. So, in form and genre the novel is written under the aegis of irony, a stance that doubles back and bites the tradition Salih has drawn upon—the bite of a poisonous snake indeed. Parry even cites the moment at the end of the novel when the narrator recounts his decision to live by "force and cunning," yet overlooks the reference to Stephen Dedalus's decision, in Joyce's (modernist) *A Portrait of the Artist as a Young Man*, to live by a code of "silence, exile, and cunning."[30] Also, her comments on the "archaic within modernity" and the "duel of voices" seem especially odd, for nowhere does she simply declare this a late-late-modernist or postmodern novel, for it is not exactly postcolonial.[31]

Turning back to her dismissal of Makdisi's argument about the possibility of a third space, or a "zone between," while Parry is correct in her view that this is not possible in the terms of the novel, the playing out of this impossibility is in fact the very substance of the novel. Now, both Makdisi and Parry are right to argue that neither Mustafa Sa'eed nor the narrator are really "from" the village, despite their separate pretensions, and so the "zone between" is not a space of choice but an uncomfortable limbo for the Western-educated intellectual from a formerly colonized country. This zone or space is not really such, more of a transition area or even a temporal notion as a phase of facilitation, like a "tax-free" or "duty-free" zone or period that makes trade possible. Most important, this zone or phase is temporary, for as a zone of facilitation it must wither away. As Marx would have it, "all that is solid melts into air" and when this "zone between" disappears, it takes with it the apparent separation between the metropole and the colony, leaving behind a sutured and totalizing global economy. Parry refers to the motorized pumps that have replaced water wheels, and the steel plows (not doors as she claims) that supplanted wooden ones, but she does not see that these are symptoms of modernization and a global economy that will sweep away the kind of crystalline cultural difference we seem to long for these days. Again, "all that is solid melts into air," and with respect to the Sudan this should be seen as the obvious trajectory of the region's history and the point of the *Season*. Salih seems to make this clear in the narrator's naïve reportage about the automobile caravanserai when he returns to the village from Khartoum.[32] Their cultural joy is pure nostalgia and calculated, if not outright silly—"How shapely is your steering wheel astride its metal stem." Most of all, it is disconnected from an earlier moment when it had meaning with respect to communal cohesion and everyday life.

Parry spends much time arguing with recourse to Herbert Marcuse's fusion of Marx and Freud, and tells us that Salih has produced a deadly cocktail of colonialism and sex in this novel. Indeed there is much mention of sex in the novel, and it is rarely "normal" as we think of it in Europe and the United States, but maybe this is the point. Through the analogy of the village elders' banter in the early moments of the novel, and then the disaster brought about by Wad Rayyes's insistence on his traditional "right" to wed and sexually possess—rape, really—Hosna, we get the sense that this is not a pristine, unchanging culture. Rather, Salih tells us that the East does change and these older traditions are incompatible with a younger generation of Sudanese and with life in the modern world, where women will insist on their rights without recourse to Western reason and justification, simply as Sudanese women. Moreover, Hosna's fight to the death with Wad Rayyes runs counter to the narrator's own values, for as Makdisi notes, he usually refers to her as "Bint Mahjoub," the daughter of Mahmoud, thereby encoding her, as Makdisi points out, "in terms of patriarchal structure."[33]

Parry is rightly fascinated with Mustafa Sa'eed, and he is certainly attention-grabbing as the Arab African intellectual who is said to have set out to "decolonize" Africa with his penis! She makes much of the Orientalist and military language with which Mustafa Sa'eed describes his sexual conquests and forays—complete with fantasia— though she sees all of this as ressentiment, deploying a word derived from Nietzsche's condemnation of Christian morality. She is right on one level, but she misses the obvious: that unlike Nietzsche's Christian moral crusaders or modern liberals, Mustafa Sa'eed is self-reflective if nothing else. Some of the most memorable moments in a most memorable novel are his declarations as when he tells the narrator that he is the drop of poison produced by the British Empire "injected into the veins of history" and then announces, "I am no Othello. Othello was a lie!"[34] Of course everything about his life was a lie, of sorts, but more than a lie, Mustafa Sa'eed realizes that he has become a living pop-culture figure, a combination of the postmodern and postcolonial protagonist. As he relates his story by day he is Mustafa Sa'eed, a successful student and then professor in the university, a lauded and published Marxist economist. But by night he is something else, seducing and abandoning English women, taking advantage of their Orientalist fantasies. To one lover's question, "Are you African or Asian?" he writes, prefiguring the statement above:

> "I'm like Othello–Arab African," I said to her. "Yes," she said, looking into my face. "Your nose is like the noses of Arabs in pictures, but your hair isn't soft and jet black like that of Arabs."

"Yes, that's me. My face is Arab like the desert of the Empty Quarter, while my head is African and teems with a mischievous childishness."[35]

That is, despite his accomplishment as an intellectual, he remains effectively trapped within the terms offered by a fantasy based in commodity culture, in this instance mass-produced versions of older and new texts about Oriental exotic and erotic peoples. While there are many articles about the relationship between *Othello* and *Season*, according to my research there is nothing about the stronger link at issue here, which is a much more powerful tradition of popular writing at the fin de siècle and in the early twentieth century. Orientalism is about more than Shakespeare and a received tradition and, perhaps, is best understood with reference to the anonymous early-nineteenth-century pornographic novel *The Lustful Turk*, followed by the publications released under Richard Burton's Kama Shastra Society imprint. By the end of the nineteenth century a mass-cultural phenomenon had developed, replete with cheap literature and tales about imprisonment, ravishment, and what we now know as predatory sexuality, including such early-twentieth-century bestsellers as Blair Hull's *The Sheik* and Robert Hichens's *The Garden of Allah*. As Gareth Stanton details in his article about sex tourism in the Berber town of Biskra, Algeria, the local culture of sexual freedom, with its lack of moralistic inhibition, when adapted to Western fantasy formations, transforms the Ouled Naïl dancers, for example, from young women who were paid for sex (money that they saved for dowries) into prostitutes as we think of such in the West.

Of course, as the novel plays out as a cruel joke, for the final irony lies with Mustafa Sa'eed and the narrator, as they too are infected by this Orientalist fantasy. Both are intellectuals, and so on subjects of the West they are rational, educated, sophisticated, and worldly, though Mustafa Sa'eed has also assumed a new role, that of the non-Western intellectual in the metropole. We know as much from his remarkable library, the "London" room reproduced in the Sudanese village on the Nile, a bookish reminder of Mustafa Sa'eed's other persona as the non-Western Marxist economist and public intellectual, the author of several books, and a man who had read widely. Moreover, whereas our narrator is also educated in Britain, and in literature, his is not the kind of engaged intellectualism that marked Mustafa Sa'eed and that in our own time has developed into a form of cultural capital. Unfortunately for Mustafa Sa'eed, he could not really "cash in" as the postcolonial intellectual and was limited to his nighttime persona, the Arab African prince and lothario. Still, both the narrator and Mustafa Sa'eed know that they are viewed a certain way, and yet they cannot establish themselves as subjects outside the given terms as, say, French intellectuals were able to do through the pages of *Les Temps Modernes* during the Algerian War of Independence. That is, they are either Othellos of Khartoum, caricatures drawn from popular Orientalist fiction, or the pawns of history, playing a part written years earlier:

> "Yes, my dear sirs, I came as an invader into your very homes: a drop of the poison which you have injected into the veins of history."[36]

Again, this is not ressentiment, for it is a most serious self-reflection upon a loss of agency. It is a good-faith analysis of living in bad faith, which is a most modernist ironic turn on modernism. In some ways the Mustafa Sa'eed of London was the consummate modern artist, a kind of modernist bricoleur, assembling an identity from the detritus of modern society and mass culture. Even more so, he is a kind of Marcel Duchamp from Khartoum, ironizing himself along with the fantasies with which others must view him. Even the narrator comes to realize his inescapable "state of irony," and so the novel ends like an existential novel of the mid-twentieth century with a most fundamental statement about human life: "Help! Help!" (169).[37]

Implications

There is, then, a kind of critical imperative that we read Orientalism—Arabia—according to a materialist-cultural paradigm grounded in the notion of a break, or historical rupture, in the 1880s when a new Orientalism emerged as mass culture in print. The implications of this position are vast and include the entirety of modernity and modern culture—that is, literature and mass culture in the broadest sense—and especially a new academic field, Postcolonial Studies. This form of Orientalist mass culture requires an investigation of the subjectivities and tactics, and in this instance new forms, of what we know today as the "Arabist"—the Western expert on the Near East whose political and personal disposition is supportive, to one extent or the other, of the people and culture of the region.

In the following chapters I will offer some examples, and in the conclusion I will address another aspect of this chapter, the status of Postcolonial Studies with respect to Orientalism as it is understood here and also the fate of the Postcolonial intellectual. Clearly, Orientalism has a special place in Postcolonial Studies and certainly casts the "post" aspect of the field in doubt. The postcolonial intellectual, at least as we encounter this subject position here as Mustafa Sa'eed, is also a complicated study, while his/her status as an insider expert is problematic by definition, as is the very possibility of postcolonial "knowledge" and "method," as some propose.[38]

3

A Refusal and a Traversal

*Robert Cunninghame Graham's Engagement
with Orientalism in* Mogreb-el-Acksa

The Swinked Tourist

THE WORK of the well-known late-Victorian-era writer, adventurer, and established commentator on North Africa, Robert Cunninghame Graham, is distinguished by his rejection of discursive forms of the time.[1] Cunninghame Graham resolutely refused to accept and then write about the Arab and Muslim world through the customary Orientalist discursive forms. Specifically, in his 1898 travel narrative about Morocco, *Mogreb-el-Acksa*, Cunninghame Graham set himself apart from his predecessors (e.g., Richard F. Burton, Wilfrid Scawen Blunt, and Charles Doughty) and contemporaries (e.g., Gertrude Bell, D. G. Hogarth, and, slightly later, T. E. Lawrence) by deliberately trying to write against this discursive tradition, which was also an established, popular literary formula. In doing so, Cunninghame Graham traversed the malicious function and forms of Orientalism.

In using the term "refusal," I refer to Cunninghame Graham's stated rejection of the discursive terms and imagery of Orientalism and Empire, in this instance print culture that appealed to a mass readership. A traversal of these discursive forms is complex, but here "refusal" refers simply to an acting out and working through of these discursive forms, resulting in a kind of mocking deconstruction. In this respect Cunninghame Graham is also part of a literary tradition, and in his persona and critical posture he is a combination of Byron and Don Quixote. In fact, he fancied himself to look like portraits of the latter, though he is especially like the former insofar as he works within and then against a literary tradition and the mass appeal of the Oriental "other."[2]

Yet I also tie these discursive forms to what I call "Orientalist fantasies," which is to say, popular ideas that ultimately transcend or exceed Orientalism. These ideas function in a murky area consisting of rumor, the felt and unstated, the imaginary, and the ideological. My engagement here, however, is with material and contingent examples of these fantasies or discursive forms, namely, Orientalist texts and Cunninghame Graham's relationship to them. So on the one hand, this is not a psychoanalytic meta-analysis; but on the other hand, and before discarding the term "fantasy," I do not want to discount the way culture functions at a specific, material level—in, say, mass-published texts—and also, at a transhistorical and ineffable, though nonetheless powerful, level.

To that end I link *Mogreb-el-Acksa* to print culture as mass culture, particularly literature about North Africa, the Middle East, and the Arab and Muslim world that was published for a mass (working-class and middle-class) readership. A comprehensive version of this project requires detailed research of these discursive forms as literary idioms within multiple genres. For now I simply want to provide some context for the text, identify the function and form of discourse with respect to Orientalism, and then demonstrate the specifics of Cunninghame Graham's refusal and traversal. Finally I will locate Cunninghame Graham's text within the mass-publication context of the late nineteenth and early twentieth centuries, so as to underline a break in the form and function of Orientalism and thus show the significance of Cunninghame Graham's refusal and traversal.

Beyond the texts and textual issues I address here, there are significant historical mediations that concern any reading of *Mogreb-el-Acksa*. We should, for example, take into account that Morocco was a place where conflicting European colonial ambitions were briefly played out, as a kind of preamble to the Great War. Morocco played a central role in the "scramble for Africa" that led to the Algeciras Agreement (1906); in the Agadir Crisis (1911); and finally in the Treaty of Fez

(1912), which brought about the deposal of the Moroccan royal family and the division of the country into Spanish and French spheres. European (including German) military and diplomatic machinations in the region kept Morocco in the public eye with much newspaper coverage, while a series of kidnappings and hostage-takings—such as the Perdicaris Affair—inflamed the British and American public in the 1880–1914 period.

Much of Cunninghame Graham's work has a political flavor, though he rarely engages in polemic about the rumblings leading to all of the above. Instead he keeps to general cultural-political insights, as in the 1904 preface to *The Truth about Morocco*, a Moroccan diplomat's book about the Anglo-French agreement.[3] In this brief text Cunninghame Graham proclaimed himself little more than a "swinked tourist" and offered a typically sardonic indictment of the recent trend in travel and exploration writing:

> In general men get up their knowledge of a country out of handbooks, or by swapping brains with other tourists, as if by rubbing two damp sticks together one could expect a blaze.[4]

Cunninghame Graham's commentary continues in this vein for several pages as he turns his attention to other types of travel writers—not "swinked tourists"—that is, those who write for elite venues and public acclaim. We might safely assume that he has the latter-day likes of Burton and Doughty in mind here. For now, however, we should simply note the extent to which Cunninghame Graham is aware of, and just how much he distances himself from, the political dimension of the pose taken by such writer-travelers to North Africa and the Arab and Muslim world. While there is a hint of aristocratic distaste for a mass readership here and elsewhere in his work, it is this pose that he rejects, for he knows well that this type of writer is not an innocent and his/her writing is not without real consequences for the lives of others.

The Exception

It would seem to be impossible, then, to find a Western writer who really "sees" North Africa and the Middle East with "fresh" eyes, but rather, in a case of "always and already," most writers of the period bring their discourses and related desires to fruition against an "Oriental" backdrop. Yet in the midst of the late Victorian era, among modern writers whom we now venerate, was Robert Cunninghame Graham, one of the "belated" British travelers to the Middle East and North Africa in the period from 1870 to the mid-twentieth century.[5] For much of this writer's career, or at least in books such as *Mogreb-el-Acksa* and his collections such as *The Ipané* and *Success*, and in newer periodical venues such as *Nineteenth Century* and the *Saturday Review*, Cunninghame Graham offered a critique of the British Empire that differed from other anti-imperialist critics.[6] Yet, if Robert Cunninghame Graham stands out now for his critique of Empire and its discourse, he is also largely forgotten. This omission is strange in other ways as well, for with regard to the history of print culture Cunninghame Graham was notable in that he wrote for and was championed by a "middlebrow" audience—an interested and engaged, but nonspecialist and largely middle-class readership—even as he maintained an antibourgeois and aristocratic public image. So, on the one hand he was writing for a new audience and in apparently new venues; but on the other hand, Cunninghame Graham wrote in a verbose and turgid style that appealed to a specific readership, an educated middle-class register. Other writers who wrote about the Empire—again, Kipling and Conrad are the best examples—were using new publishing venues though drawing from different popular literary traditions, contrary to Cunninghame Graham, a difference we will consider shortly.

Robert Cunninghame Graham a writer who not only worked in mass publication venues but also developed a mass-culture persona, hence his nickname, "Don Roberto," and his proclaimed kinship to the other "Don," the Knight of La Mancha. Indeed, from the 1890s to the 1920s Cunninghame Graham was considered by many of the most accomplished and esteemed writers and literary figures to be the "writer's writer" of the time.[7] His closest friends are now in the British literary and political pantheon, such as Joseph Conrad, whom Cunninghame Graham supported in both private and literary contexts. Both writers were part of a circle of friends that included Ford Madox

Ford and the influential editor Edward Garnett. Cunninghame Graham's other notable friends and acquaintances included Buffalo Bill, Teddy Roosevelt, George Bernard Shaw, Friedrich Engels, Ramsay MacDonald, Keir Hardie, and so on. And then there were cowboys he met in the American West, desperadoes and rebels with whom he camped in Argentina, and even various prostitutes he was acquainted with around the world. Cunninghame Graham is, then, an apt writer in this genre, for he was an avid and curious world traveler, and also he was always an outsider. He lived several years in his early adult life in Mexico, Argentina, and the Southern United States, while his ancestry was both Scottish and Spanish, surely separating him from his "English" political and intellectual colleagues.

Another part of his myth was his role in the Bloody Sunday riot in Trafalgar Square, where he and John Burns of the British Social Democratic Party charged the police and grenadiers who were blocking the streets. As part of a group of 200 workers who were promptly beaten and arrested, they were later convicted and sentenced to six weeks in Pentonville Prison (which he served and wrote about in "Sursum Corda" as well as in journalistic venues).[8] Cunninghame Graham was elected to Parliament as a liberal, but he was clearly more a socialist than a liberal: he attended the Second International of the socialist movement, supported the eight-hour workday, and was a proponent of home rule for Ireland and a Scottish Nationalist. He was also a sharp critic of the British Empire and the racism and brutality that underpinned its glamorous and triumphalist representation.

Cunninghame Graham was a prolific writer and wrote many short stories, some biography, political pamphlets, many prefaces, journalistic pieces, and several travel books. Certainly Cunninghame Graham's best effort was *Mogreb-el-Acksa*, where, in rambling and stylized Victorian prose, he recounted his 1897 trip to Morocco. The stated objective of his trip was to visit the mystical Muslim city of Tarudant, though on the way he was arrested and held prisoner by a Berber kaid, or tribal chief. Ironically, and despite the practical and grounded purpose of the trip, the valuable part of Cunninghame Graham's *Mogreb-el-Acksa* is that the voyage out, the trip "out" to Morocco and then "into" the interior toward Tarudant, is also a voyage into the mindset and ideology of a European skeptic visiting a colonized country (as with Conrad's Marlow in *Heart of Darkness*).

For Cunninghame Graham, Morocco was new and unknown or, more accurately, simply not understood or "known" in the Anglophone world, and this novelty clearly appealed to his sense of an audience and purpose. On the other hand, there was a textual mediation: the travel accounts of Walter Harris, who spent many years in Morocco as correspondent to *The Times*. Cunninghame Graham admired Harris's writing and character, though his own journey came about in the shadow of an Orientalist filibuster (in the sinister and British imperial sense of this word), that of Major A. Gybbon-Spilsbury. In 1896 Gybbon-Spilsbury attempted to establish trade links and foster a rebellion by the Berber tribes in the Sus against the Moroccan crown. He brought arms to the rebels on a hired yacht, the *S. Y. Tourmaline*. But instead he was captured and repatriated to Britain to public acclaim, and his story was told in a popular book about the matter, *The Tourmaline Expedition*. Cunninghame Graham feared that Gybbon-Spilsbury's antics damaged British relations with the Moroccan government and loyalist tribes and cast suspicion on his own journey, ultimately leading to his captivity.[9]

It is surprising that there is so little critical literature about Cunninghame Graham as both a public figure and a writer. And within the extant critical work, there is almost nothing about *Mogreb-el-Acksa*. The critical authority on Cunninghame Graham, Cedric Watts, wrote a series of books about him, and with Laurence Davies produced the most authoritative and scholarly biography to date, *Cunninghame Graham: A Critical Biography*. In the latter text, Watts and Davies dedicate a chapter to Cunninghame Graham's many visits to Morocco, attributing his interest to his attachment to Spain and particularly to Moorish Spain. They cite an 1890 comment Cunninghame Graham made, shortly after losing his seat in Parliament, that in Morocco he felt more comfortable than in England, for despite its feudalism and backwardness, injustice and inequality were not as pronounced and systemic as in the industrialized West. This kind of relativist argument is typical of

Cunninghame Graham, and we will consider other examples, but it is important to note the shift he makes from the simplicity of such points to his later rejection of Empire. It is not enough to dismiss his criticism of colonialism as lingering aristocratic thinking or an Orientalist longing for the desert as a kind of New Arcadia.[10]

Christopher GoGwilt's chapter on Cunninghame-Graham in *The Fictions of Geopolitics* is useful and interesting here, for he focuses on his involvement with the left parties of the day—the Metropolitan Radical Federation—in the 1887 Bloody Sunday march on Trafalgar Square and mass politics noted above.[11] In fact, following comments by Watts and Davies, GoGwilt notes that our writer was particularly uncomfortable with mass politics and the masses, despite his solidarity both in print and on the streets. We should not overlook the fact that Cunninghame Graham was beaten by the police and jailed following the Bloody Sunday march. Interestingly, GoGwilt makes his point through close readings of Cunninghame Graham's account of the march and riot as published in William Morris's *Commonweal* and a later short prose piece, "Sursum Corda," and selections from *The Ipané* and other short texts.

The Refusal

Again, Cunninghame Graham differed from many of the travelers to North Africa and the Middle East who preceded him. Like his antecedents in the tradition, before leaving Britain he did all of the requisite reading, poring over the accounts of Belfort Bax, Doughty, and Walter Harris as well as lesser-known explorers, adventurers, photographers, and amateur ethnographers. Cunninghame Graham set out to work against this received knowledge, specifically to rebut Doughty's Christian moralism and purpose and to spoof Burton's self-promotion— though Doughty in particular was his foil. T. E. Lawrence notes in his introduction to *Arabia Deserta* that this book "is the first and indispensable work upon the Arabs of the desert; and if it has not been referred to, or enough read, that has been because it was excessively rare."[12]

Importantly, Cunninghame Graham tells us that he was "sans flag-wagging" and "great moral purpose."[13] Again the latter comment refers to Doughty, though "flag-wagging" certainly referred to others who were overtly and covertly working for the Empire or other European imperial/commercial interests. Cunninghame Graham declares in the introduction:

> I fear I have no theory of empires, destiny of the Anglo-Saxon race, spread of the Christian faith, of trade extension, or of hinterlands; no nostrum, by means of which I hope to turn Arabs to Christians, reconcile Allah and Jahve, remove the ancient lack of comprehension between East and West, mix oil and vinegar, or fix the rainbow always in the sky so that the color-blind may scan it at their leisure through the medium of neutral-tinted glass; and generally I fear I write of things without a scrap of interest to right-thinking men: . . . but on the contrary [I write] of lonely rides, desolate camping places, of ruined buildings seen in peculiar lights, of simple folk who pray to Allah seven times a day, and act as if they never prayed at all; in fact of things which to a traveler, his travels o'er, still conjure up the best part of all travel—its melancholy.[14]

This claim to objectivity is buttressed throughout the book with increasingly sharp criticisms of British, really English, culture and politics. Even the English grass is not spared, since Englishmen take it for granted, whereas "in Morocco and Arabia green grass means life, relief from thirst."[15] He comments much later in the book that in Morocco, as throughout the Muslim world and the East, "the interest lies entirely in mankind" while the land itself has endured unspoiled, not as in the West. He proclaims:

> And so may Allah please, bicycles, Gatling guns, and all the want of circumstance of modern life not intervening, it may yet endure when the remembrance of our shoddy paradise has fallen into well-merited contempt.[16]

Though Cunninghame Graham is hard on his countrymen, both in Britain and abroad, he also criticizes the function and habits of local rulers and lords. Sherifs, various holy men, kaids, and merchants of all types do not escape his sharp observation and scathing wit, though in the last instance he is not bothered by these "types" since they are not finally as pernicious as their Western counterparts. The best known of these "types" is the Oriental despot, a major figure in Orientalist discourse.[17] Cunninghame Graham invokes this figure when he refers to the kaid who kept him captive as a kind of "Eastern Potentate of the Arabian Nights," though a page later he wonders if an English duke would similarly welcome and tolerate an Arab wandering around Britain disguised as a Christian saint as he was disguised as a Muslim hakim.[18]

Perhaps the most important part of his travel account is that Cunninghame Graham disguised himself for his journey in Morocco. He did not literally assume the Tuareg veil, but rather he shaved his head and exchanged his European clothing for an "Arab" outfit, appropriate for a wise man, Turkish hakim, or traveling doctor. In keeping with his ruse he adopted an Arab name, "Sheikh Mohamed el Fasi."[19] In addition to "traveling as an Arab" he took various packaged medicines with him, such as aspirin and quinine, which, as part of his ruse, he distributed to the local people he encountered (notably, he borrowed this ruse from Doughty, among others). The disguise was initially successful, though only because his interactions were usually with friendly people who, while not deceived, were not alarmed at the sight of a European Christian traveling as a Muslim. Yet as they approached the interior of the country, it was increasingly difficult to maintain the disguise and "role" if only because Cunninghame Graham did not speak Arabic or Shillach, the Berber dialect. Instead he avoided direct encounters and made sure that his Arab and Arabophone assistant, Lutaif, a Lebanese Maronite Christian, negotiated with all passersby. Cunninghame Graham meanwhile struck regal and aloof poses during these encounters and moved away from direct interactions.

Again, the disguise and "Arab" alter ego were key parts of the same literary tradition that Cunninghame Graham set out to subvert. The list of travelers who made similar attempts includes Richard Burton's well-known journey to Mecca and Medina and the experiences of lesser figures such the socialist Belfort Bax, Cunninghame Graham's friends Wilfred Scawen Blunt and Lady Blunt, and, of course, T. E. Lawrence. I suggest that this action, though explained as a necessity for safety and for objectivity, was about desire as such and in multiple ways as Joan Copjec and Kaja Silverman have argued.[20] There is the "fun" of shedding an identity and adopting another that is very different, as well as the pleasure of deceiving others. Still, despite the instrumental reason offered for dressing as Mohamed el Fasi, our writer is quite aware of the silly figure he casts, and so a final sort of pleasure is ironic, part of a self-critique but, importantly, the kind of self-critique that so few British travelers and colonial types were able to articulate. To the contrary, the obligatory khakis, helmet, and gun were an important part of British identity abroad, whatever the practical rationale for such clothing and accessories.[21] The following passage from *Mogreb-el-Acksa* is pertinent here:

> It must not be forgotten that in the East (and Mogreb-el-Acksa, though it means Far West, is perhaps as Eastern as any country in the world) European clothes, hard hats, elastic sided boots, grey flannel shirts, with braces, mother-of-pearl studs, two carat watch chains, and all the beauty of our meanly contrived apparel, are to Mohammedans the outward visible sign of the inward spiritual Maxim gun, torpedo boat, and arms of precision, on which our civilization, power, might, dominion, and morality really repose. A shoddy-clad and cheating European peddler, in his national dress, always suggests to Easterns the might of England somewhere in the offing, and though they laugh at the wearer of the grey shoddy rags behind his back, they respect him more than if he were attired in the most beautiful of their own time-hallowed garments, which they know no European puts on but for some purpose of his own. But if a European loses respect in wearing Moorish clothes, he gains in another way, for the Moors are constituted like other men, and, seeing a man dressed in the clothes they wear themselves, converse with him more freely, even if, as in my case, his knowledge of the language is so slight as to make conversation through an interpreter a necessity.[22]

In this passage Cunninghame Graham is clearly able to "see" himself, and alternately at least to try to see himself—clothed in different ways—through the eyes of the Moroccans (Moors). The particular vituperation here is directed toward his fellow Westerners—"A shoddy-clad and cheating European peddler"—and, of course, is really a rhetorical flourish. Such a flourish is still notable for the same reasons that, as Brian Street notes, few Westerners abroad would dare articulate and so risk their own closely protected identities.[23]

This self-critique, with the ability to question his pleasure but nonetheless enjoy it, is certainly distinctive, however, for with Cunninghame Graham the pleasure is not just about dressing as an Arab but also concerns the plot elements this attire introduces into his story. Eventually, as he and his small party approach Tarudant, they pass near the fortress town of Kintafi, a Berber community led by a kaid. At this juncture their presence has been noted and they are taken captive, though the terms of their capture are never explicit. Indeed they were not allowed to meet the kaid for a week, and then, after a successful audience, were finally released five days later. As he relates, the only reason the kaid did not torture and kill them was because Cunninghame Graham was a British subject, and they were only released when they bribed a messenger to carry a note to the British consul in Mogador. Their captivity adds to the "flavor" of the narrative—otherwise, it is a dull narrative of travel from point A to point B—and then opens a space for more narrative and description. While waiting, Cunninghame Graham listened to Arabic poetry and attempted to learn Berber—the book includes a glossary of Berber and Arabic terms and vocabulary—and there was a constant flow of characters who stopped and passed the time with them in their poor encampment (this situation of duress leading to narrative recalls the frame in *The Arabian Nights*). As Watts and Davies enumerate, they met a Persian singer traveling from Hungary to China, a Jewish peddler selling Algerian tobacco, a black African who had once worked for a Scottish company and visited London, and an array of other locals.[24] The point is that the narrative is made possible by their captivity and the deferral or putting off of their trip to Tarudant. The details of landscape, culture, and various peoples—the Jews of Mogador, the Berber tribes, the Arab rulers, and abundant comments on women (veiled and otherwise)—all entail a certain pleasure of telling and reading. (Cunninghame Graham, like many other British travelers, seems keen here to identify "minorities" and types.) The kaid would not allow them to continue on to Tarudant and sent them back to Tangier, and the story is better for their failure.

Cunninghame Graham's easy and popular response to his captivity by the kaid would have been to follow up with a self-indulgent text replete with outrage and the usual anecdotes about forced conversion and worse forms of violation. This possible story, for which there was certainly a market—consider accounts such as Wingate's *Ten Years' Captivity in the Mahdi's Camp, 1882–1892*—would have led to a penultimate moment, an audience with the all-powerful sultan or Oriental despot, a fixture of Western thought about the Near East and Arab and Muslim world. This sultan, who lazes in the luxury of the Serail, is, in Mladen Dolar's (and also Alain Grosrichard's) Lacanian formulation, the Subject who is supposed to enjoy. Yet we cannot allow such pleasure to persist and so the sultan is revealed to be impotent, and the Serail is actually the scene of lesbian, homosexual and otherwise perverse trysts, rather than "proper" phallic domination (notably, the well-endowed Dey of *The Lustful Turk* is castrated by one of the harem women, ending the narrative—though it has been published in many editions for the last two centuries!). In Cunninghame Graham's text, however, we do not find a trace of such discourse. When he meets the kaid, he notes, for example, that he is served coffee by slaves in cheap clothing, that the coffee glasses are all mismatched and of varied origin, and that the kaid keeps his official sealing wax—from Europe—in a broken cardboard box. Thus:

> By race and language he was a Berber, but speaking Arabic tolerably fluently, and adapting all his habits and dress to those in fashion amongst Arab Sheikhs. His clothes white and of the finest wool, and clean as is a sheet of paper before a writer marks it black with lies. . . . The sealing-wax was European, and kept in a box of common cardboard, which had been mended in several places with little silver bands to keep the sides together, as we should mend a lacquered box from Persia or Japan.[25]

The focus here is on our writer's refusal to see the usual or "expected," the Oriental despot, a position entailed, for example, in the way he views and represents the kaid amidst his bric-a-brac not as a parody of Western power, but as a kind of mirror of the reality of Western power, a pile of garbage. For contrast compare this scene of colonial litter and bric-a-brac to the scenes in *Heart of Darkness* where Marlow describes the rivets, the upside-down train tracks, and the wire the colonists and traders exchange for ivory. Yet here we have something different—consider the following passages from *Mogreb-el-Acksa*:

> Slave boys, in clothes perhaps worth eighteenpence, served coffee, rather an unusual thing in visiting a Moor, for all drink tea. The tray was copper, beautifully chased, and adorned with sentences from the Koran, the service varied, and consisting of a common wine glass, one champagne glass of the old-fashioned narrow pattern, three cheap French cups, and a most beautifully engraved old Spanish glass goblet out of which his Excellency drank. The coffee pot looked like a piece of "Empire"; the coffee most excellent, and brought most probably by some pilgrim from Arabia, and used only on great occasions such as the present was.[26]
>
> An Eastern potentate of the Arabian Nights, with all the culture of the Arabs of the Middle Ages absent, but as he was, the arbiter of life and death in a wide district. A gentleman in manners, courteous to those whom he had all the power to treat with rudeness or severity; a horseman and a fighter; a tyrant naturally, as any man would be if placed in his position; but no more tyrannical in disposition than is some new elected County Councillor, mad to make all men chaste and sober, because he himself is impotent and enjoys a never to be satiated thirst for ginger beer.[27]

The note of disgust is apparent, and perhaps the point is the same, that Empire brings junk with it, a clutter of useless commodities. Yet this point is made for different ends and with different consequences, and it bears repeating here, that with all of their faults and weaknesses, none of the local rulers and scoundrels can match colonialism and its "people." Indeed, Cunninghame Graham refuses a false parallel here with the colonizers. He comments at the end of the book:

> For myself I need hardly say I should prefer to see Morocco as it is, bad government and all, thinking but little as I do of the apotheosis of the "bowler" hat, and holding as an article of faith that national government is best for every land, from Ireland to the "vexed Bermoothes," and from thence to Timbuctoo.[28]

The Refusal in Its Literary Context

It is important to look at other texts by Cunninghame Graham in order to demonstrate the consistency of his stance toward racist and imperial discourse. Just as important, Cunninghame Graham's rejection of racism and colonialism is instructive in order to separate him from his peers (such as Conrad), and to demonstrate that while these views and racist language were widespread, they were by no means deemed normal and acceptable.

In one of his many short stories set in Morocco, "At Torfaieh," he describes the goings-on at a nonfunctioning trading post "run" by armed Britons who refuse to trade with the local traders and who, when they do not shoot at them, even give them payments in order to keep them within a potential (future) trading circuit. Thus:

> Outpost of progress, now, alas! Submerged once more in the dark flood of Islam; portion of Scotland, reft from the mother country and erratically disposed in Africa in the same way bits of Cromarty are found scattered sporadically about the map. Torfaieh was as Scotch, or even more Scotch, than Peebles, Lesmahagow, or the Cowcaddens, for the setting went for nothing in comparison with the North British composition of the place. . . . Order and due precision of accounts, great ledgers, beer upon tap, whiskey served out "medicinally," prayers upon Sunday, no trifling with the Arab women ever allowed, a moral tone, a strict attention to commercial principles, and yet no trade, for by a cursed fate the "doddering" English directors who controlled the cash had sent an order that no trading should be done, as they were waiting for the time when a

paternal Government order should equip them with a charter. . . .
Therefore the order ran, "Let no one bringing trade approach the
place." . . .

The legend grew about the mad Christians, who fired on traders, but yet paid good allowances to chiefs to encourage trade, and
welcomed every one so that he came with empty hands.[29]

As with Conrad's outpost in "Outpost of Progress," these British colo-
nials use a "native" intermediary, in this instance a Lebanese (Syrian)
Christian, Najim, who is reminiscent of Cunninghame Graham's
guide in Morocco, Lutaif.

When not on duty he [Najim] wore the Arab clothes, talked with
the tribesmen, learned their lore, rode in the powder play, heard of
the "ould el naama" (son of the ostrich), the child, who, lost by his
parents, had found a foster-parent in an ostrich, and in whose capture
three good mares were tired, and by degrees insensibly grew to think
the desert life the best which it has pleased Allah to show to man.[30]

The contrast is striking, for whereas Conrad's Makola and the fireman, two well-known racist caricatures from "Outpost of Progress" and
Heart of Darkness, are (respectively) suspect and ridiculous, Cunninghame Graham attempts to represent the conflicted mindset of someone
who represents difference within the colonized people. He takes care
to explain that Najif speaks the same language, approximately, and has
an understanding of the local culture, though he is not Muslim and is
not from a nomadic culture, and is in many ways as much an outsider
as the British. Still the story renders the powerful pull of identification
that Najif experiences. As Cunninghame Graham sees this part of the
world, the population of the Arab world is not an undifferentiated mass
stretching from Antioch (formerly in Syria) around the Mediterranean
to the Maghreb and down the Arabian peninsula, but a world where
huge differences separate people within the racial and demographic des-
ignation. Clearly what he sees is an expanded and differentiated Arabia.

Cunninghame Graham's countervision also entails seeing the people differently and finding new ways of addressing or knowing them.

By contrast with *Heart of Darkness* and much of Conrad's work, we find the replication of what is given, drawn from the pool of popular culture. Following Said we might read much into the author's use of the framed tale and double narrative—debts to the nineteenth-century translations of *Arabian Nights*—and make even more of the irony and hollowness of Marlow's narrative. Yet none of these features really explains Conrad's recourse to racist language or imagery and fully answers Achebe's denunciation of *Heart of Darkness*.[31]

Cunninghame Graham, by contrast (and remarkably for his time), directly takes on the epithet and those who use it. In his ironically titled "Niggers," he writes:

> In Africa, Australia, and in America, in all the myriad islands of the southern seas inferior races dwell. They have their names, their paltry racial differences, some are jet black, some copper coloured, flat-nosed, high featured, tall, short, and hideous or handsome—what is it to us? We lump them all as niggers, being convinced that their chief quality is their difference from ourselves.[32]

This short text was intended as a kind of journalistic critique of both the use of the word and the imperial and oppressive purpose the word serves; that is, the performative function of epithets and racist language and their importance for the maintenance of Empire. As a performative, the epithet "nigger" is not just a word but a kind of call to action or, from the standpoint of the victim, a pointing to one's vulnerability and the onset of violence. And so, Cunninghame Graham clearly understood that words have material bearing with material consequences. He adds near the end of the piece:

> The Ethiopian cannot change his skin, and therefore we are ready to possess his land and to uproot him for the general welfare of mankind. . . . Niggers who have no cannons have no rights. Their land is ours, their cattle and their fields, their houses ours; their arms, their poor utensils, and everything they have; their women, too, are ours to use as concubines, to beat, exchange, to barter off for gunpowder or gin, ours to infect with syphilis, leave with child, outrage,

torment, and make by contact with the vilest of our vile, more vile than beasts.[33]

It is surprising that Conrad and Cunninghame Graham were close friends, for this last passage runs so counter to the ambiguous (at best) use of the epithet and imagery that so angered Achebe.[34]

Don Roberto and the Star Turn

Cunninghame Graham is exceptional as an anti-Orientalist and anti-imperial voice, yet there is another dimension to his work that we must explore, a dimension that, I maintain, yields insights, albeit discouraging ones. This other dimension concerns print culture, specifically the venues where he published. First, apparently far removed from the world of fiction and what we now know as creative nonfiction (and both are Cunninghame Graham's favored modes of writing) were emergent popular literary forms such as cheap daily newspapers (mostly illustrated) and the "boys' story magazines." Of the latter, and as noted earlier, the notable examples are the *Boy's Own Paper* founded by the Religious Tract Society for the promotion of Empire and Christian morals, and the jingoistic *Union Jack* edited by G. A. Henty, the author of many tales of Empire and Oriental adventure. The newspaper venues included *The Daily Telegraph* and others that ran frequent accounts of heroic explorers and imperial adventurers (again, Stanley, Gybbon-Spilsbury, and Lowell Thomas's *With Lawrence in Arabia*). Indeed, Stephen Donovan argues that Conrad's "unholy recollection" realized in *Heart of Darkness* was probably derived from these same sensational accounts of Livingston and Stanley.[35] Furthermore, I argue, they are probably mediated by the language—imperial slang and "common sense"—of boys' magazines.[36]

Second, though these new venues might seem removed from the world of serious writing, the discursive field upon which their success hinged greatly influenced all writers in the period. The use of epithets and the reinforcement of racist, Orientalist, and imperialist "knowledge" is only one aspect. It is interesting to note here that Conrad first published *The Heart of Darkness* (with the definite article in the original title) in an established literary journal, *Blackwood's Edinburgh Magazine.*[37] "Maga," as it was popularly known, published many authors who gained fame in its pages, notably Walter Scott, Thomas De Quincey, George Eliot, and Anthony Trollope. Founded in the early nineteenth century as a Tory counterpart to the Whig-aligned *Edinburgh Review*, Maga eventually set the standard for literary publishing in the Victorian period. By the end of the century, just as Conrad was preparing to publish his novella in the 1,000th edition, Maga was beset by competitors representing the new journalism movement, yet it held onto its established publishing format. Two notable examples of these upstart venues were *Nineteenth Century* and *The Saturday Review*, and significantly Cunninghame Graham published his work in both. Also of note here, Wilfrid Scawen Blunt's *The Future of Islam* was compiled from a series of mid-1880s articles that initially appeared in *The Fortnightly Review*. Counter to Maga, and in the same period, *Nineteenth Century* was publishing much "harder" journalistic pieces about far-off places, but with a contemporary political cast. For example, following the battle at Omdurman and General Gordon's death at the hands of the Mahdavists in Khartoum, *Nineteenth Century* published a series of articles in its October 1897 and October 1898 issues by a Muslim scholar, Rafiuddin Ahmad, about the new conjunction of Islam, nationalism, and politics. This was very different material from that of the staid Maga.[38]

As the name of the movement suggests, the New Journalism publications were venues for what in the twentieth century came to be known as "middlebrow" opinion pieces, as well as articles by experts. In many ways these journals are akin to today's *New Statesman* and *The Nation*. Laurel Brake identifies the *New Review*, a competitor of *Nineteenth Century*, as an exemplar of this movement.[39] This journal broke with established patterns and proclaimed that its audience was railroad travelers who appreciated carefully selected images and appropriate production values (one could read them while traveling), as well as news and opinion pieces. There was a widespread recognition in the 1890s that the older publishing venues and forms, especially quarterlies, were outdated and that a new market, which traveled by railroad and through other distribution points, demanded new forms of text.

As Brake also notes, the New Journalism was, as the name suggests, rooted in the "quiddity" and politics of the day and followed a tradition of political writing.[40] New Journalism, then, was found in newer and more upscale publications such as *Yellow Book* (where Henry James published his story about New Journalism, "The Death of the Lion"), *Nineteenth Century*, and *New Review*, as well as in daily and weekly news outfits such as *Saturday Review*. Following the lead of the older literary journals, these publications pushed the star-writer system further, advertising their stable of writers and contributors in ways not seen before.[41]

Again, in the 1890s Robert Cunninghame Graham was publishing a variety of work in these new venues. For example, in the December 1890 edition of *Nineteenth Century* he published "Idealism and the Masses," a socialist opinion piece about the nature of idealism, faith, and hero worship with respect to the "masses" and the rich. By the mid-1890s he was publishing shorter pieces in the weekly *Saturday Review* about a range of topics, such as "Bloody Sunday" ("Sursum Corda" as mentioned above), and a creative text, "The Ipané." Given his life experience in Argentina and South America he also published related work through the same period into the late 1890s in *Review of Reviews* (W. T. Stead's publication) and *Badminton Magazine*. Indeed, as he tells us in *Mogreb-el-Acksa*, Cunninghame Graham's trip to Morocco was on behalf of *Saturday Review*, and he was released from captivity following pressure from the British government who were in turn pressured by the editor of the journal (among others).

Also of note, Robert Cunninghame Graham frequently published in what we now call alternative publications. For example, he wrote an anti-imperialist text, *The Imperial Kailyard*, which he originally published in the London anarchist publication *Justice* (where other well-known writers also published work) and then, in 1896, reprinted the text as a pamphlet with a newly founded and activist Twentieth Century Press. We might deploy Raymond Williams's (Gramsci-derived) terminology to see, in the 1890s, Cunninghame Graham working in a very particular print culture context, which, like Conrad's situation, combined elements of the residual and the emergent. Indeed, like

Conrad, there is also an element of the popular here, at least insofar as Cunninghame Graham published with these alternative presses as a kind of pamphleteer. Yet for the most part we can establish that his venues were emergent and directed toward a readership of the new middle class, the railroad audience that the writer for *New Review* noted above.

Conrad worked, then, in a "residual" venue, the literary journal, but under the influence and aegis of an emergent and soon-to-be-dominant form of popular writing, while Cunninghame Graham was engaged with the (near) dominant, though still somewhat emergent, monthly journal and middlebrow press. Thus he wrote for a new, moneyed readership yet with an appeal to rationality and propriety, contrary to the visceral language and appeal of more popular venues and forms of print culture. On the other hand, Cunninghame Graham's dominant influence, as noted above, was in the newspaper and pamphlet of a much earlier era. Of course, newspapers and pamphlets were used for scandal-mongering in earlier times, but the tradition of writing to which Cunninghame Graham belongs is at the genteel end of the spectrum. Following George Orwell's vaunted tradition of the pamphlet, we might set aside the rumor-mongers and libelers and identify Cunninghame Graham in a tradition of pamphlet writing with Defoe and Swift.[42]

Style, I argue, is important, not only for its relationship to form—the pamphlet, for example—but also in the way style engages a readership. Perhaps better than engagement, we should consider the relationship between style and interpellation (in Althusser's sense) where an audience is "hailed" or drawn in by a certain way of writing, imagery, and phrasing.[43] Both writers are verbose, and perhaps this a bland way of describing Conrad's penchant for adjectives, as Leavis pointed out in a well-known essay, or Cunninghame Graham's rhetorical flair and love of the multiclaused—all dependent and adjectival—denunciation. This last tendency, or stylistic marker, is probably due to the writer's roots in the tradition of the pamphleteer, as noted earlier, and then an oral mode of discourse, here again the pamphlet's dual role as text and textualization of a political speech or something related (and Cunninghame Graham was a politician and noted for his oratorical skills—see his "Maiden Speech" in Parliament). Consider the following remarkable (for rhetorical as well as ideological reasons) passage from his introduction to *Mogreb-el-Acksa*:

> It may be, that my poor unphilosophic recollections of a failure, may interest some, who, like myself, have failed, but still may like to hear that even in a failure you can see strange things, meet as strange types, and be impressed as much with wild and simple folk, as any traveler who thundered through the land, Bible and gun in hand, making himself no spiced conscience, but putting into practice the best traditions of our race, confident that the one way to win a "nigger's" heart "is to speak English to him," and doing so even at the rifle's mouth.[44]

Cunninghame Graham piles noun upon noun, short clause upon short clause, and uses colloquial words and phrases, all building and building to a rhetorical crescendo, his opponents obliterated![45] Moreover, while Conrad represents a newer imagistic way of writing grounded in the colloquial and slang prose of the popular press—again, boys' magazines and cheap news dailies—Cunninghame Graham is a "man of the word." Despite his verbosity here, words on the page have a value as a mediation or bargain with the reader, or remain as language, simply noises and sounds. With Conrad the word, the phrase vanishes and the thing itself, the presence of the "other," is conjured up as though in the flesh where the word on the page and the thing, say, the "African," is that epithet. The word is a kind of vanishing mediator, for finally what difference is there between the cannibal or the insolent black man and their words, realized in the way they speak in *Heart of Darkness*? For Conrad's audience this is blackness itself; stamping and grunting on the banks of the Congo River, and the image is the thing, realized in the moment of enunciation and with the act of reading.

The Emergence of the "Arabist" Brand

Much of Edward Said's work concerns Joseph Conrad, whether as the reclusive individual who wrote interesting correspondence—and some of the most interesting exchanges (letters) were with Robert

Cunninghame Graham—or as the novelist who has been a ranking member of the Anglophone literary canon for over fifty years.[46] Today Conrad is famous and Cunninghame Graham is simply his forgotten interlocutor, and while modernist style has something to do with their separate fates as writers, this is only incidental when we reconsider the structural features and resilience of the Oriental fantasy for the modern Western writer and reader. For Said, writing in the last days of the Cold War, the modern artist is an outsider, an excluded, exilic consciousness surveying the machinations of modernity from the outside, removed from the factory floor, or excluded within the imperial world. Said has written a good deal on the figure who assumes this pose as the writer, artist, or intellectual, and he includes a diverse group of names ranging from Julien Benda to Antonio Gramsci and Erich Auerbach, among many others.[47] As for literary examples, Said explicitly points to this pose as proof of modernism's ambivalence toward its imperial context when he writes the following:

> Conrad, Forster, Malraux, T. E. Lawrence take narrative from the triumphalist experience of imperialism into the extremes of self-consciousness, discontinuity, self-referentiality, and corrosive irony, whose formal patterns we have come to recognize as the hallmarks of modernist culture, a culture that also embraces the major work of Joyce, T. S. Eliot, Proust, Mann, and Yeats. I would like to suggest that many of the most prominent characteristics of modernist culture, which we have tended to derive from purely internal dynamics in Western society and culture, include a response to the external pressures on culture from the *imperium*.[48]

Much of this passage is possibly mediated by Raymond Williams's comments on modernism and the metropolitan experience, that of immigration and the movement of labor, and in this sense it is an attempt to save modernism from its well-known racist, fascist, and imperialist tendencies.[49] Implicit here, as I read the passage, is an acknowledgment of the racist and quiescent character of much modern art and literature, which Said saves with a certain sympathetic and dialectical reading. Yet it is a move to save modernism and its forms nonetheless, particularly where these concern the pose of the artist and, strangely, the autonomy of the text. The autonomy of the text seems strange with regard to Conrad in particular, as Said wrote in an earlier essay that the author considered the text "a produced thing, the produced thing. . . . The text was the never-ending product of a continuing process."[50]

In fact, as farfetched as this insight might seem at first, it is perhaps the very basis of modernist aesthetics or style, as some might refer to the "look" of modernism. The outsider, the alienated one, the rebel, the underground man, the exile, the outcast, the vagrant, the flaneur, the deracinated one; these are all poses assumed by modern artists as the pose of the artist or, in a few cases, the lives they lived. As a group, however, these constitute a critical position valorized by most of the literary and cultural experts of the twentieth century, particularly those clustered around various midcentury American left-wing journals. In this respect Said was no different from most academics who emerged from the intellectual milieu of the Cold War (this might have something to do with Said's relationship to Freud's work as well), though for our purposes here, this pose or positioning is related to his interest in Conrad. In his later book, *Culture and Imperialism*, he writes that Conrad's position as an outsider, like that of his narrator, Marlow, is crucial with regard to his understanding and representation of imperialism. He writes, "[Y]our self-consciousness as an outsider can allow you actively to comprehend how the machine works, given that you and it are fundamentally not in perfect synchrony or correspondence."[51]

I have stressed this aspect of Said's commentary on Conrad, modernism, and Empire because it is central to his theory of secular criticism and "worldliness" and the role of the intellectual. It is not coincidence that each passage I have cited is related to a comment on Julien Benda's *Treason of the Intellectuals*. In his appraisal of Said's work on Orientalism, and of the book itself, Aijaz Ahmad made much of this championing of Benda, and perhaps rightly so in one respect, but without respecting the shading with which Said used Benda's argument.[52] Ahmad writes:

One does not have to read far into *Treason of the Intellectuals* to see that the "treason" of which Benda speaks is none other than the intellectuals' participation in what he calls "the political passions"; and (b) that "class passions" and "racial passions" are for him among the worst, so that "anti-semitism" and "socialism" are said to be equally diabolical, while "the working classes who, even in the mid nineteenth century, felt only a scattered hostility for the opposing class" are castigated because in Benda's own time (the 1920s) "they form a closely-woven fabric of hatred from one end of Europe to another."[53]

Of course Ahmad is correct in his assessment of Benda, but not fine enough in his reading of Said's comments on the latter. Within the totality of the essay where Benda is mentioned, "Secular Criticism," Said clearly sees Benda as an intellectual who has deliberately removed himself/herself from the political fray for the better. He is taking Benda at his word here, and later in his essay "Swift as Intellectual" he makes it clear that what he takes from Benda is his insistence that "the intellectual's obligation [is] to adhere to absolute values and to tell the truth regardless of material consequences."[54] Perhaps Said is naive with regard to Benda, or perhaps (and more probably) he is just reading his text dialectically, carrying the premises and promises of liberalism to the bitter end.

The problem with Said's ideal intellectual is the very notion that anyone who takes public positions as a public intellectual must and can do so without compromises or obligations of one form or another and of course, in a more fundamental sense, that this neutral and pure position is even possible. You do not have to be a structuralist to find this a dubious claim, albeit a cornerstone of liberal journalism in the United States despite the obvious mediations of media ownership and powerful lobbies. It is strange, though, that Said invokes Gramsci in his defense, and Ahmad also faults him for this reference as well, for the Italian Communist and committed intellectual gave us critical concepts and terms such as "hegemony" and the "organic intellectual," which surely preclude the kind of apolitical purist Said valorizes, despite his protests to the contrary. Foucault, who with Gramsci is an important influence on Said's work, was blunt about the relationship of the intellectual to power:

> The intellectual's role is no longer to place himself "somewhat ahead and to the side" in order to express the stifled truth of the collectivity; rather it is to struggle against the forms of power that transform him into its object and instrument in the sphere of "knowledge," "truth," "consciousness," and "discourse."[55]

Given the sustained criticism Said has given us of Orientalists such as Bernard Lewis, I have to read his comments on Benda with Foucault to best understand how he sees the intellectual today, as an engaged academic and as a critic of a most destructive form of clerical treason, Orientalism.

Yet to get this point and to tie the debate about the intellectual in the late twentieth century to Orientalism in more substantial ways, we have to return to the pose of the modern artist-critic and the persona of Robert Cunninghame Graham. More so than Conrad, who was reclusive and otherwise hid his personal life, and whose work was not intertwined with a public image, Cunninghame Graham followed in the tradition of Burton and flaunted his private life in order to develop his personae, Don Roberto and Sheikh Mohamed el Fasi. These personae are travelers' identities, the names of outsiders, exiled or on the run, and are like some of the characters Cunninghame Graham met abroad in far-flung places. Most important, we see here a link to the modernist pose, in the same way Said links Erich Auerbach and the story of *Mimesis* to secular criticism, for these travelers are able to view a given culture as an outsider and make comparisons and draw analogies, or not, to a "home" culture as an outsider. It is a putative, objective point of view, or if we consider that modernity/everyday life is a decisive mediation here, it is a point of view from outside the culture and the routine of the working day.

We should be aware of several factors in play, the first of which is the opposition of the Orient to the modern West, whether it is the opposition of the desert or the serail to the modern metropolis of the West, or the "pastoral" life of the Arab (of the desert) opposed to the working day of a British office functionary. The Orient is clearly an "oasis," albeit a mirage of fantasy, but it serves a purpose in the social and political imaginary nonetheless. As for Cunninghame Graham, another factor is class. Despite his links to radical politics, and even his brief imprisonment and the text he wrote about the experience, "Sursum Corda," Christopher GoGwilt's analysis of his politics is correct.[56] Don Roberto was just that, an aristocrat in fact and fantasy, with little meaningful concern for capitalism as such and the struggles of the working class in particular. In this sense, in his suspicion toward the "masses" he was not much different from many other liberal or progressive writers of his time—and throughout the twentieth century—as John Carey argues in *The Intellectuals and the Masses*.[57] What we must note here is that this class politics, this conflation of everyday life with the abject and defeated consciousness of ordinary people, working-class and middle-class, is a key component to the pose of the Arabist and the modern artist. The links are not coincidental, given the influence of Burton and Doughty on modernist writers such as Joyce and Eliot, while the earlier Orientalists' disdain for the Arab cities, particularly Beirut, as a hybrid mess suggest the same disdain felt for London and Manchester and the "seething masses." I am reminded of the Penguin paperback cover of Salman Rushdie's *Midnight's Children*, a photograph of "Oriental" men charging into the frame, the masses of the East replacing the masses of the West.[58] I believe at a fundamental level this book cover did indeed tell more about the truth of the novel and Orientalism today than we might want to accept.

Perhaps one way to draw together the role of the intellectual today and the Arabist, the Orientalist as intellectual, is to briefly consider an influential group that directly contributed to the new Orientalist scholarship, that of the U.S. State Department and related institutes and think tanks: the group of writers and pundits commonly known as the "New York Intellectuals." In his thoroughly researched and sharply written book on this group, Alan Wald introduces them as follows:

> In popular usage, the term [New York Intellectuals] usually refers to a loose circle of intellectuals whose preeminent forums have been

Partisan Review, Commentary, and *Dissent.* Contributors to these journals who were old enough to be politically active in the 1930s tended to become, like [Sidney] Hook, not only anti-Stalinists but also revolutionary Marxists of one persuasion or another. . . . In the 1980s, many—including not only Hook but also many other former Trotskyists and Trotskyist sympathizers such as Lionel Abel, Saul Bellow, Irving Kristol, Melvin J. Lasky, and Seymour Martin Lipset—are associated with the neoconservative "Committee for the Free World" led by Midge Decter and her husband, *Commentary* editor Norman Podhoretz.[59]

Interestingly, Wald includes Lionel Trilling in this group. Trilling was of course a significant cultural critic and literary scholar and, importantly for our purposes, Edward Said's former colleague and the major scholar and professor in the English Department at Columbia University from the 1950s to 1970s, where he taught Norman Podhoretz along with many others who gained fame in American political and cultural life. It is unfair to smear all of the writers associated with the group with such occasionally distasteful and virulent politics and machinations. Indeed, Wald concedes that some distinguished figures such as Dwight Macdonald, Mary McCarthy, and Philip Rahv "eventually broke free of their Cold War liberalism or political quiescence and moved unexpectedly back to the left."[60] Two others never really left, as it were, and this would include Irving Howe, who was a key figure in the 1960s debates between the "Old Left" and the "New Left," and Daniel Bell. Yet Wald makes an especially interesting comment given the place of Benda in this debate, asking:

> Was it not the very ideology of becoming "independent critical thinkers," indeed intellectuals beyond the blinding grip of ideology itself, that became the chief means by which the New York intellectuals masked their shift in political allegiance?[61]

Citing Raymond Williams—and he might have referred to Gramsci as well—Wald points out that "independence of thought" preserves other ideas such as "free will," which in turn sustain "dominant institutions" and thus hegemony.[62] Moreover, the independent thinker is a kind of witness, standing outside the circle peering in, the latter-day kin of the modern artist and the critical attitude of the nineteenth-century Arabist towards the Orient and the West.

Still, "independence of thought" was a powerful idea during the Cold War, and we live with the legacy today. Perhaps it was most powerful in the arts, where the art critic and theorist for *Partisan Review*, Clement Greenberg, almost singlehandedly pushed the cause and rise of abstract expressionist art as the consummate representation of American values such as freedom and liberalism. Interestingly, for Greenberg, this type of abstract art is only achieved through the "isolation" of the artist, a familiar idea:

> The American artist has to content and brace himself, almost, with isolation, if he is to give the most of honesty, seriousness, and ambition to his work. Isolation is, so to speak, the natural condition of high art in America. Yet it is precisely our more intimate and habitual acquaintance with isolation that gives us our advantage at this moment. Isolation, or rather the alienation that is its cause, is the truth—isolation, alienation, naked and revealed unto itself, is the condition under which the true reality of our age is experienced.[63]

In his influential book *How New York Stole the Idea of Modernism*, Serge Guilbaut picks up the thread of the New York intellectuals' cultural project and ties them—especially Greenberg and Harold Rosenberg—to a Cold War aesthetic that was rhetorically close to the military and economic policies of the United States.[64] And so abstraction and abstract art, they argue, is a long-standing American and modernist tendency that is also international in its appeal and claims. It was destined to supplant Europe in its role as the standard bearer of the Western tradition. As Guilbaut comments, American abstract art, not the *kitsch* Greenberg denounced, "was placed on the same footing as American economic and military strength: in other words, it was made responsible for the survival of democratic liberties in the 'free' world."[65] To bring this point home, Guilbaut later cites comments by the New York intellectual, historian, and presidential adviser Arthur

Schlesinger, who made much of the "anxiety and frustration that the individual feels when faced with a choice."[66] This last word "choice" is surely a keyword in Cold War discourse, while "frustration" and "anxiety" are feelings associated with alienation.

It was not surprising, then, that the *Guardian* published an article in 1995 stating for the record that the Central Intelligence Agency, through various fronts, notably the Congress for Cultural Freedom, funded exhibits of abstract expressionist art and was deeply enmeshed in New York City's Museum of Modern Art's curatorial decisions and programs at the highest levels.[67] Most of all, this front funded "two dozen magazines, including *Encounter*." The *Guardian* article does not mention that the editor was Irving Kristol, a former Trotskyist and member of the New York intellectual circle.

All of the above makes for great conspiracy narratives, tales of political intrigue if not political and academic gossip. But there is a substantial connection here to the trajectory of the Orientalist in the twentieth century and the kind of Orientalist that Robert Cunninghame Graham was outlining for himself, or at least for his persona at the fin de siècle. The best way to grasp the argument here is through Pierre Bourdieu's idea of cultural capital. As Bourdieu explains in several texts, capital is accumulated and functions in three forms, especially in modern society.[68] The principal form is economic capital, and its simplest form is money. We usually think of banks in this respect. The other two forms are social capital and cultural capital, which have become especially important at the end of the twentieth century and in our own time for various reasons related to social networking tools, such as Facebook, and the homogenization of culture as such within a global context. Social capital is simply the set of social connections one establishes that give one power and place within a given community and/or larger society. Social capital might entail marriage relations, membership in a given club, or a proper name that resonates with others. It is all marketable these days, as advertising agencies quickly realized in their exploitation of mass media. Cultural capital is a bit more elusive, but the best example has to do with education. It is at once the school from which one earned a degree, the reputation of the professor with whom one worked, the length of time it took to earn the degree, perhaps the book that was the result, and the reputation of the university press that published the book. As any academic knows, this is how the contemporary job market works. What is most important is how social capital and cultural capital are converted into economic capital. Again, today this is fairly obvious, as Facebook and other social networking sites have demonstrated that "friends" can be the basis for making money, while most prestigious American liberal arts colleges understand the value of a faculty member who is from a prestigious graduate school and has published a book with a prestigious university press on a politically acceptable topic. This is why many colleges give special place to their faculty pages and recruit accordingly.

Again, we might seem to be far from Orientalism, Robert Cunninghame Graham, and the question of the Orientalist as intellectual, but here is the connection. The small political and cultural journals for which he was writing in the 1880s and 1890s—*Saturday Review, Cornhill Magazine, Nineteenth Century*—were a form of print culture that continued through the early twentieth century. It was even adopted by leftist groups and (modern) artists as the "small magazine." The New York intellectuals were the heirs to this form and founded their own examples, notably *Partisan Review*, which persisted through hard times because it published engaged and well-written articles by writers who were respected by the readership or who established themselves as respected writers. The point is that this form was not profitable at first, but what it accumulated nonetheless was cultural capital. These venues and the writers concerned were only able to convert this cultural capital in the 1970s and, especially, the 1980s when many supported Ronald Reagan and moved into sponsored positions in mainstream universities (such as Irving Kristol's position at New York University) or were absorbed into think tanks such as the American Enterprise Institute.

The connection to Orientalism lies not just in the extent to which this tradition is grounded in a form of print culture that emerged and blossomed in the 1880s, the era of the Anglo-Egyptian war, and which early on featured work by Orientalists and about the Orient. No, the very pose adopted by these magazine editors is, as I have pointed out, that of the Orientalist, later that of the modern artist. And it is not surprising that the legacy continues today with the work of think tanks and grants specifically directed toward the Arab and Muslim world, whether this is the work of, say, the Washington Institute for Near East Policy or the allocation of special funds to universities that teach "strategic languages," with Arabic being a primary interest.

Finally, with regard to Middle East studies and the way the Arab/Muslim world is understood, taught, and discussed—Orientalism as a discourse in the broadest sense—the pose of the Orientalist and the connections to modernism, the Cold War, and the intellectual are connected to popular culture once again. The ultimate irony is that the modernist pose of the removed and distant intellectual, the Orientalist who is an objective and acute observer of both the East and the West, is a feature of popular culture today. After all, this is the stance of the "rebel," the "loner," and the "renegade," which is common in sports (think Andre Agassi, maybe even Eric Cantona) and on the movie screen. Sylvester Stallone and Clint Eastwood have had successful careers playing such characters.

As for Conrad and Cunninghame Graham and the traversal of the Orientalist fantasy, the link here is grounded in the difference between irony and sarcasm. Much of the critical literature on Conrad's work makes much of irony as a persistent characteristic of his writing. Indeed, this is Said's central point about Conrad's "two visions" and the way we can read, say, *Heart of Darkness* as anything other than a racist text.[69] And the roots of this position lie in the Cold War and the role of the artist. Cunninghame Graham, as I have argued, distanced himself from the Orientalist fantasy with a clear and stated form of irony far more explicit than that of Conrad, and sometimes more akin to sarcasm. So if we are truly to subvert, critique—or, better, traverse—the fantasy of Orientalism or any part of the colonial legacy, is irony enough, even when it is as pronounced as we find it in Cunninghame Graham's *Mogreb-el-Acksa*? There is an attempt to traverse the fantasy here, but it is so deep and constitutive within our culture that the effort falls short and the fantasy survives, albeit in newer, perhaps muted forms.

4

Orientalism from Within and Without

Marmaduke Pickthall

From Marmaduke to Muhammed

MARMADUKE PICKTHALL is a most interesting figure among British writers of the late nineteenth and early twentieth centuries, a period punctuated by the Great War. In literature, the era was marked by the rise of what is now known as the modernist movement. Pickthall, today, is largely forgotten. Yet other modern and modernist writers are still celebrated, even though they did not achieve the same kind of commercial success and broad readership, nor gain recognition for their skill and intellect, as Pickthall did in his time

To understand Pickthall's place among writers in his time, consider the respected journals where he published reviews and serialized versions of his works during the fin de siècle period: *Cornhill Magazine*, *Nineteenth Century*, and *Academy*, *Athenaeum*. These journals held a prominent place for their educated middle- and upper-class readership.[1] *Cornhill Magazine* also stands out because of its connection to so many well-known authors who formed the tradition of the nineteenth-century novel.

Pickthall worked hard to break with Orientalist discourse about the Arab and Muslim world. His deep roots in the discourse of British culture—the novel tradition—brought about a crisis of thought and representation. It is on this crisis that I wish to focus this chapter and, with reference to several early-twentieth-century texts by Pickthall, figure out what this crisis of thought and representation meant for our author as well as for the legacy of liberal and progressive Western thought and discourse about the Arab and Muslim world.

Marmaduke Pickthall was one of twelve children born to the Reverend Charles Pickthall and his wife Mary. The family had some social standing, given his father's position in the church. But after his father died in 1881, the family experienced a great deal of financial hardship. Still, Marmaduke attended the Harrow School as a day student, where his fellow students included Winston Churchill and L. S. Amery. Following his failure to gain a position in the Levant consular service as a young adult, and at the invitation of a family acquaintance, Pickthall visited Syria for an extended stay from 1894 to 1896. Syria included modern Lebanon at that time as well as Mandate Palestine. Young Marmaduke traveled the countryside and explored the major cities of the region—Beirut, Jerusalem, and Damascus.[2] He also spent a good deal of time traveling off the usual tourist routes while making friends and contacts among the local populations wherever he went. Pickthall learned Arabic and much about the culture of the region, to the outrage of his fellow countrymen, and he even shunned the company of fellow Britons, Europeans, and Christians. This was the formative experience of his life, launching him as a writer and eventually as a major figure in the Islamic world of the time.

Pickthall was a moderately successful writer in the early twentieth century, specifically from 1903 to 1922. Most of his novels and short stories from this period concerned the Near East. His collections of short stories such as *Pot au Feu* (1911), *Tales of Five Chimneys* (1915), and *As Others See Us* (1922) also concerned the Near East to some extent. But the bulk of his oeuvre consists of the Near East novels, which include *Said the Fisherman* (1903), *The House of Islam* (1906), *Children of the Nile* (1908), *The Valley of the Kings* (1909), *Veiled Women* (1913), *The House of War* (1916), *Knights of Araby* (1917), and *The Early Hours* (1921). *Oriental Encounters* (1918) is an autobiographical travelogue from the same period. These works were published mostly by established houses such as Methuen, Collins, and John Murray in Britain and Knopf in the United States. Considering that Pickthall wrote approximately fourteen novels and numerous short stories as well as literary reviews and journal articles on politics and culture, it is clear that he was an accomplished and prolific professional writer.

However, perhaps Pickthall is a significant intellectual figure today mainly because he converted to Islam in the middle of his adult life and quickly gained an important status with the Muslim community in Britain and subsequently in the Muslim world as a whole. To identify him as a British Muslim, as Peter Clark does in the title of his biography, *Marmaduke Pickthall: British Muslim*, is not to diminish his work as a writer but to emphasize that he converted in a time when such a move was still viewed as a scandal. As an example, during the siege of Khartoum, Gordon angrily rejected the Mahdi's surrender terms simply because they required him to convert.[3] Or consider Gordon's deaf ear to Pasha Slatin's pleas for help because as a captive of the Mahdi he had converted to Islam.[4] Gordon was certainly an extreme and devout Christian, and perhaps atypical if not singular in many ways, but his special opprobrium for British converts to Islam was far from unique, making Pickthall a singular and notable figure in this regard. We must consider also that our writer was neither an anonymous middle-class wage earner nor an eccentric aristocrat, but rather a middle-class intellectual with a significant body of work to his name and a distinguished reputation as a man of letters.

Pickthall announced his actual conversion in 1917, though there were early indications of a slow rejection of Christianity in some of his prior work. In 1914, for example, he walked out of a church gathering when the congregation sang "For the Mahometans," the hymn of Charles Wesley (#443 in the 1875 *Wesley Hymnal*) that contains racist lines about an "Arab Thief."[5] As Clark notes, in the summer of 1917 Pickthall "gave a series of talks to the Muslim Literary Society in Notting Hill, West London, on 'Islam and Progress.'"[6] It was during the last of these talks that Pickthall told the audience of his conversion to Islam, explaining that only Islam could be considered a progressive religion, hence the title of his lecture. Indeed, he underlined his commitment to Islam by taking "Muhammed" for his first name in lieu of the very English "Marmaduke."[7]

From this point on, Islam was at the center of his spiritual and intellectual life. Again, Clark's excellent biography provides a detailed account of the writer's conversion and related activism. In these two chapters Clark makes interesting comments on the ways Pickthall argued for Islam to both Muslim society and the West in the shadow of the fall of the Ottoman Empire and the Caliphate, yet he did so in ways that were unique. With regard to political notions of tolerance and the rights of women, and a more general supportive relationship to the sciences and modernity, Pickthall always cast Islam as more Western than the West or more English than England in this respect.[8]

The circumstances surrounding the book for which Pickthall is best known today, and which (even now) is available for purchase worldwide (unlike most of his fiction), are relevant here. I am referring to Pickthall's well-known translation and commentary, *The Meaning of the Glorious Koran*. He started the project in 1928 with a series of consultations and meetings with notable figures in Islamic and Arabic literary studies at the Islamic Al Azhar University in Cairo. The book was first published in 1930 by the publishing house Alfred Knopf of New York City. From the start the project was controversial, since it is a translation of a sacred text, though the sharpest critic of the book, Taha Husayn, was not a religious figure but rather a professor of Arabic literature at the University of Cairo. Still, what we should take from this controversy and the aftermath is that Pickthall survived the critical storm, and even today *The Meaning of the Glorious Koran* remains a significant text—it is more than a mere translation—around the world.[9]

For our purposes we should consider that, after 1921, Pickthall turned almost entirely toward the Islamic world and left behind his career as an established British novelist.[10] Now, some might be most intrigued by the Islamic second part of Pickthall's career, and with good reason. Still, I have focused in this chapter on the preconversion period, for several reasons. First, though it is remarkable that such a figure from British letters and culture converted, his position as a Muslim is not as interesting simply because he moves away from an oscillation between worlds and shifts entirely to one side, that of Islam. His work in the 1903–1916 period is most relevant due to this back-and-forth activity, the kind of oscillation associated with both an ideological and a spiritual rupture. Moreover, I focus on *Said the Fisherman*, and to a lesser extent *Oriental Encounters*, because of the themes they produce—the city and the masses—and also due to what I refer to as the "problem of standpoint." My point is to trace how Pickthall's disenchantment with British thinking about the Near East—in both formal commentary and everyday discourse—moved from that of an insider, with connections outside in the East, to that of an "inside outsider" who could move easily around the Arab and Muslim world. I will give some attention to Pickthall's writing about Turkey and the Armenian genocide in order to tease out the contradictions of his position. In the last part of the chapter, I discuss Pickthall's position as an outsider when he converted to Islam and dedicated his life to the Muslim world and culture.

The gist of my argument and this tracing is to show that ideology, or "discourse" in Foucault's sense of the word, is not so easily given the slip. My point is simply that the most pernicious of ideologies—and Orientalism is surely one such system of thought—survive and flourish in the most unsuspecting quarters, following the lessons of modern hermeneutics and interpretive techniques after Freud. With reference to Marmaduke Pickthall, perhaps we might better understand how and why this is so, for this same form of "progressive" Orientalism is the basis of so much apparently liberal and otherwise supportive thinking, and writing, about the Arab and Muslim world today. Pickthall's discursive dilemma is emblematic with reference to the last century as well as our own moment.

Standpoint, or the Writer Takes a Position

In a 1909 review in the *Athenaeum* of Hall Caine's popular novel *The White Prophet*, we see Pickthall's skill as a reader and writer, and most of all his stance as a British writer who can write about the Near East and Islam from within the culture. I will address culture as an issue in Pickthall's work in the conclusion of this chapter, but for now we should simply note that he was aware that culture was a critical factor in thinking about—and "doing," to echo Matthew Arnold—social issues at the fin de siècle. Aptly, *The White Prophet* is set in Egypt. The novel is about a nationalist Islamic figure and his white British female captive, and so it fits with the common genre of captive and harem literature and also the subgenre of Orientalist melodrama (softcore erotica akin to a Harlequin romance). Unlike readers today who might read this novel as a cultural artifact and part of a genealogy of Orientalist thought, Pickthall, on the eve of the Great War, is ruthless in his assessment of what we might call the "false ideology" of the novel.

The novel purports to support the nationalist cause, and on this matter Pickthall pinpoints a few pages and references in the novel. But overall, he finds the novel clumsy and simplistic. Thus, the English characters constantly "ejaculate" expletives, such as "damn" and "fool," while the Egyptian characters offer Arabic expressions that are either mistranslated or misused by the author of the novel. There is one part toward the end of this review, which I should add has a certain crisp tone overall, where Pickthall declares:

> The author's picture of the fanaticism of the Mohammedans is much exaggerated, as concerning Egypt at the present day; and his suggestion of a return to the bare Coran as preaching tolerance, sounds the depth of his ignorance of the whole subject. In this context we may note in the author's favour, that he avoids the common error of confusing civilization, in the modern sense, with Christianity.[11]

I have quoted this passage because it certainly addresses Western fantasies that persist today, and also because here Pickthall tells us several things about himself. He is clearly knowledgeable about Islam and Muslims, and he is a critic of the way the West—specifically Britain—conflates this vision of Muslim fanatics and global politics with suggestions for possible Muslim reform. Indeed, this is familiar territory.

Pickthall's journalism placed him in the public eye, though his novels and other texts earned him a reputation as an accomplished man of letters. His best-known novel, *Said the Fisherman*, was published in 1903. In 1918 he published the autobiographical travelogue *Oriental Encounters*, and then in 1921 he published many other texts of all types, including the novels noted earlier. The decline of his reputation is easily ascribed to two factors in his life that both drew him away from the life of a popular writer and made him unpopular. In the first instance, Pickthall converted to Islam and for the rest of his life dedicated more and more of his time and writing to Islam and the British Muslim community. This turn was brought about by religious conviction and necessity, and at least initially did not harm his reputation. That is, it is not clear that his public life as a British Muslim affected his readership. But his pro-Turkish writing and activism of the period, both before and during the Great War, certainly damaged his reputation and public standing. These factors comprise what I call "standpoint," an idea that I will explain shortly. For now, we should think contrarily and consider that Pickthall's assumption of a standpoint, while it places him outside the mainstream as a matter of opinion, is still very central (as an action or gesture) to the way a writer and intellectual should act according to the protoliberal paradigm.

In a 1903 review of *Said the Fisherman*, the reviewer makes the following comment:

> If Mr. Pickthall be a Briton, he is an artificer of astonishing cleverness. Into this Mahommedan romance, covering the period from March 1860 to July 12, 1882, he has breathed a spirit so Oriental as almost to persuade his reader that Said is as real as Sindbad. . . . His is a Damascus of massacre, and in the noon of his prosperity his womenkind call each other mothers of nothing and daughters of dogs. They and he are lifelike and shapers of artistic meanings without any obtrusion of British sentiment to show their creator in the act of assisting them.[12]

Now, that Said is "as real as Sindbad" should certainly make us all pause, if not laugh, while the comments about the behavior of Arab women—of course Said has two wives!—and sectarian massacre certainly fit other Orientalist fantasy paradigms. However, my interest here is really that the writer has identified Pickthall as an authentic, almost Arab writer, yet still a Briton. Taking us back to Burton, and even further into the past, and then forward to T. E. Lawrence and the present, this idea of the (white) Briton who enters into and becomes a part of the world of the Arab other is both scandalous and a guarantor of commercial success. Titillation about crossing over—the pleasure of being mistaken for the "other"—is certainly a popular publishing ploy and an exciting idea for British readers, perhaps even today.

But at a deeper and more significant level, this passage is about what I call "standpoint." By "standpoint" I refer to the position taken by the writer, in this case the position of the outsider on the inside, or the Westerner with the privileged view from the interior of the East, a view that might even be from within the cloistered and privileged space of the harem. So standpoint (that is, the position(ing) of the writer) is not just about politics but also entails Desire in its most obvious form (the harem, the dancer, and privileged access)—yet it also gets to the heart of all Orientalist writing. Indeed, all of these writers make some claim to special knowledge, whether attained as a matter of erudition or through guile, luck, or good looks. Moreover, standpoint is a key idea when we consider much critical writing—fiction and nonfiction—in fin de siècle Britain and Europe, for it is clearly the basis for the modern artist's aesthetic. Simply put, the modern artist, the modernist, is a singular artist with a unique view from without into the inside of modernity. So the modernist/modern artist stands on the periphery, isolated in the midst of modern life, and from this position—this standpoint—is able to see and represent modernity in ways that defy the efforts and abject consciousness of those who live within the rhythms of modern everyday life.

Standpoint and *Oriental Encounters*

Oriental Encounters is a later text with which to begin this exegesis of standpoint in Pickthall's work, but it is also a clear expression and articulation of Pickthall's intellectual and creative persona. Though it is ostensibly a travelogue of the author's first visit to Syria and Palestine, the book is also a very personal reflection on how this visit changed Pickthall in spiritual, cultural, and intellectual ways. The book is, like his other work (especially *Said the Fisherman*), a kind of picaresque tale of his adventures in the company of two roguish companions:

Suleyman, his adviser, and Rashid, his guard and personal servant. He also had a cook, an atheist from Jerusalem, as we learn in one chapter, but the former two are his principal friends and interlocutors. Each chapter is a separate tale; some are more amusing or serious than others. "Bastirma" is about a cured piece of meat that turns out to be all that is left of the father of a Jewish traveler, who they meet as he is en route to bury him in Jerusalem. Of course there is a disgusting mishap. In other chapters they encounter fellow (hostile) Europeans, bitter Christians, and crazed Bedawi who variously challenge them to jousts and brawls, and otherwise produce amusing stories.

Again, Pickthall's book functions as both a travelogue and popular entertainment, but it is clearly a text of rigorous self-scrutiny about the situation of a Briton in the Arab and Muslim world during the fin de siècle era, as is evident from the first page. To that end, the author's introduction to *Oriental Encounters* is relevant here given what it tells us about the author's state of mind both with respect to his book and the Arab-Western encounter as such. Two passages from this introduction bring out an interesting discourse with which he recounts the origin of the book and his passion for the "East." Pickthall planned for a career in the consular corps in either Turkey or the Levant, yet he did poorly on the competitive exams; when turned down for these posts, he felt condemned to "the drab monotone of London fog." He "dreamed of Eastern sunshine, palm trees, camels, desert sand, as of a Paradise which I had lost by my shortcomings."[13] Still, he left anyway at the age of 18, ostensibly to find a way into the consular corps, though actually seeking a more authentic experience. He writes:

> [T]he European ceased to interest me, appearing somehow inappropriate and false in those surroundings. At first I tried to overcome this feeling or perception which, while I lived with English people, seemed unlawful. All my education until then had tended to impose on me the cult of the thing done habitually upon a certain plane of our society. To seek to mix on an equality with Orientals, of whatever breeding, was one of those things which were never done nor even contemplated by the kind of person who had always been my model.[14]

He goes on to describe his "Eastern" desire as a sneaking wish to "know the natives of the country intimately." The points we should draw from this passage are, first, the remarkable clarity of Pickthall's prose. There is no awkward phrasing, archaic usage, or even euphemism. Without shame the writer is telling the reader that his desire for the East was just that, a desire for intimate relations, and though the book is without sexual content, and we do not know anything about Pickthall's sexual "encounters" in the Near East, it is nonetheless a sensuous journey for him, a structure of feeling following Raymond Williams's critical terminology. Yet it is sensuous mostly by contrast with the West, that is, the "drab monotone of London fog." What we find here is, of course, a well-known stereotype but, and this is important, it is wrapped up with the life of a somewhat middle-class writer. Remember, he visits Egypt and then Syria as a very young man, having failed his diplomatic exams, which is surely a different itinerary from that of his forebears in the British Orientalist tradition. Yes, the East might be a career, but here the East is also the opposite of a career, and in fact offers sensuousness, life in and for itself, contrary to the routine and sacrifice—the disavowal of desire—intrinsic to everyday life in twentieth-century Britain.

Later in the same section he writes about how he adopted "semi native garb," which with his avowed "love for Arabs [his friends] . . . I was made to understand, was hardly decent."[15] Again, is this a well-known narrative, the same story that British writers had written for over one hundred years? Or is there more? I think the latter, and so I return to the circumstances that Pickthall offers as the origin and impetus for his journey: the failed exam, his dashed career ambitions, and his disillusionment with Western attitudes toward the Arab and Muslim world. Now, he might sound like many who preceded him and some who followed, but this much is different: he conflates the East with the sensuality of life itself, and the West with an inhuman routine, and so his rejection of England and Englishness is an affirmation of life. Pickthall, unlike almost all of the others, is a true believer.

Two points in the body of the text are of interest here. In a late chapter the narrator and his companions come across an unattended grape arbor laden with fruit. Rashid and Suleyman stop and immediately start to cut bunches of grapes, passing some to the narrator to eat. He refuses and lectures them about stealing, only to be told by Suleyman that his morals do not apply in this context—in Syria, a non-Western culture.

The book ends with a moving account of the narrator's last day in Beirut, when he receives a visit from an older Christian gentleman who had arranged for a tailor to make for him a special set of clothes of traditional design and the best cloth. This older Beiruti was very learned, and from the narrator's first days in the city had helped him to learn Arabic. When he brought the clothes he also brought a gift and a bill. The narrator reviewed the bill and spoke harshly to the gentleman about the cost. Though the latter mildly protested that the cost was due to the quality of the cloth, and was not much for a European, he nonetheless left quietly after giving the narrator a gift. The narrator unwrapped the packet to find an especially rare version of *The Thousand and One Nights*, a key text for British Orientalist fantasy and also an ironic gift given the way he had mistreated this man. The narrator recounts how he tried in vain to contact the tailor subsequently to explain his rude behavior but was not able to do so; he eventually discovered that the old Beiruti had died in the interim.

Standpoint and the Lumpenproletariat

Said is no Sinbad. Indeed, the eponymous protagonist of Pickthall's best-known novel, *Said the Fisherman*, is a kind of lumpenproletariat, someone who lives at the lowest level of society with respect to labor and everyday life. I will elaborate on the lumpenproletariat and the novel form shortly, but for now we should simply consider just how odd it was that Pickthall chose to build his novel around someone we might kindly call a "lowlife." In popular American literature, Edith Wharton's *House of Mirth* features Lily Bart, a female character who only a few decades earlier would have been denounced on moral grounds; while in Britain, the characters of major novels by Hardy, Wells, and Bennett, and even Conrad's Kurtz, were flawed, but they were not as abject as Pickthall's Said.

Consider briefly the outline of the novel. We first meet Said when he is a fisherman somewhere on the Syrian coast—probably within modern Lebanon—albeit not very successful and barely making ends meet. Due to a theft of his small savings, he and his wife, Husna, must leave the village and find work in Damascus. He tells those whom he meets that he is going to collect an inheritance from a deceased brother. En route he commits various petty crimes, though without planning or intent, and in the same mindless way abandons his belea-guered wife when she is injured due to his fight with someone on the road. Once in Damascus he meets a donkey driver and other urban types, in particular a most devious beggar, Mustapha. The latter urges him to help with the murder of a wealthy Christian and the abduction of his daughter, whom Said desires. Said agrees and the plan is real-ized as both participate in the 1860 massacre of the Damascus Chris-tians and use the turmoil as cover for their crime. The friend dies in the process, and Said is left with the ill-gotten treasure. He and his other friend develop a prosperous business but he is finally undone and robbed by his young wife—Husna has returned in the interim—who flees to Greece with the treasure, his son, and another man. A beaten man, Said wanders back to his village, and then to Alexandria (with a London detour), gradually losing his mind and his life in the riots that accompanied the Colonel Arabi–led nationalist uprising in the Anglo-Khedive–ruled Egypt during the early 1880s.

This novel is remarkable, again, because while it appears to be a novel in many ways, it is not such in other important ways. While the protagonist develops as in a bildungsroman, his rise to wealth and prosperity is both ill-gotten and accidental, running against the narra-tive and ideological trajectory of the nineteenth-century British novel, though with some kinship to the French novel, particularly Flaubert's work (e.g., *L'Éducation sentimentale*). Still, Said is not even a crafty thief! Also, though the text has a picaresque quality, it is inaccurate to dub it a picaresque novel. I mention this because the picaresque has proved useful to some twentieth-century writers, such as Emile Habiby in his *Said, the Ill-Fated Pessoptimist*. First, the picaresque is not a genre but rather describes a character type who might feature in all forms of narrative. Also, the picaro is foolish, and worse, but not as malicious or negligent as Said. Moreover, the picaro does not change, nor is he expected to change. We might expect Said to improve in some ways, though he remains much the same throughout the novel.

For Karl Marx and for many others in the tradition and without, this category of the lumpenproletariat—and the people therein—is the object of suspicion and stigma. These are the people who, in Marx's view, form the counterrevolutionary mob, the forces of reaction. Pickthall traces Said's life journey as a kind of anti-bildung, where his protagonist starts with nothing, gains much, then loses it. Yet as with Dickens's Pip in *Great Expectations*, Said's gains are ill-gotten, so the process of bildung, or development in an affirmative sense, is reversed here, for ill-gotten wealth cannot be the source of social elevation. So Said suffers a social and material fall and eventually death at the conclusion of the novel, all due, we are led to infer, to his selfish and nasty behavior toward others, especially those who love and trust him.

Pickthall sets his character up from the start, offering an unsavory, nearly abject portrait:

> The house of Said the fisherman nestled among the sandhills of the seashore at a long stone's throw from the town, in whose shadow it lay at sunset. Within it was a single room, very dirty, the abode of many aged smells; without a squat cube with walls of stone and roof of mud, sun-baked and rolled to a seemly flatness. Hard by was a fig tree, the nearest to the sea in all that coast. Here, in the crotch of the branches, Said would place his mattress in the stifling summer nights and snore two deep bass notes in peace and coolness, while his wife trumpeted a treble from her couch upon the housetop.[16]

This description with which the novel begins, and with which we meet Said, is laced with notions foul to the senses: bad smells, a tree "crotch," snoring, and the suggestion of domestic filth.

The next paragraph confirms the worst, as we find out about Said's work and work habits:

He [Said] was not a great fisherman, such as is to be found in Europe, with a sailing boat of his own, who will go far out to sea with his nets. If there were any such in all the coasts of Arabistan, Said had never heard of them. Sometimes he would row out in a friend's boat to a little distance from the shore and drop his nets, a great circle of bobbing cork and driftwood to mark their whereabouts. But mostly he would go to some river-mouth or promontory where flat-topped rocks stretched far into the sea, promising safe foothold. And there, mother-naked, save for a huge turban, he would paddle and flounder all day long with his cast-net, sometimes alone, sometimes with several comrades.[17]

This is hardly a flattering portrait, with a subject whom even Thomas Eakins might not render well.[18] The detail about the turban confirms the sense we have that Pickthall is keeping his character at a distance, again, a kind of anti-bildungsroman "hero" or abject subject.

That the protagonist is worse than an antihero is hardly the only aspect of *Said* that suggests that Pickthall is attempting to subvert certain Orientalist tendencies. Contrary to most nineteenth-century British writing about the Near East, and with the exception of Edward Lane's *An Account of the Manners and Customs of the Modern Egyptians*, this novel is set in an Arab city, not the country, that is, not in a mountain village or a desert encampment. I argue that this is at first remarkable and an intervention on Pickthall's part, demonstrating his attempt to subvert novelistic discourse about the Arab and Muslim world. Yet our author cannot escape the rhetoric and frameworks—the discourse of the nineteenth-century British novelist—within which he must work or represent his ideas. So Pickthall turns to an established binary of British literature, the city and the country, which introduces a related discourse of the masses.

Street Arabs: The Arab Country and the Arab City

Before we move forward, and because we are addressing the Arab city, I argue that a brief genealogy of the phrase "street Arab" is most instructive as to the situation of the Western reader. The *Oxford English Dictionary* entry for "street Arab" is as follows:

> A homeless child or young person living on the streets.
>
> Now generally regarded as offensive.
>
> 1853 M. HILL in M. Hill & C. F. Cornwallis *Two Prize Ess. Juvenile Delinquency* vi. 240 Can it be believed that these children are street *Arabs*, street *vermin*, thieves, [etc.]. 1875 *Punch* 6 Mar. 108/2 Irregular crossing-sweepers, unlicensed boot-cleaners, and street-Arabs generally.

Clearly street Arabs are children, and usually boys, who are found in the streets of the poorest and oldest slum areas of the United States and Britain. These boys are also orphaned or otherwise detached from a traditional family structure, and they are engaged in menial if not illegal work. Street sweepers, shoe shine boys, and thieves—street Arabs all. Like Said, they are truly lumpenproletariat.

Jacob Riis's *How the Other Half Lives*, an early-twentieth-century book about the slums, tenements, and tenement dwellers of New York City, is also of interest here, for prominent among his chapters on waifs, prostitutes, and "the common herd" is a chapter on "the Street Arab." Riis not only provides a definition of this creature but photographs as well.[19] It is notable that this book and this writer were considered key to liberal reform in their time, while the documentary text and photographs comprise a kind of proto-sociology of the American and British slum that was fully realized in midcentury studies such as that of Michael Harrington and others. Riis tells us that the street Arab is usually a runaway boy and represents a peculiar New York institution:

> The Street Arab has all the faults and all the virtues of the life he leads. Vagabond that he is, acknowledging no authority and owning no allegiance to anybody or anything, with his grimy fist raised against society whenever it tries to coerce him, he is as bright and sharp as the weasel, which, among all the predatory beasts, he most resembles.[20]

Riis's use of the term "street Arab" entails much of the *Oxford English Dictionary* definition and also some aspects of late-nineteenth-century liberal reformist ideology. The street Arab, for Riis, is still a miscreant, a vagabond, who inhabits the older parts of cities, but now he is at once a rebel and a devious rodent. Riis's characterization of the street Arab as a rebel is important, for clearly these boys are seen as a social threat to some degree, though not a serious threat to established authority. Yet their organization as a band of brothers is also interesting, for it is a lateral bond, one without a "father," leader, or leader class. The band of brothers is central to, say, Freud's theory of patricide and social organization.[21] It also mediates how British travelers view Arab society, especially that of the Bedouins.[22]

The street Arab is also interesting in that for the most part, at least through the second half of the nineteenth and into the twentieth centuries, most British writing about the Arab world valorized the desert and the Bedouin at the expense of the city and city-dwelling Arabs. Indeed, most of the narratives were clearly travelogues about journeys though the mountains and desert, so there was little point in focusing on the cities of the Arab world, which were considered too well known in any case. Again, the desert and the people of the desert were of greater interest, especially in the remote parts of the interior of the Arabian peninsula. This last point is key to the success of the Blunts' books about their voyages into the interior and especially Doughty's *Travels in Arabia Deserta*. As noted earlier, this is a book that melded ethnography with archeology, adventure literature, and moral discourse and offered a vision or image of the region that inspired later writers of all sorts and in many ways. At the least, and referring to this strain of British Orientalist writing as a kind of displacement, the desert and the Bedouin function at once as a kind of pastoral respite from the ravages of the industrial cities of the West, and also as a kind of nostalgic realization of the lost classical world.

Still, for all of his valorization of the desert and Bedouins, Doughty never displayed the contempt for Arab city dwellers that we find in the work of Gertrude Bell and her pupil turned pop-culture hero, T. E. Lawrence. Early in *Seven Pillars* the latter writes:

> In his [the Bedouin's] life he had air and winds, sun and light, open spaces and a great emptiness. There was no human effort, no fecundity in Nature: just the heaven above and the unspotted earth beneath. There unconsciously he came near God.[23]

Clearly Lawrence, like so many before him, finds something pure in the figure of the Bedouin, almost pastoral, but definitely preindustrial and untouched by modernity and capitalism; the contrast with city dwellers is implicit and clear. The desert and desert dwellers represent an alternative space for a dissatisfied upper-middle-class Briton, while the Arab city and urban Arabs are somehow corrupted by the West and of no interest.

So, by contrast, the Arab city was not as represented, which makes Pickthall's Damascus novel so unique despite its flaws. Indeed, a word about the Arab city and modernity is needed here. First, the country and the city paradigm does not really work when we consider the history of the Arab city. Importantly, the Arab city and the Arab country should not be seen as two entirely separate spheres and cultures. For the most part the division of the city and the country, or between urban and rural Arabs, was a constant until the middle of the twentieth century. That is, the respective populations did not merge as they did under the pressures of industrialization in Britain with proletarianization of agricultural workers and peasants. To the contrary, Bernard Hourcade comments:

> The mass of the rural population generally remained on the margins of the cities, and the massive waves of rural to urban migration did not appear until rather later in the "urban revolution."[24]

In fact the movement from the country to the city in the Near East was very specific in its moment and consequences. As Leila Fawaz and Robert Ilbert point out:

> One result was that when a civil war engulfed large parts of Mount Lebanon in the mid-nineteenth century, the rural population that fled came to Beirut, the politically safest and economically most secure port. However, they brought with them their fears

and prejudices about the other communities with whom they had clashed with [*sic*] in their home villages.[25]

So the Christian and Druze refugees from the 1860s mountain war brought their respective prejudices into the heart of an ancient city, Beirut, where, to this day, they persist in muted form.

Said is not a street Arab, but the streets of the street Arab, the dank and dirty urban space of the old slums of the West, and the chaos and hubbub we also associate with them are reproduced in this novel: the East End of London is Damascus. These older spaces are the same tumbledown and dirty areas that reformers such as Riis argued should be torn down and replaced with modern, clean, and healthy housing and factory buildings. Consider the following passage from *Said*, as the protagonist is led across Damascus by his beggar friend.

> Mustapha led on by unfrequented tunnels and passages avoiding as far as might be the main streets, where professional pride obliged him to put on an appearance of extreme feebleness and whine despairingly as one in the clutch of a devil. At last, in a narrow lane between high walls, with never a lattice, he stopped before a low door which was open. . . . A narrow passage turned at right angles after a few yards, so that the interior of the house could not be looked into from the street. . . . On turning the corner Said was quite unprepared for the scene of splendour which burst upon his sight. There was a small quadrangle of two storeys high, its walls inlaid with arabesque figures as a frieze under the roof and as medallions under the windows. . . . A few lemon trees in the centre formed a bower over a tank of clear water fed by a freshet that flowed through the midst of the court in a toy channel.[26]

This account of the movement across the Oriental city, Damascus, is akin to key moments in Dickens's *Oliver Twist* and probably many other nineteenth-century novels of the city, especially London. Unlike, say Coketown in *Hard Times*, London is an ancient city where the premodern and irrational persists in twisting, nearly unmapped, and impenetrable older sections of the city. Consider this passage in *Oliver*

Twist when Sikes leads little Oliver across the city to Fagin's roost, through Smithfield market, in the early hours of the day as the working classes prepare for the working day.

> They walked on, by little-frequented and dirty ways, for a full half hour: meeting very few people: and those appearing from their looks to hold much the same position in society as Mr. Sikes himself. At length they turned into a very filthy narrow street, nearly full of old-clothes shops; the dog, running forward, as if conscious that there was now no further occasion for keeping on guard, stopped before the door of a shop that was closed and apparently untenanted. The house was in a ruinous condition; and on the door was nailed a board, intimating that it was to let: which looked as if it had hung there, for many years.[27]

Later on in the novel Fagin also leads Oliver across the city in order to commit a crime. And the quarter where they wind up is clearly a kind of ghetto, replete with casbah-like small streets and suspicious characters who furtively dart here and there.[28] Bluntly put, since Fagin is a Jew, and thus of the "Orient," then his crew of child thieves are surely "street Arabs," while even the slums they frequent assume an "Oriental" character.[29] By the early twentieth century Joyce has caught on to this idea, and so in "Araby," a selection from *Dubliners*, the traveling bazaar is imbued with the Orient as our young protagonist ventures forth like a knight-errant from a Walter Scott (Orientalist) romance to obtain a prize for his love object (since this is a Joyce story, he fails). And certainly in the Nighttown sequence in *Ulysses,* as Bloom and Stephen move through the red-light district of Dublin, the social space assumes a kind of Orientalist air, bringing these tendencies to a peak, as the equation of sex and the East/Orient is finally resolved.

In *The Country and the City*, Raymond Williams documents how a pair of ideas, the binary of the country and the city, figured so largely in the English social and political imaginary of the nineteenth and twentieth centuries. Of course with the end of the nineteenth century we expect a paradigm shift as the Empire is imperiled and then crumbles, yet when it comes to the social imaginary Williams notes a good deal of continuity. And so he writes about the genealogy of the country and the city in the social imaginary over the course of two hundred years, linking the fantasy of the English village to exoticized locales of the Empire:

> The effects of this development on the English imagination have gone deeper than can easily be traced. All the time, within it, we have seen so many examples. But from at least the mid nineteenth century, and with important instances earlier, there was this larger context within which every idea and every image was consciously and unconsciously affected. . . . The lands of the Empire were an idyllic retreat, an escape from debt or shame, or an opportunity for making a fortune. An expanding middle class found its regular careers abroad, as war and administration in the distant lands became more organized. New rural societies entered the English imagination, under the shadow of political and economic control: the plantation worlds of Kipling and Maugham and early Orwell: the trading worlds of Conrad and Joyce Cary.[30]

Developing this reference with regard to psychoanalysis we might see Williams's genealogy of "the country and the city" as a process of displacement in the broadest sense. With displacement the form of the fantasy persists, albeit in an altered—even new—guise. And yet with Orientalism other powerful fantasies come into play, turning a paradigm from the English social and political imaginary, as well as the British literary tradition, into a renewed and revitalized ideological form.

Lately, in the mainstream American press, the street Arab has been "inverted," literally, and so we frequently read about the Arab street in articles that concern public debate about politics in the Arab society, with the same set of associations and results.

Now, with reference back to Dickens's Fagin, it is perhaps an instrumental understanding and application of Freud's notion of displacement, but what we notice here is that the "street Arab" and "the Arab street" are gradually conflated with a discourse of class and social space. Then finally the latter drops out, leaving the Arab as at once the figure of the Orient and the urchin and schemer of the teeming, crowded metropolis of modernity. If the Arab is the ultimate signifier of modernity, or at least its necessary nemesis, then, finally, the signified of the attendant language and textuality of proto-urbanism and philanthropy is eclipsed by the visceral appeals of this ideologeme.

Arabs in the Street: Sectarian Violence and the Mob of "others"

"Street Arab" is clearly too racist for use in the contemporary mainstream press, but the idea of the Oriental masses will not die so easily, and so here we see its second life today. While the discussion might concern nuclear weapons and human rights, what is really at stake is a certain fear of the wild fanatics and dirty denizens of Arab cities who support Oriental despots. Of course this is the established discourse of the mob. It is hardly controversial today that modern British literature, or more broadly textuality of the eighteenth through the twenty-first centuries, is decisively mediated by a discourse of the mob and the masses.

Perhaps this discourse is clearest in Matthew Arnold's key text of the period, *Culture and Anarchy*, where he argues for the primacy of culture in modern society. Culture—the vaguely defined "sweetness and light"—is part of the English tradition that must be extended, surely in the same way that the franchise was to be extended following the Chartist protests that marked most of the nineteenth century. Arnold wrote this important text—for reasons far contrary to his vision—on the heels of a series of disturbances in Hyde Park. Workingmen gathered to demand the franchise and other rights, again as part of the extended Chartist movement, and when troops were called the calm and flower beds of Hyde Park were disturbed. As silly as this might seem to us now, there is some urgency in Arnold's program, for it is only with the extension of culture as he understands it that anarchy might be forestalled. In addition to his career as a writer and influential intellectual of the late Victorian era he was also a school inspector, and he argued that through schools the working classes might be brought into the fold. Now, this is a less-than-brief account of this text and Arnold's program, but it is key to the discourse of the masses in the period, and note that "culture" is the pivotal term. Pickthall too recognized that culture was the problem. British culture was a problem, and a misunderstood Arab and Muslim culture was also a problem. And like Arnold, as we shall see, Pickthall could not let go of his distaste for the masses, a distaste he carries over to his work concerning the Near East and the Islamic world. In Said we see this clearly, for, after all, it is a novel about the masses in the street, a Muslim mob of homicidal fanatics. The masses are a mob, even in Damascus.

Indeed, Raymond Williams's first major work, *Culture and Society*, makes just this point, that the masses are part of the discourse of the mob, which he underlines with a special eloquence in the conclusion of this monumental book:

> Yet, masses was a new word for mob, and the traditional character-
> istics of the mob were retained in its significance: gullibility, fickle-
> ness, herd prejudice, lowness of taste and habit. The masses, on this
> evidence, formed the perpetual threat to culture. Mass-thinking,
> mass-suggestion, mass-prejudice, would threaten to swamp consid-
> ered individual thinking and feeling. Even democracy, which had
> both a classical and a liberal reputation, would lose its savour in
> becoming mass-democracy.[31]

Culture and Society was followed by an equally important work of cultural history, E. P. Thompson's *The Making of the English Working Class*, while the work of the Birmingham Center for Contemporary Cultural Studies carried the project into the 1960s. These writers brought analysis that was sometimes nuanced and subtle, but always engaged, showing how the obvious class prejudices of, say, Dickens or Hardy were in turn the basis for law and everyday life in the nineteenth and early twentieth centuries. And the list does not stop or start with Dickens and Hardy but must also include Cobbett and Carlyle, and then Eliot and Woolf and other significant writers of the twentieth century.

Turning to *Said*, we find the novel producing a now-familiar historic context, that of social upheaval and the rampage of the mob, yet in a new locale and with new players. We read about a mob of Arab Muslims rampaging through the streets of Damascus, while in the background, and ostensibly motivating their actions, however irrational these might be otherwise, is the 1866 Druze and Christian war of the Lebanon mountains. So the third difference from the British literary tradition of writing about revolutionary mobs is that these Arab Muslims in the street are engaged in a sectarian conflict.

In the following passage we see some of the usual language and imagery from our tradition, sprinkled with references and words that mark this as a non-Western context and narrative of mob violence. Here, Said follows Mustapha into the streets, where the latter is anxious to take advantage of the sectarian conflict to rob the wealthy Christian merchant he believes has robbed him. Said follows simply because he is malleable and also because he hopes to rape and abduct the pretty young daughter of the rich Christian merchant. While they are in the Christian quarter of the Old City of Damascus, where there are churches, monasteries, and convents, they come across the mob, led by a crazed old man filled with religious zeal and energy:

> "Din! Din! Din Muhammed!"
>
> The words of the saint were drowned in a shout which thrilled Said to the marrow and made tears start in his eyes. . . ."Din! Din! Din Muhammed!" The mob thus reinforced set to work once more. "To the French convent!" someone shouted. "Let the nuns be ravished and then slain!" The cry was taken up on all hands with laughter and coarse jibes. "The nuns! The nuns!" "Aha, the nuns are sweet!" "They have kept their flower for us, the darlings!" "Let us see how the nuns are fashioned!"[32]

Given the sectarian massacre and the preceding mountain war in Lebanon, it is perhaps apt that a historic figure makes an appearance and saves the day. Just as Walter Scott might insert Richard Coeur de Lion into one of his crusader novels, so Pickthall inserts Abdelkader, the legendary leader of the Algerian rebellion against French colonial rule. Interestingly, this narrative is based on a true account, as Abdelkader and his small Algerian force did in fact intervene and save a group of nuns from the mob.

Indeed, the novel ends as Said, now seemingly infected with sectarian zeal, is swept up in a similar event in Alexandria, Egypt, during the famous 1882 nationalist revolt of Colonel Arabi and on the eve of the subsequent British bombardment of the city and defeat of Arabi at the battle of Tel Kebir. The mob scene is much the same, as we see in the following passage:

> Suddenly on turning a corner he found himself in a yelling, furious mob, all rushing in one direction. Fierce eyes, brandished weapons, curses and a roar of shouting. It was as though a door swung open in Said's brain, admitting light into a chamber long shut up. Understanding flashed in his eyes.
>
> "Din Muhammed!" he cried, and rushed forward with the rest, only more fiercely, with more of frenzy. Even in that turmoil men looked at him and looking made way for him to pass. There was something awful in his face, a light of madness or inspiration beyond their ken. He was a prophet and would bring them good fortune. They pressed on behind him, shouting louder than before. On he ran, tearing a way through the crowd. At length he led them, was at their head, still rushing on.[33]

Setting the author apart momentarily, I find this novel remarkable insofar as it is about sectarianism in the Arab world, a non-Western context, yet it produces this conflict in terms, language, and imagery entirely derived from the British literary tradition. Now, initially, it might seem that Pickthall—as a British writer—is simply working with the forms available. The British literary tradition is what he knows, and as for his ideology, well, he is British after all. So much is obvious, but consider the larger ideological consequences of the way this conflict is recorded and produced for a Western market of readers. Indeed the conflict was nasty, as Ussama Makdisi notes in his important book on the conflicts in the region:

> When Muslims in Damascus rioted soon after [the Druze-Christian war in Lebanon] to protest increasing European influence in their city, thousands more Christians were slaughtered in the ugliest urban violence of nineteenth-century Syria. The Sultan of the Ottoman Empire was made to hear what one chronicler described as the "sighs of Syria."[34]

Yet Makdisi, as a historian and a scholar of Lebanese origin is careful to advise as to how sectarian conflicts should be understood.

> Sectarianism can be narrated only by continually acknowledging and referring to both indigenous and imperial histories, which interacted—both collided and collaborated—to produce a new historical imagination.[35]

Indeed, he underlines this point later and insists—and here is his major intervention—that sectarianism is modern:

> Sectarianism is a modern story, and, for those intimately involved in its unfolding, it is the modern story—a story that has and that continues to define and dominate their lives.[36]

Still, Makdisi laments that a Western readership and compliant press wanted to understand these sectarian events in a certain way.

> For their part, Europeans who took any interest in the affairs of the Ottomans fused the Damascus outbreak in July and the Lebanese massacres which preceded it in June into a single indication of the primordial passions of the local inhabitants.[37]

I agree with Makdisi that sectarianism is modern, as is so much of the classification and typology that accompanied British and French colonialism of the nineteenth and twentieth centuries. As Said notes in *Orientalism*, Napoleon's conquest of Egypt was brought about with rifles and scholarship as the French documented and excavated their new conquest and finally gave "Egypt" to the Egyptians. This documentary and scholarly activity is of course right out of the Enlightenment, bringing rational inquiry to a land of sand-obscured antiquity, which is important for how the West constitutes itself and for sweeping aside obscurantism.

In *The Intellectuals and the Masses* John Carey offers his own take on the literary tradition of the mob. In most contentious terms he persuasively argues that the theoretical basis of writers of the late nineteenth and early twentieth centuries, moderns and modernists, hinged on fear and loathing for the working classes, the mob, and the masses. Carey's book reads like a well-informed diatribe, but he brings together the nineteenth-century theories of LeBon on the crowd with early-twentieth-century revisions by Trotter and others, and then tracks these ideas, oddly, through the work of Freud and Nazi ideology. For our purposes I think here we see once again the notion of displacement that we inferred from Williams's *The Country and the City*, and importantly a little bit more. He comments about Pound and Forster:

> This [Pound's "In a Station of the Metro"] fusion of pastoral and historic pageant to provide a cosmic version of the mass becomes the dominant motive in the fiction of E. M. Forster. Repelled by what he saw as the coldness of the English middle classes, and especially their coldness to homosexuals, Forster looked southwards to Italy for more congenial life forms. . . . When he went to India Forster found a mass that was even more primitive and colorful than the Italians. . . . He invented an India in which the masses, unlike those of industrialized Europe, are surrounded by a romantic aura of primitivism and naturalness.[38]

With this last comment about Forster and the eroticization of the peoples of the East—the brown masses of the Orient, as Carey might put it—I think we have joined displaced anxieties about the masses of the British working classes with Colonial Desire.[39] Again, perhaps this is finally a displaced wish, one that cannot be fulfilled or even fantasized in Britain with British subjects, yet the racial aspect and the related network or strains of other fantasies of the erotic and exotic make the new masses of the Empire a special knot for interpretation.

If we turn to D. H. Lawrence's *Women in Love* and the equation of the primitive (primitive sculpture and primitivism) with raw sexual power (perhaps Gerald), we see that this is not a startling idea. Indeed, whether in Picasso's painting or the novels of Conrad or D. H. Lawrence, or even the cultural paranoia of Eliot's theory, modern art and especially modernism as an aesthetic intervention is nothing without projections and fantasies about the natives of the Empire.[40]

Standpoint, Prejudice, and Genocide

Before and during the Great War, as a Muslim and as a critic of the Christian West, Pickthall was openly supportive of the Ottoman government, defending its foreign and domestic policies. Then, in 1913, during the Turkish-Balkans war, a preamble to the Great War, Pickthall wrote a series of reports from Constantinople for *The New Age* about politics and everyday life in Turkey at that time.[41] He subsequently published these reports as a book, *With the Turk in Wartime*. Of note here, Pickthall hoped for a position in the Arab Bureau in Cairo but was passed over for a young soldier, T. E. Lawrence. Pickthall particularly despised Lawrence, having spent much time in Damascus and the region and believing the war hero to be a charlatan.[42]

In this context, standpoint is used sharply, first to defend the Ottomans during the Great War and then to rebut and deny Turkish atrocities and genocide against the Armenians and Christians. The following passages about the latter groups are notable. In Constantinople, Pickthall stayed with a German woman who had lived there for many years and adopted a Turkish persona, Miskut Hanem. She often received guests, and among some of these were local young Greek women who felt comfortable enough in that context to discuss social matters with Pickthall. He records these conversations to show their prejudices toward Turks and Muslims:

> I had many subsequent opportunities of studying the point of view of ordinary Greeks, for these girls were often in the house and our cook was also Greek and fond of argument. I never ceased to marvel at its pure fanaticism. They really liked the Turks of their acquaintance; that is to say, their own experience would have made them tolerant, but for the instruction which they had received from priest

and parents, in which they hurriedly took refuge if accused of such a liking.[43]

There is really nothing wrong with Pickthall's point here, that it is largely social pressure that produces bias and not individual ignorance and impulse. The exception is his repeated use of "fanaticism" to describe this bias, which he fully understands has a social origin in each case. Initially, we might suppose that he is simply giving the word a rhetorical turn, using it to describe Christian bias against Muslims, just as so many Muslims were (and are) described as "fanatics." Yet we have to take the writer at his word, literally, and assume that he believes them to be fanatic. The problem is that this notion also fits neatly with some Western prejudices toward Arab Christians. Even as European and British travelers were interested in Arab minorities, especially non-Muslim minorities, they were not especially impressed by Arab Christians. Pickthall makes this clear in his accounts of encounters with nasty prejudiced missionaries and other Christian functionaries in *Oriental Encounters*. In an earlier time, Burton was also disdainful toward Arab Christians and missionaries, bringing about complaints and scandal during his tenure as consul in Damascus, and while visiting Jerusalem.[44]

As for Pickthall's disposition towards Armenians, one of the oldest of the Eastern Christian groups and antagonists to the Ottoman regime, the following passage needs little explanation:

> [A] race of traitors, spies, blacklegs, perjurers, lickspittles, liars, utterly devoid of shame or honor. That is the Armenian nation in the eyes of Asia at the moment. To kill them is as good a deed as to kill scorpions. They defile the globe. It is not a pleasant thing to write but it is true.[45]

We should note that the visceral and hateful aspect of this passage is conflated with Pickthall's defense of the Ottoman regime. Clark documents and explains Pickthall's support, even love, for the sultanate, but he does not really tell us why this was so. I suggest that Pickthall's attachment was not really at odds with his thinking as a Westerner, that is, he valued the regime for its modernizing and revolutionary potential, which he believed to be a frightening prospect for Europe and especially Russia. Indeed, in a May 1, 1919 article in *The New Age*, Pickthall points the finger at Russian intervention in Turkish affairs, with European collusion, as the source of the trouble with respect to the Armenians and Eastern Christian minorities.[46] He blames the massacres of these groups on "indignation" among the local Muslim populations against these "traitors" (and these two words are his!).

Clearly Pickthall is an apologist for genocide, though we should not doubt his sincerity here. Also, in Pickthall's view (as expressed in most of his writings on the massacres), the Armenians were a contrary, if not archaic and troublesome, minority hindering progress, a political characterization that quickly changes into a grotesque aestheticization of an enemy. This position is not unlike the way minority groups are often perceived or cast today in the face of a given government project, albeit with a special racist venom.

My point here is that Pickthall's Turkey was not really a negation of the West. As I noted earlier, and citing Clark, Pickthall's take on Islam was always presented in British terms, where Islam is understood as the realization of British democratic and egalitarian tendencies. So it is not surprising that there is a chapter in *With the Turk in Wartime* dedicated to the Woman Question. The Woman is of course the Muslim woman, and a veiled one at that. And we might assume that this woman is a city dweller since, even today, women in the countryside do not wear the veil or even a hijab, since it inhibits their work-related movements.

Pickthall's standpoint here is that of the British insider on the outside, but then inside "with the Turk." As Geoffrey P. Nash summarizes Pickthall's Turcophilia in *The New Age*, he believed that "duplicitous European diplomacy," the "perversion of European public opinion" by Eastern Christians, and "the betrayal of the auld alliance with Turkey by the British political establishment, were the main causes behind the anti-Turk tendency."[47] The "auld alliance," as Nash explains at various points in his book, is derived from the pro-Ottoman policies of Disraeli, upended by the likes of Gladstone, Cromer, and Sykes. Pickthall supported the Young Turks—and, implicitly, the rise of Kemal

Attaturk—and their vision of a dominant and modernizing Turkish role in the Muslim world, contrary to the atavistic Arab model that was promoted by the British political establishment.[48]

Of course by 1917 Pickthall's standpoint was to shift away as an insider-on-the-inside-of-the-outside to that of an outsider of a special sort, a British Muslim. Since we started with his early novel, *Said the Fisherman*, it might seem that we have tracked a break, as Pickthall does, and indeed to attempt to settle his accounts with his culture and upbringing. In an interesting article titled "Tory Muslim: The Conversion of Marmaduke Pickthall," Lawrence M. Stratton offers a close reading of the 1917 lecture wherein our author proclaimed his new faith. Stratton interprets this lecture, and Pickthall's vision of Islam, as a modification of tendencies already present in Christianity, with some notable exceptions. One is the beauty of the language of the Koran, which Pickthall cited at key moments, while the other is Islam's relationship to both human spirit and nature. He casts Islam as a religion of tolerance grounded in this life, indeed an avowal of human life by contrast with Christianity's complicity with greed and commerce.[49]

Clearly there is a thread connecting *Said* to the Islamic writings of Pickthall's second career—as a spokesman for Islam—which is worthy of consideration here. Moreover, the point that needs to be made is that his liberal view of Islam flows from the criticism of the West in the early work, as well as the biases we have tracked in the novel—the discourse of the masses and related problems—and reaches a final moment of development in his writing on Islam. Briefly, to demonstrate my point, consider the argument, even the terms used, in the opening lines of Pickthall's 1927 essay "Islamic Culture":

> Culture means "cultivation" and, generally nowadays, when this word is used alone, it means "the cultivation of the human mind." Islamic culture differs from other cultures in that it can never be the aim and object of the cultivated individual, since its aim is not the cultivation of the individual or group of individuals, but of the entire human race. No amount of works of art or literature, in any land can be regarded as the justification of Islam so long as wrong,

injustice and intolerance remain. No victories of war or peace, however brilliant, can be quoted as the harvest of Islam. Islam has wider
objects, grander views. It aims at nothing less than universal human
brotherhood. Still, as a religion, it does encourage human effort after
self, and race, improvement more than any other religion and since
it became the power in the world, it has produced cultural results
which will bear comparison with the results achieved by all the other
religions, civilizations and philosophies put together.[50]

We should note the emphasis placed on culture, since, for a British
readership, this is an overdetermined idea. Again, culture for the British reader, whether in the writing of Matthew Arnold or in British
imperial and domestic legislation concerning education, is critical for
what it means to be British and also for how Britain coheres within the
immediate boundaries of the British Isles all the way to the periphery
of the Empire, to India under the Raj. So Pickthall's invocation of culture in the defense of Islam is confrontational and also, in strange way,
dialectical. That is, Pickthall looks to that which most Britons would
define as the "not British" to propose that Islam is in fact more British
or Western than Britain or the West. He goes on to drive this point
home by noting that art in the West is alienated from human life and
human values, and in this context an expression of decay in values. Art
is valued over human life, and this is a valuation that no Muslim or
Islamic society would ever propose. Indeed, he pushes further, and as
though to answer the tradition of Arnold he argues that Islam's emphasis on human life entails political and intellectual tendencies, which,
while the West espouses them, are in fact contrary to history and fact.
In particular he argues that with Islam there is no opposition to sci-
entific inquiry as there is in Christianity, while the democracy of the
West is a sham of the priesthood, unlike the priest-free brotherhood of
the Muslim world. Again, the band of brothers.

Pickthall and Where We Stand Today

Standpoint is key to understanding the trajectory, consistency, and
ruptures within Pickthall's work. Yet most important, and bringing the

literary into the larger social and political realms, it is an idea critical to the ways we articulate ideas such as democracy, freedom, and citizenship in the West today. That Pickthall's standpoint is intertwined with a tainted discourse of the mob and masses, and that it is then central to his role as a spokesperson for the Islamic world, is certainly of interest for literary and cultural studies. On the other hand, Pickthall's writing shows us the twists and turns taken by certain ways of thinking about the Arab and Muslim world and gives us some idea of how and why these ways of thinking have persisted.

Our author's emphasis on massacres—either as a feature of his novel (representation) or in his journalistic writing during and after the Great War—leads us to the discourse of the masses and, most important, a related discourse of injury. By injury I refer to, say, a rumor of murder by a person or group of outcasts, or a conspiracy such that the mob feels, and it is felt here as a structure of feeling, that each individual member has somehow suffered due to this alleged deed. So, as in the United States in the twentieth century, a lynch mob forms because of a rumor about a rape of a white woman by an African American man, or the murder of a young white girl by a Jewish factory owner—Leo Frank of Atlanta—and each member of the mob feels injured, as though "it was done to them." Clearly, this is both the process of interpellation in its crudest terms, as explained by Althusser, and perhaps more to the point, it is a mark of modernity. In the late nineteenth century Nietzsche noted this aspect of modernity. Here, as Wendy Brown argues, as in the events represented in *Said*, lie the roots of modern, Western social movements, upheavals, and disasters. Brown writes:

> But in its attempt to displace its suffering, identity structured by ressentiment at the same time becomes invested in its own subjection. This investment lies not only in its discovery of a site of blame for its hurt will, not only in its acquisition of recognition through its history of subjection (a recognition predicated on injury, now righteously revalued), but also in the satisfactions of revenge, which ceaselessly reenact even as they redistribute the injuries of marginalization and subordination in a liberal discursive order that alternately denies the

very possibility of these things and blames those who experience them for their own condition.[51]

By the late twentieth century this politics of injury, rooted in the mob discourse of the nineteenth century, is the basis of identity politics and movements and a key feature of both right-wing and, importantly, liberal political and social discourse.

Perhaps Pickthall was onto something here in both a conscious and an unconscious way. In a conscious way, in his recourse to the discourse of the masses and the mob, the country and the city, Pickthall at once represents the Arab and Muslim world in forms and ways that the West can understand. And yet, with his recourse to these discourses, he replicates, through a process of displacement, the same prejudices but with new life. This is the unconscious aspect of Pickthall's project, in some ways the most interesting for us today. That is, the working-class mob and the Oriental mob—angry workers and fanatical Muslims— share much, but we must note how these discourses shift and morph. Simply put, for this project I have chosen Marmaduke Pickthall in part because of the way his writerly and critical ambitions are confounded by his métier, that is, the mode and the forms with which he must work. Marmaduke Pickthall was a British novelist, and as we have established, one who was steeped in the British literary tradition. What is interesting is that he tries to use the tradition to militate against itself, in this instance using the British novel to undo the prejudices toward the Near East that are so much a part of the same tradition. Again, my point here is that the mob and the masses of the city are now fully displaced from the cities of the West to the cities of the Arab and Muslim world. In this sense we have traced the genealogy of an ideology and cultural form, but just as important we have demonstrated a kinship, as it were, between the pro-Arab and Muslim view of Pickthall and the neoconservative writers of the late twentieth century.

Perhaps Pickthall was aware of his predicament, and his entry into the service of Islam was also a retreat from the West and its ideology. Remember, after 1921, as Clark notes, Pickthall did little writing for the usual British journals and newspapers and did not produce another novel. Instead he wrote for and edited *Islamic Culture*, functioned as a kind of ambassador for Islam to the West, worked for figures from the Islamic world, and supported the British Muslim community. And, of course, he published *The Meaning of the Glorious Koran*.

Again, I have presented a genealogy of standpoint, traced from this earlier transitional period in Pickthall's career, for reasons significant today, especially as a problem of ideological crisis and rupture both then (the fin de siècle) and now (the late twentieth and early twenty-first centuries). By the middle of the twentieth century this pose of the modern artist is a key idea, even an ideal, for Western liberalism, particularly in the United States. The modernist canon coalesces and is theorized here in this period, as the writers from these early years are valorized as intellectuals and alienated heroes. Yes, this is the return of the politics of the masses, where mass-man is part of the herd or mass of everyday life, while the alienated writer and his or her standpoint, which is decisively and rationally assumed, are immune and outside of the danger of such a fallen consciousness.

In another sense the Pickthall dilemma—wanting to be progressive and different in thought about the Arab and Muslim world—is magnified in so much liberal writing today. I am referring here to the journalist Thomas Friedman, the longtime reporter and Middle East specialist for the *New York Times*. Of course the latter is an easy target of criticism, as Edward Said famously criticized his representations of the Arab and Muslim world, and thus his neo-Orientalist point-of-view. Yet, Thomas Friedman is relevant here because, despite the trenchant criticism of Said and many others, he appears on television and other public venues as an otherwise respected voice of the liberal establishment.[52] Clearly, the fantasy, or at least the version of the Arab and Muslim world that Friedman offers his readers, cannot be exorcised with traditional forms of rational critique.

Like Pickthall, Friedman writes in venues that reach the educated middle-class audience. Also like Pickthall, Friedman would have his readers believe that he is rubbing against the Orientalist grain and writing from a unique outsider position, telling "hard truths" as an educated witness. This example of standpoint as a key discursive element in American liberalism is evident throughout his writing on the Arab and Muslim world, such as in his earlier book of 1989, *From Beirut to Jerusalem*—for which he was awarded the National Book Award!—and more recently in an article about the 2009 Lebanese elections.[53] Just a glance at the first two pages of the former book tells us of Beiruti Armenians tossing bricks of gold on a Middle East Airlines flight as well as of Jerusalem alleyways filled with humanity. We also read of the author himself, who in an earlier life "must have been a bazaar merchant, a Frankish soldier perhaps, a pasha perhaps, or at least a medieval Jewish chronicler."[54]

Unfortunately many agree with Friedman's analyses of Middle East politics and his comments on Arab culture, though many also reject them for what they are: prejudiced, ignorant, neocolonial, and self-righteous. With this latter sentiment we might also bring Friedman's critics into the fold as well, for self-righteousness is an end in itself, a cause, and it is as prevalent among Western defenders of the Arab and Muslim world as it is among liberals such as Thomas Friedman or neoconservatives at the American Enterprise Institute. To this end the success and failure of Marmaduke Pickthall, British Muslim and writer, holds implications for anyone today who might move to the Middle East, live in an "authentic" neighborhood or village, speak the language, and one day find that his story and life's purpose has been already written a century ago or more. Again, we cannot give ideology the slip, nor can we escape our very ways of being in the world, even as effects of language, and we take all of this with us to the remotest Kurdish village or a Bedouin camp in the Nedj.

Perhaps the answer to the Pickthall dilemma lies with James Clifford's acclaimed essay "Travelling Cultures," where he argues against a tradition of anthropology and ethnography that was hitherto blind to the biases and limits of its discourse, whether as a matter of epistemological foundation; the positivist emphasis placed on language; or simply the fundamentals of the disciplinary method, where the anthropologist arrives from without to observe what is within. Hence, the importance of "travelling" in the essay title. He writes that with his countervision "what is at stake is a comparative cultural studies approach to specific histories, tactics, everyday practices of dwelling and traveling: traveling-in-dwelling, dwelling-in-traveling."[55] He continues to urge studies that take into account borders and localities, with "here" as much as "there," and with attention turned toward Brooklyn today as much as the Caribbean and other places where one finds the "other." While there is much to admire and follow in Clifford's argument, and despite his skepticism about ethnography and writing as such, nonetheless there is a lingering idealism, as though it were just a matter of changing this or adjusting that. The problem is worse, however, since it is ideological and therefore constitutive for the West (and for Western academics).

I now turn back to Edward Said's Gramscian injunction that we must inventory the storehouse of Orientalism. I suggest that this storehouse is not really a place we can easily enter, as though through the open front door. Moreover, the storehouse is not one where the contents are readily available for viewing and assessment, that is, the rational and ethical procedures of the Enlightenment and the West. Instead, as with Freud's method and the unconscious, our inventory procedure must work in unexpected places and with unexpected figures and texts. Simply put, from the first we do not expect to see Marmaduke Pickthall in a genealogy of Orientalists, since he worked so hard to negate these same writers and discourse. Yet the very terms of his struggle only contributed toward a displacement and reinforcement of these same ideologies. Moreover, in order to understand the Arab and Muslim world we do not have to turn to more "authentic" and arcane knowledge to counter the prejudices of Orientalism, as though now we were honest and ethical experts. Perhaps the Orient is not really over there after all, but already with us, nestled in our hearts and minds, as it has always been, rooted in the Orientalist unconscious of the West.

5

The Arabist as Abject Modern

T. E. Lawrence

AN EARLIER VERSION OF THIS CHAPTER, titled "The Hidden and the Visible in British Orientalism," was originally conceived with the intention of discussing the "visible" Arabist, T. E. Lawrence, and the "hidden" double agent, Harry St. John Philby, father of Kim Philby, one of the most famous double agents of the twentieth century. But with further development of my thoughts, I have chosen to limit my focus in the present chapter to the "visible and hidden" in the Lawrence legend, primarily by discussing his well-known account of the Arab campaign of the "Great War" (World War I), *Seven Pillars of Wisdom: A Triumph.* For it turns out that we do not need Philby to investigate productively the "hidden" in British Orientalism. The legend and writing of Lawrence is sufficient material for an instructive analysis and intervention that addresses the relationship between British Orientalism and mass culture, a legacy we confront today.[1]

Yes, there was plenty hidden by Lawrence, not least his sexuality. I say this not for petty titillation or a reactionary "outing" of a twentieth-century British cultural hero. What I argue, with reference to Michael Warner's recent book *Publics and Counterpublics*, is that the sexual aspects of the Lawrence legend (the "hidden") are inextricable from any meaningful analysis of the relationship between British Orientalism and the politics—in the broadest sense—of everyday life in modern Britain.[2] Moreover, the conflation of illicit sexuality and the masses brings out a certain attitude toward power, a certain abjection. Part of the process of becoming and being an Orientalist entailed a bodily experience—Doughty-derived asceticism of one extreme or another—and a certain obeisance before patriarchal authority. I think we live with this tradition today. In the late nineteenth century and into the first decades of the twentieth century, this "Oriental" experience was for the most part understood as a mass cultural fad, derived, say, from the Orientalist films that brought fame to Hollywood stars of the silent era such as Rudolph Valentino and Theda Bara. Yet quickly the asceticism of Doughty crossed over from the realm of the popular to that of the cultural elite, this time as a form of existentialism. In some ways it is the T. E. Lawrence legend, as it unfolded through the twentieth century, that made this transition possible as his character and inner turmoil continue to appeal to a broad public and scholars alike. Yet we cannot overlook the place of mass culture, hence the emphasis here.

The Hidden and the Visible

It is worth noting at the outset just how the hidden/visible paradigm is interpretively useful within much British Orientalist writing of the modern period and how it functions at multiple registers. Following Edward Said's understanding of the binary function and form of Orientalist discourse, consider how the hidden and the visible bleed into more familiar pairings of ideas: private and public sectors, elite culture and mass culture, moralism and sexuality. And for much of modern Middle Eastern history the hidden–visible binary refers to a covert American or European agenda on the one hand and overt/stated (and possibly contradictory) policies on the other hand.

Imperial culture at home, in the metropole, brings us around to the role of fantasy, and how fantasy serves as a mediating and indispensable screen through which we in the West must see the Orient. As for how we see and know the Orient, I turn to two metaphors that are key to much psychoanalytic thought: the screen and the mirror. Although these metaphors are usually at odds, with one school promoting the screen and the other the mirror, I maintain that both are useful here to demonstrate the function and form of Orientalist fantasy at unconscious and conscious/manifest levels. Orientalism is a preexisting discourse that the subject encounters as an "always already." To that extent, Orientalism is a screen or, perhaps better, a filter through which the subject sees or knows the Arab and Muslim world. And yet, just as importantly, the process of knowing is not dialectical, for the already-knowing subject in turn is vetted or certified through this process. The subject "is" due to the function of a kind of Orientalist mirror in which the subject is reflected back; that is, the West in key ways is "produced" through the mimetics of Orientalism. I will develop these ideas shortly and also discuss the historical mediations that make this period, 1880–1930, so important for literary production as such.

T. E. Lawrence's international fame as Lawrence of Arabia developed from this moment and this literary tradition, and to this extent he is a pop-culture hero. We can ascribe Lawrence's status as such to Lowell Thomas and his multimedia stage show, which I will describe shortly, and also to a key figure in British Orientalism in the 1880s, Richard Burton. The latter along with Charles Doughty comprise the two tangents of British Orientalist writing in the period, with Burton's the ascendant tangent but Doughty's still influential. In this period Burton shifted his writing attention to the translation and publication of Orientalist erotica, such as the *Kama Sutra* and his own ballyhooed translation of *The Arabian Nights,* working with the pornographer and lawyer Leonard Smithers. Through a series of editions of his translation of the latter book, Burton contributed to a shift in Orientalist writing, feeding a popular market for tales of harems, captivity, sexual deviance, exotic practice, and the like. I will return to Smithers, for I maintain his influence as a purveyor of Orientalist pornography on British Orientalism still has to be accounted for.[3]

In the same period Charles Doughty gained fame and status as an Orientalist with the publication of his *Travels in Arabia Deserta*, where he describes his journey on the Muslim haj disguised as Khalil, a Christian.[4] Ostensibly on a geological trip, his book blends descriptions of the desert topography with requisite comments on Nabetean (pre-Islamic) inscriptions and ethnography. Also notable was the violent reception Doughty received when he visited Kheybar, a town that has some significance in Islam. The result is a book that was a favorite of Lawrence's; he wrote the introduction to a later abridged edition edited by David Garnett. As more editions emerged, Doughty's influence spread, albeit to a smaller market than that of Burton's, but still very influential. By comparison with Burton's Kama Shastra oeuvre, Doughty's text is moralistic and has a certain abstemious and pious view of the Arabian landscape—the desert—and its people.

In Lawrence's text we find all of these tendencies: the elite bourgeois Orientalism of the Royal Geographic Society (the hidden) in tension with Orientalism as mass culture (the visible); and then Burton and the text of Oriental excess (sex) versus Doughty's moral agenda in Arabia. The result is what I call a "knot," for the strands are crossed and tied together but never fully intertwined to form a unified cord. I argue that this is the best way to read *Seven Pillars* and the Orientalism we encounter today.

Lawrence as Action Hero, Savior, and Martyr

This interpretation of the legend of Lawrence can be easily buttressed through several quotations from *Seven Pillars*. I have divided these quotations into two groups. The first group concerns the public Lawrence and his brush with mass culture; I have dubbed this the "Lawrence as Action Hero, Savior, and Martyr" group. The second group is about the private Lawrence and concerns the Deraa incident and other tortured aspects (excuse the bad puns) of his account in *Seven Pillars* and, of course, the now infamous flagellation sessions with John Bruce. The latter is the hidden Lawrence. In an odd twist, I will link it to his antipathy to mass culture, his quietistic politics, and his great love for handmade, fine press books. I have dubbed this second group "Lawrence Amidst His Complexes and Fine Books." Also, with both groups I plan to pull Lawrence away from hagiography and psychobiography, and with attention to the production of his legend to set him squarely in a political and historical context.

In the preface to the 1926 George Doran edition of *Seven Pillars*, Lawrence offers a brief, well-known history of his text. It was already a legend prior to mass publication. There were three original prepublication versions of the book, which Lawrence calls texts 1, 2, and 3. Text

1 was written in 1919 in London and Cairo and then lost somewhere at Reading Station. Some writers have disputed whether this story of the lost text was true, but the lost version was followed by text 2, which Lawrence wrote from his notes and diaries and the issues of the *Arab Bulletin* that he had edited during the war. He improved this version with a third in 1921, written largely in Jeddah and Amman. This version was the basis for the first published edition of *Seven Pillars*, the famous Oxford edition of 1922 of which only a handful of volumes were published. The Oxford edition was in turn, with some modification, the basis for the subscribers' editions of 1926 and 1927, of which more than one hundred copies were published at a loss to Lawrence. For that reason, in 1927 he published an abridgement, *Revolt in the Desert*, with Jonathan Cape in London and George Doran in New York. I will return to the special editions of the book later, but for now, please take note of Lawrence's fetish for the book and for small-scale publication. This mode of production is contrary to the mass-culture legend that boosted interest in—and the value of—*Seven Pillars*, and it is notable that it eventually led to mass-published versions of the same in one form or another anyway.[5]

In the opening pages of *Seven Pillars*, Lawrence, looking to the end of his book and toward his legacy, proclaims his cause in a good example of the stilted prose that marks key moments in the book:

> All men dream: but not equally. Those who dream by night in the dusty recesses of their minds wake in the day to find that it was vanity: but the dreamers of the day are dangerous men, for they may act their dream with open eyes, to make it possible. This I did. I meant to make a new nation, to restore a lost influence, to give twenty millions of Semites the foundations on which to build an inspired dream-palace of their national thoughts.[6]

As to the language of this passage, it certainly is contrived in a pretentious voice and archaic phrasing. It is a register at odds with other moments, the better part of the book, which are either in the style of spare reportage and description or written in an enthusiastic style akin to that of contemporary boys' literature. As for what he states, it is fairly obvious that Lawrence's posture here fits into a tradition of imperialist patronizing—we call it "tutelage" these days—though it is especially weird in that he inserts himself so distinctly: "I meant to make a new nation" and "to give twenty millions of Semites the foundations of their dream palace."[7] Now, Lawrence admits he failed in this last effort, but the language and posture surely detract from this key admission, sweeping the reader along with the gesture and its terms, the signifiers as it were, while the signified, the loss of Syria and Palestine, are buried beneath.

Guerilla Warrior and Secret Agent

In the second and third quotations I have selected, we find the guerilla warrior (asymmetrical warfare) and secret agent (double agent)--that is, Lawrence, the man who will become the international star and cult figure, Lawrence of Arabia. Here he is in action later in *Seven Pillars*:

> Just at that moment the watchman on the north cried a train. We left the fire and made a breathless race of the six hundred yards downhill to our old position. Round the bend, whistling its loudest, came the train, a splendid two engined thing of twelve passenger coaches, travelling at top speed on the favoring grade. I touched off under the first driving wheel of the first locomotive, and the explosion was terrific. The ground spurted blackly into my face, and I was sent spinning, to sit up with the shirt torn at my shoulder and the blood dripping from long, ragged scratches on my left arm. Between my knees lay the exploder, crushed under a twisted sheet of sooty iron.[8]

This last passage is from the second part of *Seven Pillars*, yet early on in the book is an equally important moment for the development of this new pop-culture hero, Lawrence of Arabia. It is this scene that David Lean made much of in his film version of Lawrence of Arabia, when Peter O'Toole as Lawrence changes into Arab garb:

> Suddenly Feisal asked me if I would wear Arab clothes like his own while in the camp. I should find it better for my own part, since it

was comfortable dress in which to live Arab-fashion as we must do.
Besides, the tribesmen would then understand how to take me. . . .
If I wore Meccan clothes, they would behave to me as though I were
really one of the leaders; and I might slip in and out of Feisal's tent
without making a sensation which he had to explain away each time
to strangers.[9]

By now it is well established that Lawrence of Arabia, that is, the celebrity guise of T. E. Lawrence, was not a "natural" development. This
persona did not emerge organically as news of his exploits spread. In
fact this very persona deliberately was created by Lowell Thomas, the
Princeton professor turned war correspondent and later impresario of
travelogue and Cinerama fame. In 1919, with the help of Harry Chase,
a photographer who accompanied him to the Middle East and who
had worked with a certain Frank Roberson in an earlier stage venture, Lowell Thomas produced a multimedia show, known as an illustrated travelogue, about the exploits of Lawrence for sellout audiences
in Covent Garden and Royal Albert Hall in London and venues in
other cities in Britain. In the show Thomas told the story of the whole
desert war, and so it was titled *With Allenby in Palestine and Lawrence
in Arabia*. Later, realizing that Lawrence was the aspect of the show
that produced audiences of more than one million, Thomas changed
the title and adjusted the material. To do so he asked Lawrence to
pose for him at his house with Orientalist props and in his "Meccan"
clothing. Lawrence obliged, and these are the photographs that made
the image of Lawrence of Arabia. Chase was a top photographer who
understood the idiom. With so many different hand-tinted images, a
series of projectors, and, by contemporary standards, elaborate dissolv-
ing effects, these images remain a landmark accomplishment in the
history of mass culture.

Though Lawrence attended the show several times in 1919, sometimes in disguise, and though his mother, brother, friends, and comrades all saw the show and approved of it, he spent the rest of his life
disavowing it and heaping opprobrium on Thomas. There is an interesting example of Lawrence's disavowal of the Thomas myth from the

Metcalf Collection at the Huntington Library. A former comrade and fellow British soldier asked him to annotate a copy of Lowell Thomas's book *The Boys' Life of Colonel Lawrence*, and the hero obliged. Still, some of the inaccuracies and myths about Lawrence, which later were exposed, in fact were fed to Thomas by Lawrence himself. A good example is his alleged title of "Sharif of Mecca." According to Thomas's notes and diaries, Lawrence's claim to be "the only white man who ever had or ever will have this title," as well as comments about his special ability to survive in the desert, were all told to Thomas by Lawrence himself, though the latter went out of his way to disavow these comments to friends such as George Bernard Shaw and Robert Graves.[10]

There were other shows like this and, like Thomas, some of his comrades also produced books with photographs, including one by a lower-level soldier, a driver of one of the Rolls-Royce armored cars.[11] Yet, as I stated earlier, Lawrence repeatedly disavowed Thomas's show and its creator, which made him an international star. In *Seven Pillars* he comments,

> There was a craving to be famous; and a horror of being known to like being known. Contempt for my passion for distinction made me refuse every offered honour. . . . The eagerness to overhear and oversee myself was my assault upon my own inviolate citadel.[12]

It is easy to follow Richard Aldington and others and denounce Lawrence as a liar and hypocrite, and to engage in moralistic critique.[13] But Lawrence's disavowals are far more interesting and exceed such ad hominem commentary. First, consider that it is the visible, public, mass-culture image of Lawrence that is dominant, and it is the private and troubled Lawrence who disavows this other persona to a small circle of friends. Second, we should emphasize the cultural aspect, that is, that this mass--culture persona frightens the private Lawrence, the one his friends know, and he retreats to the shelter of his cottage and his fine books. More on the fine books later, but for now, we simply can leave it that mass culture for Lawrence is associated with excess and deception; it is something common but nonetheless attractive and a source of pleasure. Perhaps there is an important sustaining dialectic then, between the public and private Lawrence, the visible and the hidden, for as we shall see, both are apparent in *Seven Pillars*.

Moving beyond the Lawrence personae (warrior, savior, and martyr) to the masses and mass publication, there is a link here between the Lawrence legend and an established tradition and market of popular fiction and nonfiction about the Arab world. I refer here again to the literary outburst that started in 1894 and continued on and off past the turn of the century and that was certainly the Orientalist context within which the Lawrence legend and *Seven Pillars* were conceived and produced. Folded in with General Gordon martyrology are many examples of popular fiction about the Sudan Campaign of the 1880s through 1898, all of which certainly prepared the market for the Lawrence story and influenced his account in some ways. Also, consider that some of those who led the Sudan Campaign, such as Churchill and Kitchener, were significant figures in the British military and foreign office by World War I. The titles I have in mind are G. A. Henty's *Dash for Khartoum*, the oft-filmed (six times by my count) *The Four Feathers* by A. E. W. Mason, and a short political adventure novel by Arthur Conan Doyle, *The Tragedy of the Korosko*, all discussed in earlier chapters. Also, John Buchan, the early-twentieth-century adventure-story novelist, was working in Cairo in the war propaganda office (they called it the information office), where he played an especially key role in facilitating Thomas's tour with Lawrence. It is striking to think that the author of *The Thirty-Nine Steps*, among the first modern double agent and spy stories, in turn was involved with the creation of another kind of agent, a British soldier who disguised himself as an Arab, our Lawrence.

The Desert of Men

So far I have examined the "visible" in British Orientalism and the Lawrence of Arabia legend—how in the 1880s certain discourses became staples of popular culture as politics and culture combined in new mass formations. But there also is the "hidden" Lawrence, one with similar roots in British Orientalism, roots that predated the 1880s but survived in underground forms, also crossing from elite audiences to common consumers. I am referring here to Orientalist pornography, and it is through this tradition that we might see the Lawrence story—his sexuality in particular—in new ways, moving away from the formalism of psychoanalysis and the moralism of other interpretive modes.

Richard Aldington perhaps is known best for the bitterness of his *Lawrence of Arabia: A Biography of Enquiry*, and especially his sensational "outing" of Britain's twentieth-century hero.[14] Of course, there were obvious signs and indications of one form or another in Lawrence's work indicating his homoerotic, if not homosexual predilections, material that was extant even during his lifetime and more obvious and legible than some sort of code. Thus, in some ways it is remarkable that such a fuss was made over Aldington's book, as though this news was "shocking, so shocking!" In the following passage Lawrence makes it fairly clear what went on in the desert, though the description makes it seem tortured and guilt-ridden, where sexuality is a burden to be sloughed off:

> The public women of the rare settlements we encountered in our months of wandering would have been nothing to our numbers, even had their raddled meat been palatable to a man of healthy parts. In horror of such sordid commerce our youths began indifferently to slake one another's few needs in their own clean bodies—a cold convenience that, by comparison, seemed sexless and even pure.[15]

Lawrence refers in this same passage to "souls and spirits in one flaming effort," as well as the pain and the "degraded" body and "filth," but his use of the verb "slake" is notable and surely anachronistic, even in the early twentieth century. As for a literary source, the most prominent example appears in Andrew Marvell's poem, "Clorinda and Damon" ("Damon: Might a Soul bath there and be clean, / Or slake its Drought"),[16] where we find the same pastoral elements that imbue so much of Lawrence's representation of desert life (following Doughty). And to describe sexual urge as a "thirst" and something to be rid of suggests a troubled disposition toward human sexuality as such and the ooze and excess of the human body. Most critics now feel that Lawrence in fact did have homosexual encounters during his war service and before. Moreover, Lawrence was very up-front about his relationship with Dahoum, whom most consider to be the "S. A." of the dedicatory poem of *Seven Pillars*. Lawrence met Dahoum in Syria before the war during his time at the Carcamesh dig and scandalized the locals with his, in their minds, unthinkably close relationship. Lawrence even brought him to England before returning with him for the Arab campaign. Dahoum died in 1918 in Damascus, and some feel that his presence there played powerfully in Lawrence's conscious and unconscious thought as he plotted the entry to Damascus with Feisal. Unfortunately Dahoum had died by the time Lawrence arrived in the Syrian city.[17] Other liaisons might have included the two young men whom he retained as servants, Faraj and Abdullah, who were in turn inseparable in suspect ways. But the point is that the signs of his sexual tendency were always there, and never fully hidden—it seems for several decades readers just could not see, or read, the signs, or perhaps they simply refused to acknowledge them.

Deraa

The Knightley and Simpson biography with its sensational accounts, as well as John Bruce's later confirmation of the whipping sessions at Clouds Hill cottage, are another matter. The latter's account is especially compelling, if this is the right word, because of the cover story Lawrence gave him and then the account of one session. As Bruce recounts, Lawrence told him that the "Old Man," to whom he owed a debt, required that he be punished, hence the flagellation sessions. After one session Lawrence told Bruce that the Old Man—clearly a fictional figure—demanded that he be whipped again, since the first session was not sufficient. So Bruce laid a rug—Oriental?—over his back and birched his "small buttocks," which brought Lawrence to orgasm. Lawrence even asked Bruce to sign up with him in the Tank Corps, which he did, and they shared a room during this period.[18]

All of the above served to confirm suspicions prompted by the infamous "Deraa" section of *Seven Pillars*. Around the middle of the book Lawrence recounts how he went off one day with only an old man to accompany him. He planned to spy on the Turkish battalion stationed in Deraa, and so disguised himself as a Circassian worker. He was stopped, however, by Turkish troops, who turned him over to the commandant. According to Lawrence's account, the commandant propositioned him for sex, and though he refused, the commandant started to touch and kiss him. Lawrence kneed him in the groin—he describes this as "jerking" his knee up into him. Writhing in pain, the commandant called the guards and ordered them to beat Lawrence. After a beating while stretched over a bench, the guards pulled Lawrence to his feet. He continues:

> I remember the corporal kicking with his nailed boot to get me up; and this was true, for next day my right side was dark and lacerated, and a damaged rib made each breath stab me sharply. I remembered smiling idly at him, for a delicious warmth, probably sexual, was swelling through me: and at that he flung up his arm and hacked with the full length of his whip into my groin.[19]

After his beating, Lawrence was bloodied and dirty, and the commandant no longer was interested him. He was locked in a makeshift cell from which he escaped, slinking and broken, back to his camp.[20]

So, where do we go from this point, and what does this have to do with Middle East studies? For some readers, the Lawrence legend might have finished right there, given the sordid or possibly disturbing aspects of the story, and what this means for an up-to-date reading of, say, the Deraa narrative in *Seven Pillars*. I have selected three different responses to this that build on this new Lawrentia, which are representative of recent trends in literary and cultural studies and explore the sexual, cultural, and textual dimensions of his book. Indeed, far from pounding the last nail in the coffin of his reputation, these books of prurience instead enrich it further. Indeed, we late moderns or postmodern readers now find a level of complexity and compelling contradiction in Lawrence and the near-tortured prose of *Seven Pillars* that in some ways elevates the significance of the book to an even loftier level than before.

A "standing civil war" is Lawrence's self-critique in one of those introspective moments we find in *Seven Pillars*, and it is a comment upon which Edward Said seizes for his brief essay in *Reflections on Exile*. I cannot account for the motivations, but Said draws our attention to the salacious accounts of Lawrence's sexual life and then sidesteps the implications, or public significance, of these same accounts. Instead, Said brings us back to the text with this idea, with which he subsumes the excessive sexual aspects of the Lawrence legend. This textual emphasis might be due to the fact that Said did not want to lose this interesting and important figure to the gossips. Yet Said makes more of Lawrence—he is not just any writer. Moreover, the activity of writing, as Said reads Lawrence, is central to understanding the man, his work, and what he wrought for the British Orientalist of the twentieth century: the bricoleur modern and Arabist as existentialist. In his writing, Said tells us, Lawrence found a pied-à-terre, a small and temporary foothold. Of course the final house was realized as *Seven Pillars*, hence the metaphor, but Said is not so certain, for as he reads Lawrence, writing was a process of reconciliation, of making things fit in a way they did not in the world around him. He comments in the Lawrence essay:

> What attracted Lawrence to the act of writing was what paradoxically frustrated him, although he was able to recognize how perfectly writing itself, viewed either as tight order, as mechanism, or as having no conclusive force over things, was an analogy for his own personality.[21]

I think what we should make of Said's commentary on Lawrence is first the emphasis on his writing, that he wanted to be known as a writer, and then the kind of writer he wanted to be known as. I will get to this kind of writing shortly, but we also should consider that if writing is a "tight order" that frustrates, it is also a form that conceals, hence the way the corners of truth and motive are rounded with such craft in *Seven Pillars*.

Yet writing—textuality—is not without its sexual dimension, and so even as Said fends off this libidinal dimension of a writer whom he admires, he and we cannot excise such stories fully from the postmodern Lawrence of Arabia legend. To that end, Kaja Silverman, the Class of 1940 Professor in the celebrated Department of Rhetoric at Berkeley, proposes an intriguing psychoanalytic interpretation of the Lawrence legend in a chapter of her book *Male Subjectivity at the Margins*. The chapter, titled "White Skin, Brown Masks: The Double Mimesis, or with Lawrence in Arabia," explores what she calls an "inverse desire" as, in this instance, the white Lawrence goes "Arab."[22] On the way to unwrapping Lawrence from his Arab garb, Silverman comments on his masochistic predilections, which, she argues, call into question his ability to lead. She asks, how can we understand Lawrence's success? She explains, a few pages later:

> If the Lawrence of *Seven Pillars* is able to participate psychologi-
> cally in Arab nationalism, that is in large part because his particular
> homosexuality promotes an erotic identification both with its lead-
> ers and its servants.[23]

Yet the key point Silverman makes is that Lawrence's masochism is not feminine, since it is not resolutely passive, but is sacrificial, to such an extent that he knows he must fail as a leader. And so his donning of Arab garb is related to his mediated, partial identification with his Arab comrades and is a key to Lawrence's military strategy and notion of Arab nationalism. A change of clothes necessarily follows a change of heart, as Lawrence is engaged in an identification with the Arab Other that, as Silverman writes, will end with a rewriting of his own subjectivity. In some ways Lawrence actually does that with which Burton and Blunt only titillated their audiences, and which Gordon resolutely refused. In important ways for an Englishman, Lawrence crossed over to the other side. A parallel could be drawn to Marmad-uke's conversion to Islam.

As for being English, I should be precise here, and point out that Lawrence was born in Ireland, and so his nationalism always was shadowed by the contemporary colonial situation in Ireland and the bloody struggle for independence that peaked in 1916 as Lawrence was preparing to wage war in Palestine and Syria. Also, back to the birch-ings, it is unfortunate that Silverman overlooked some obvious aspects of this story, specifically that the Anglo-Irish Lawrence, of muddied upper-class background, was birched by a Welshman, John Bruce, who was working-class, while on holiday in a sparse cottage in a remote and harsh corner of Scotland. And for good measure, this same Lawrence was introduced to the Arab world through his interest in the Crusades, which leads us to knight-errantry and medieval romance. Parsifal, Galahad, and many other legendary knights and the accompanying chivalric code demonstrate that Lawrence's military profile and posture, while not phallic as Silverman, or an American, might have it, is certainly well grounded in British and European lore and is neither unusual nor weak.

There is something else lacking in Silverman's otherwise smart psychoanalytic reading of the book and the issues it concerns. It is too formal, and history is simply tacked on. So, if a cultural and historical—and pointedly political—interpretation of the Lawrence legend is needed, then Jonathan Rutherford's chapter on Lawrence in his *Forever England* (1997)would fit the bill. The gist of Rutherford's argument is that after the Great War, and the wartime death of the writer and public figure Rupert Brooke, mainstream English notions of masculinity changed in radical ways due to the horrific losses associated with the conflict. To the contrary, Lawrence was a *Boy's Own* story, he comments, full of pageantry and exotic appeal. Indeed Lawrence seemed to appeal to everyone, for after all he had a good war, unlike so many. Rutherford goes further, however, and links Lawrence's image to now unseemly politics—imperial and otherwise—of that time. First, Rutherford links Lawrence to the "indirect rule" crowd in the foreign ministry. This was a group with links stretching back to Lugard and his book on how to govern Nigeria through local forms of leadership and rule, that is, using "brown" people to rule for a "white" empire. This is a familiar idea now, and we even see it in Iraq these days—and I do not apologize for such direct political commentary—but it was a theory also known as the "Punjab Creed" and was most successful in application in India. Of course, this was how Lawrence and his superior, Winston Churchill, saw Feisal and the Hashemite kingdoms of the Middle East, and this view was inextricable from his advocacy of air power. Under the mantle of a discussion of Lawrence's sexuality, Rutherford brilliantly brings together this theory of the Punjab Creed with the RAF and finally Lawrence's dalliance with the British Union of Fascists (BUF). Indeed, the day he died he was returning from a trip to the post office, having mailed a letter politely declining an invitation to speak to the BUF annual gathering.[24]

I maintain that these three writers, Kaja Silverman, Jonathan Rutherford, and Edward Said, have offered us the most interesting critique of Lawrence as the most influential Orientalist of the early twentieth century. Also, I maintain that the way I understand Lawrence brings all three strands—psychoanalytic, cultural historical, and cultural literary—together for the most powerful critique of the tradition then and now. Indeed, I read the homoerotic and Deraa sections of *Seven Pillars*, and the accompanying documentation of Lawrence's predilections, as just what a man in his tradition might do. Lawrence, after all, is a latter-day Cannibal. By this I refer to the Cannibal Club, a mid- to late-nineteenth-century secret subsection of the elite London Anthropological Society, which, as Lisa Sigel documents in her remarkable book, *Governing Pleasures*, was at the center of Britain's imperial venture.[25] The poet Swinburne and various members of the ruling class and government *nomenclatura*, such as Lord Houghton, General Hodgson, and Lord Penzance, all were members with, of course, Richard Burton. Their central activity was the production and distribution of colonialist pornography for their circle and other elite "consumers." However, and this is key for the formation of colonial and imperial ideology, they justified their activities as the pursuit of science and art, where pornography, or their pseudo-scientific combination of sexology and anthropology, would help to understand better the specific sexual practices and culture in the far-flung reaches of the Empire.[26]

Sigel points out that the Cannibal Club kept its pleasure for its members and in fact made a point of policing them, even as it helped them make a pretense of flaunting obscenity laws. The latter would include Richard Burton's frequent invocation of Mrs. Grundy, the fictitious Victorian prude, censorious authority, and enemy of his Kama Shastra Society. But in so many ways this pretense and pose was in bad faith, and worse—and this is where Sigel's analysis is most interesting, for far from challenging the letter of the Law, which they merely skirted using diplomatic pouches and other avenues, their activity actually reinforced the extralegal authority of the bourgeoisie, the Cannibal Club. In this way, and taking us back to Silverman's reading of *Seven Pillars*, we can better understand, say, Burton and others when they dally with the other, going Arab or assuming native garb and darkening their skins. Their gesture is a complete cooptation of the other in body and clothing.

As the nineteenth century ended, the viewing privileges of the Cannibal Club and other such elite groups was overturned as French and British companies began to mass-produce "dirty" postcards, many of which had a colonial or imperial image. Thus, "[t]hese nature-oriented postcards stood at the intersection of pornography, science, and tourism and were less censorable because ideas implicit in them had been completely naturalized in late nineteenth and early twentieth century Britain, thanks in part to the early work of the Cannibal Club."[27] Moreover, and this point should be emphasized, these cards were affordable for working-class consumers, bringing about a whole new audience for colonialist and imperialist culture and ideology. Indeed, in her groundbreaking book *Imperial Leather*, Anne McClintock calls these postcards and other such imperialist cultural forms—especially soap advertising—"commodity racism."[28] Sigel reiterates this point but takes it further, noting that now the subordinated, the masses of Britain and Europe, could view forbidden images, something that the authorities found very unsettling.[29]

Fine Books and the Dirty Masses

In addition to the flagellation sessions and his military duties, Lawrence's life at the Clouds Hill cottage mostly involved working on book projects. Indeed, Vyvyan Richards, his close friend and collaborator, notes early on in his *Portrait of T. E. Lawrence* that fine books and printing projects were his lifelong preoccupation, more than anything else:

> His eagerness for fine printing never left him. It occupied plans in the early Oxford years, and just after, till the war filled the whole horizon. And at the last, when his longed-for leisure was at hand, he

was planning a little printing shed by his cottage at Clouds Hill. He formed a good collection of well-printed and finely bound books, mostly from private presses.[30]

Lawrence truly believed in a William Morris–inspired notion of the small press, hand press books, hence the early editions of *Seven Pillars* and the care he took with the illustrations by Kennington and Augustus Johns (for the limited editions of *Revolt in the Desert* too), as well as the production materials and process. This task entailed a great deal of labor, obvious when one opens one of the early limited editions. There is a vast difference between these and the later mass-produced copies. One special project was Lawrence's translation of Homer's *Odyssey* for a New York small press owned by the American Bruce Rogers.[31] It is amazing, not a book but an object, with scented vellum pages and gold embossing and special type. The checklist of books from Clouds Hill includes many by renowned artisanal presses such as Golden Cockerel, Whittington, and Corvinus, as well as parts of a press and rare type from defunct small presses.[32]

Some mention of Leonard Smithers is also necessary, if only to cement Lawrence's connection to the underground publishing scene of the late nineteenth and early twentieth centuries. As noted earlier, in this period Smithers, a middle-class lawyer, set himself up in London as a discreet and discriminating publisher and seller of fine books and sophisticated erotica. The conjunction of the two is important, of course, since the elite associations of fine books with special and small press work and materials, coupled with content for a "discriminating" consumer, all served as a marketing device and a shield against the anti-pornography censors. Again, Smithers is important for our tradition of Orientalism because he worked so extensively with Richard Burton, and with Lady Burton after her husband's death, and brought out a memorial edition of the great Orientalist's work, as well as erotica such as Catullus's *Carmina* and an edition of *Priapeia* (which eventually was published with a disclaimer concerning Burton's role in the publication of the book). The list of books at Cloud's Hill does not contain any editions published by Smithers, although it is quite possible that

Lawrence owned some, for not all were pornographic and most were printed in small numbers and with the features Lawrence admired. The point I want to make is that our hero's interests fall into a paradigm that some would like to see in distinction, separate from the sordid and effete reputation of Smithers. However, the latter, while married and otherwise a heterosexual man, published authors who were associated with the sexual scandals surrounding Oscar Wilde. The brief and brilliant run of the Art Nouveau and "decadent" journal *Savoy* is the best example here.[33]

As to Lawrence's dialectic of public and private space, or, here, between mass-produced books and fine hand-printed editions, and then the connections to sexuality, Michael Warner's work, especially his recent *Publics and Counterpublics*, helps us find our way through these oppositions and disconnections and move toward new insights into what Lawrence and his branch of British Orientalism means today. Warner's work has always centered on the relationship between print culture, sexuality, and politics—formal and informal—and he is especially interesting with regard to Walt Whitman's life and writing. So it is not surprising in his chapter "The Mass Public and the Mass Subject" in *Publics and Counterpublics* that he makes the following point at the outset:

> In the eighteenth century, as I have argued elsewhere, the imaginary reference point of the public was constructed through an understanding of print. At least in the British American colonies, a style of thinking about print appeared in the culture of republicanism according to which it was possible to consume printed goods with an awareness that the same printed goods were being consumed by an indefinite number of others. This awareness came to be built into the meaning of the printed object, to the point that we now consider it simply definitional to speak of printing as "publication." In print, understood this way, one surrendered one's utterance to an audience that was by definition indefinite.[34]

Warner continues to point out that at the time this indefinite audience was a "badge of distinction," in much the same way bloggers and others vaunt the numbers of visitors to a website today. He also points out that this transformation, as he calls this print phenomenon, was a cultural "rather than a technological one."[35] I would add, and this is a point I will address shortly, that the conjunction of pleasure and anonymity is also important with regard to Lawrence's work and persona/subjectivity, though Warner nicely dubs this a "principle of negativity," where the writer surrenders who he/she thinks he/she is, the "realities of their bodies," to a sort of utopian space of abstraction.[36]

It is particularly notable when, further along in Warner's argument, he comments that this negativity of abstraction has historically meant the elimination of the body, the writer's body especially. Today, he points out, the body figures largely in the "mass-cultural public sphere" in a new turn of "iconicity." He mentions Muammar Qaddafi and Karen Carpenter, and we might also consider Andy Warhol's silkscreen series of pop icons such as Marilyn Monroe, Chairman Mao, and others in this regard. This, some might argue, is the postmodern turn. But we see it in incipience with Lawrence, and perhaps this begins to explain the lasting and "tropic" fame which marks his persona. Warner argues that this turn, the "iconicity" of mass publicity, promises a "reconciliation between embodiment and self-abstraction."[37] Of course, if we substitute "market" for "public" and "alienation" for "self-abstraction," we might see this moment as the heaven, or hell, of a most alienated culture, where subjectivity outside the terms of the commodity and its market is impossible. Indeed, Warner states clearly that "a fundamental feature of the contemporary public sphere is this double movement of identification and alienation," which, he adds later, is part of the "legacy of the bourgeois public sphere's founding logic."[38]

Shock and Awe

I have suggested that Lawrence took a certain pleasure in mass culture, in the visibility of public space. Yet it is here that Warner's analysis of publics and counterpublics apparently veers away from relevance to the case of Lawrence and the legacy of British Orientalism. Warner is clearly interested in the queer public of the United States and how this public makes a queer private space within American civic life a possibility, albeit tenuous. That is, in the chapter "Sex in Public," written with Lauren Berlant, they emphasize that the Christopher Street clubs, bars, theaters, and tawdry and dirty features of queer public life in New York City's West Village make "mainstream" private queer life elsewhere possible, far from the waterfront and pier scene.[39] In a way, the West Village, Castro, and areas like it serve as a disavowed point of origin for some without which their "normal" lives might never have been possible.

Warner's interest in the erotics of public and private space, and the possibility of counterpublics, is relevant here nonetheless. In a general sense, and in our own time, public institutions, public spaces, and being public are often associated with immoral or suspect behavior. Single mothers, politicians, government workers, public school teachers, even college professors are all suspects as they act as public actors. It was not long ago that political campaigns hinged on dubious stories about welfare recipients driving Cadillacs and spending welfare checks on alcohol and other nonessentials associated with bodily pleasure, while school budgets are determined by tales of teachers sexually abusing children or teaching "dirty" ideas. This is a tradition, in Britain, which we can link to George Orwell's essays on popular culture (dirty postcards, for example), so it is not simply the purview of the demagogic right wing.

As for Lawrence, consider again that in his own life story there is clearly a certain secretive pleasure that he associated with mass culture, with the Thomas show, and with the fame that he achieved. Yet it is clearly a shameful pleasure that he could never avow. Consider also, then, that it was only in the desert that he could avow anything. Only in *Seven Pillars* could he have the relationship with Dahoum which he desired, despite local objections, and feel free and alive in all respects. The story of his rape at Deraa is strange then, for while he is forthright about what happened, and he even recounts the strange pleasure of orgasm which accompanied the brutal violation and assault he suffered, it is hard to point to this moment and declare that it is simply about his hidden or repressed sexuality. Indeed it might be, but the way this moment marks for Lawrence, by his own telling here, and by the accounts of Bruce, the beginning of a pattern of violent sexual encounters that are completely infused, even determined, by geopolitical events and discourse is remarkable for our attempt to trace the genealogy of British Orientalism. The betrayal of the Arab cause and the false entry into Damascus is one example, but that it was always his relationship to the "Old Man" that made his birchings meaningful is where we should focus.

This is a story and line of inquiry that has to do with sexuality, but I stress that there is indeed more about the legacy of British Orientalism and the persona of the Arabist today. Still, to continue with this line of inquiry concerning Lawrence would necessarily entail some sort of statement about his sexuality, which would in turn require biographical detail and a sharp critique of sexuality and gender; this is the kind of masculinity study of early-twentieth-century British culture that Jonathan Rutherford has offered.[40] I am reluctant to "go there" primarily because it is hard to separate oneself from the scandal-mongering and prurient—and homophobic—legacy of the likes of Aldington, among others. As I stated earlier, Lawrence is a most interesting case for the kind of trenchant sexual and cultural analysis, queer theory, that Warner and others have developed over the last twenty years. My interest here, however, lies with Lawrence's place in the tradition of British Orientalism, so while I must bring in some aspects of, say, psychoanalytic critique and queer theory, my objective is to explain how the Lawrence of Arabia story marks both a continuation of a tradition and something radically new.

The continuation of the British Orientalist tradition is clear. Lawrence never hid his admiration for Doughty, with whom he maintained a correspondence and for whom he even raised money when the older man was nearly destitute in his final years. Moreover, as noted earlier, Lawrence promoted an abridged, inexpensive edition of Doughty's *Travels* and wrote the introduction. As for what he took from the older man, it seems obvious that Doughty's ascetic or prophet persona was very attractive to Lawrence. Leaving Oxford and England, he must have felt that it was in the desert that he must experience something pure and uncomplicated, different from life amongst the masses of the

imperial city, London, and this would be achieved through bodily suf-
fering. Thirst, filth, heat, abstinence, hunger, and pain: All were part of
the process that made the British Orientalist and his (rarely her) tradition, and all were espoused by Lawrence's hero Doughty in the desert
of the Arabian peninsula.

The Old Man.

Yet, this aspect of the indications that Lawrence gave to Bruce, to give
him directions and also to "explain" the birchings, tells us many things.
It is undeniable that the birchings were about sexual pleasure, though
not the sort of pleasure that most are willing to accept. It is a secret raw
pleasure accompanied by pain. It is the pleasure Žižek describes, drawing on Lacan, and it is a pleasure-pain that is only achieved by following rules.[41] It is the pleasure of the pervert, the lover of the Law, the Old
Man. My point is not to dub Lawrence a pervert, though some might
do so; that is the tactic of the moralist. My point is what the lover of
the Law, Lawrence, who takes a certain pleasure in private, then acts in
public, means for British Orientalism and for the history and legacy of
colonialism and neocolonialism in the Middle East.

What it means in the first instance concerns what Lawrence did
after the Great War. He served his country two times, first briefly in
the RAF, enlisting under the name of Ross. When his cover was blown
by a local newspaper he was discharged, though shortly thereafter he
signed up for service in the Tank Corps, with Bruce, this time under
the name of Shaw. At a psychobiographical level, indeed, there is much
to consider here: changing the family name; the need to enlist in the
military, a most fundamental "family" order; and entering at the lowest rank. Moreover the assumed family names, Ross and Shaw, looked
like a shelter from public view but also provided anonymity. I suggest
then, that for Lawrence, and for the tradition of the British Orientalist,
his personal story, the birchings and psychological travails, were about
his relationship to power—again, the Old Man.

In this postwar period, the Old Man (who really is the superego)
could be identified with Winston Churchill, if we must give "him"
a name. Of course the Old Man is patriarchal authority of a most

fundamental type. Yet for this project, and for our American link to this legacy, it is important that it was Churchill, who we know largely as a hero of World War II, who cut his teeth as a young officer with Kitchener during the Nile War against the Mahdist Khalifate of the Sudan. And, just as important for our own time, it was Churchill who oversaw the use of air power to successfully suppress the Arab uprising in Mesopotamia, a conflict obviously linked to Lawrence's own war activities and political machinations with Feisal. Moreover, these machinations did not end with the Sykes-Picot agreement and end of the Great War, but they carried on through the early 1920s in the face of a nationalist Arab uprising in Mesopotamia, now known as Iraq.

During this period Winston Churchill, an advocate of air policing and the use of poison gas for such purposes, had made the transition from a successful military career to politics and served as the Secretary of War and Air under several Conservative administrations.[42] In his capacity as a cabinet minister Churchill used the nascent Royal Air Force as part of what David Omissi calls his "coup," that is, the consolidation of more power over the armed forces as a whole and political and public acclaim and capital.[43] The uprising was costly for the British because on the one hand they wanted to withdraw forces to save money, though the area was increasingly important for its still-unexplored oil reserves, particularly in the north, around Mosul, where the Turks, now under Attaturk's nationalist leadership, had massed forces and successfully used covert operations to disrupt British rule in Kurdistan and the north.[44] Working with Hugh Trenchard, the head of the RAF, Churchill devised a plan for the use of air policing and indirect rule. He called in the war hero T. E. Lawrence to serve in situ as an adviser. Lawrence did so despite his vehement 1920 public denunciation of the way the uprising was being handled, published in the *Sunday Times* (August 22) where he warned of a "disaster" and a "trap," all of which came true when British forces were surrounded and forced into a humiliating surrender at Kut. Churchill's policy was apparently effective, for the air force was successfully used to gather information and destroy Turkish and nationalist advances in support of smaller ground forces fighting rearguard actions. Also, Feisal was brought in as the king of Iraq, while his brother Abdullah ruled in Transjordan, which satisfied Lawrence's personal commitments and his support for Lugard-inspired indirect rule. Feisal was a weak puppet who would fall within years, but by July 4, 1922, in a letter to Sir John Shuckburgh that was also published, Lawrence resigned his position and stated that "if Mr. Churchill permits, I shall be very glad to leave so prosperous a ship."[45]

It is not apparent in the public version of Lawrence's story, but with his obedience and near-fawning behavior toward Churchill, combined with his Arabist take on indirect rule and other private behavior, then what we see in Lawrence, perhaps in exaggerated form, is abjection before power as a necessary aspect of the British Orientalist position. I understand abjection here as a self-destructive set of behaviors that entail an internalization of subservience to external force, a symptom of guilt and fealty to the power of the Father or patriarch, perhaps, which finds its way back "out" as actions that once again demonstrate loyalty.

Thus, it is not so much what the British Orientalist reads, writes, and says; this is the obvious discursive tradition we hold up for interpretation. But it is also how this is internalized in a most corporeal fashion, and how this internalization plays out as a deference to power. Julia Kristeva's *Powers of Horror: An Essay on Abjection* provides a most useful description and analysis of abjection in this respect. On the first page of the book she writes:

> There looms within abjection, one of those violent, dark revolts of being, directed against a threat that seems to emanate from an exorbitant outside or inside, ejected beyond the scope of the possible, the tolerable, the unthinkable. It lies there, quite close, but it cannot be assimilated. It beseeches, worries, and fascinates desire, which, nevertheless, does not let itself be seduced. Apprehensive, desire turns aside; sickened, it rejects.[46]

If we turn to Lawrence, and back to Doughty, and then move forward to the desert romances discussed earlier, this description of abjection seems to be apt. Perhaps of most interest, it shows how this corporeal and psychological condition is almost a rite of passage, where the frailties of the body are conflated with discovering true knowledge. This last point suggests Doughty, though filth is also a necessary component of abjection as Kristeva understands it, which certainly brings us back to the modern world of illicit sexuality, the quickie in a city alley—the world Lawrence conflated with mass culture. Kristeva writes:

> It is thus not lack of cleanliness or health that causes abjection but what disturbs identity, system, order. What does not respect borders, positions, rules. The in-between, the ambiguous, the composite. The traitor, the liar, the criminal with a good conscience, the shameless rapist, the killer who claims he is a savior.[47]

Only pages later she follows up with a point that seems most appropriate for Lawrence:

> It follows that *jouissance* alone causes the abject to exist as such. One does not know it, one does not desire it, one joys in it [*on en jouit*]. Violently and painfully. A passion.[48]

Toward the end of the first chapter she makes a point that demonstrates what I am trying to establish about Lawrence, abjection, and the tradition of British Orientalism:

> The abject is perverse because it neither gives up nor assumes a prohibition, a rule, or a law; but turns them aside, misleads, corrupts; uses them, takes advantage of them, the better to deny them. It kills in the name of life—a progressive despot; it lives at the behest of death—an operator in genetic experimentations; it curbs the other's suffering for its own profit—a cynic (and a psychoanalyst); it establishes narcissistic power while pretending to reveal the abyss—an artist who practices his art as a "business."[49]

A business indeed, for how else can one explain the continual betrayals of a whole region of millions of people? This was and remains a business, the oil business.

For Kristeva, abjection is about the subject caught in a dialectic between a dominant patriarchal authority and a residual maternal authority that is never fully synthesized or entirely eliminated. To some extent the abject, as Kristeva argues through Freud and Lacan, is always with us, all of us. It is a part of subjectivity. I do not disagree, but it is important to note here that this dialectical drama, the dance between the Father and the Mother, is exaggerated in modern life, where mass culture, popular forms of government, and new forms of subjectivity threaten the kind of absolute power and loyalty that the Father demands. Also, consider again the public and private of Warner's analysis. In today's terms, the public is that of modern life, with the anonymity of mass production and the commodity, and the secret yet public pleasures that are now possible—cruising in parks and malls or even watching a film in a large theater surrounded by strangers; while the private is like Lawrence's cottage, Cloud's Hill, something thatched and vestigial, like a vintage letterpress type set. Perhaps this is the basis of fascism today, in one form or another, but Lawrence's own dance is first an integral part of what British Orientalism entails, and second it is a part of modern subjectivity.

Slouching toward the Orient

I want to conclude by reemphasizing the general theoretical points I made at the outset, which take this project beyond Lawrence and underpin my project.

First, there is the importance of studying mass culture and the 1880 break in British Orientalism. With the advent of mass culture and mass politics, policy and colonialization is "sold" differently. Importantly, it is also sold to a new mass audience. This mass audience is not the working class, or not exclusively so, but also includes middle-class and civil service employees, both at home and abroad in the colonies. It is important that war and colonial policy be sold to new voters, and it is an electoral process that finally is underpinned by a commodity culture—Pears soap and Jaffa Cakes—that appeals to these new masses in a most visceral and somatic manner. Also, there is the tension between mass culture and private elite culture in the 1880–1920 period. Again, the culture of this period is for the most part a culture of Empire as well as a mass culture that determines home life in the crowded city space of London and elite Oxford; labor; economic factors; gender formation (masculinity); and political discourse, as well as life overseas. And let us not forget that the Great Strike of 1921 is a backdrop against which the Lawrence narrative and geopolitical machinations in the Middle East take place. Mass production, mass culture, the masses, or public things in general, as Warner would have it, were surely both fascinating and disgusting for Lawrence and so many like him (and there are many modernist writers and artists we might include here). Oil is also a factor at play here, if only as an ominous portent, though it became an actuality only a decade later as the House of Saud consolidated power and ARAMCO entered the picture, setting the stage for a new economy and new forms of colonial control. And so, even in their complaisance and lack of engagement with colonial policy, the working classes are complicit in more immediate and "hidden" ways.

The second point concerns Middle Eastern studies and its erstwhile companion, American foreign policy. For me, the area and problem at hand must entail the study of fantasy in the popular culture of the West—a study of how it functions today, here and in the popular culture of the Arab Muslim world. Examples include the audiences for the sexy divas of popular Arab music, ranging from Rouby to Yasmin Hamdan; the popularity of TV dramas such as *Homeland*; and the neoliberal (and neoconservative) discourse around films such as *The Kite Runner* or the ballyhooed *Reading Lolita in Tehran* and other films of their political ilk. Even the place of accomplished writers from North Africa and the Middle East, such as Assia Djebar and Ahdaf Soueif, is in question. While their work is of top caliber, perhaps we need to recognize that this is culture in a form—the novel—which has a global appeal and consumer base and also entails a way of seeing and representing the world, and life as such, through a history that is in turn overdetermined by the history of capitalism in the West. Just saying "No!" to Orientalism will not make it go away, while the future of the legacy—and mass culture—might lie as much within "Oriental" countries and non-Western consumers as anywhere else.

This brings us back to the mirror and screen of Orientalism. It is with great precision and rational procedure, the markers of Western scholarship and academic discourse, that we might carry out Said's Gramsci-influenced injunction to inventory Orientalism and colonialism in general. Just as important, we need to consider this discourse as not only a screen but a kind of mirror of Western subjectivity. The persistence of anti-Arab and anti-Muslim prejudice at the deepest levels of Western and American political and cultural discourse suggests that there is something more than mere ignorance and fear that must be cured. We have to consider that here we find enjoyment, in a sense as perverse as that of our Orientalist hero, Lawrence of Arabia.

Conclusion

How to Read the Orientalist Archive

ORIENTALISM is pervasive in the culture and everyday life of modern Britain. This has certainly been so since the 1880s during the British occupation of Egypt and the Sudan War. Yet Orientalism in this sense is not about foreign policy debates, human rights, or the fear of a clash of civilizations. Rather it concerns the taste and appearance of packaged sweets, the scent of a bar of soap, and the lure of advertising images and jingles for other mass-produced consumables. Most of all, however, British Orientalism as a current in mass culture is rooted in words and phrases that produce and then evoke a fantasy, which in turn is a feature of the larger British public imaginary. It concerns texts—that is, the exotic, lascivious, and fantastic stories found in popular mass-produced textual culture, with related films and photographs, that provided the market context for so much consumer culture of the fin de siècle. Indeed, none of the mass-produced sensory delights mentioned in the preceding chapters would have been sold or expanded into a global market without this popular textual context.

And so, for nearly a century every Briton knew something about the harem and the oppression of Arab women—who are nonetheless seductive and wily—and about the streets of the Middle Eastern city and the dark alleys of the North African casbah and, of course, the despotism of Oriental governments. Together these narratives comprised, and still form the basis of, an Oriental fantasy with roots in mass-produced texts that, again, mediated much of the political and social life of Great Britain in the 1880–1930 time frame. To reemphasize a point made several times, the stake here is not that the fantasy is wrong, that it is wrong-headed, or even that it serves the purposes of imperial domination, all of which are true. No, the stake here is what I have identified as the constitutive function of the Oriental fantasy in British mass culture and the ways this fantasy has mediated the most intimate, private, and indeed personal (subjective) aspects of British life and identity with regard to sexuality, gender (especially masculinity), religious faith, and nationalism and citizenship.

To demonstrate such a broad claim about texts and mass culture, I offer a selection of photographs that were published as a supplement to popular books, newspapers, and journals of the time. The photographs included as illustrations in this chapter depict four of our writers: Richard Francis Burton, Robert Cunninghame Graham, Marmaduke Mohammed Pickthall, and T. E. Lawrence. It is notable that, except for Pickthall, these writers chose to include images of themselves appearing in "Arab" or regional clothing and guise, yet presented for a mass audience of readers. The Pickthall image was published in an early-twentieth-century newspaper as well as an Islamic journal, which still serves as a mass-publication context but in a slightly different way, as I will explain through a reading of the image. These images condense the issues, ideas, and contradictions that I have discussed in this book and yet they suggest more, taking this project beyond its time frame and into the present. Once again, the works of Slavoj Žižek, and specifically his development of the Lacanian terms/concepts of the ideal ego, ego ideal, and fantasy within a larger political dimension, provide a series of most useful insights. To that end I offer a few final points about the constitutive function of the Oriental fantasy in an analysis that exceeds the ideological limits of related academic fields such as postcolonial studies and world literature.

Burton, a Man of Eastern Pleasures

There are many wonderful photographs, drawings, and paintings of Burton as an Arab at various points in his life. Even those of the "real" man suggest someone who is not quite British, due to his hairstyle,

Fig. 1. Studio photograph of Richard Francis Burton. First printed in Edward Walford, *Representative Men in Literature, Science and Art*, 1867. This item is reproduced by permission of the Huntington Library, San Marino, CA, from a copy in the Metcalf Collection.

"Oriental" mustache, and perhaps darker complexion, all of which he was quite proud. Taken as a group, these images suggest a man who had a definite idea of the contours of his persona, and who was a master at manipulating the latter, in image and text and as a kind of multi-media ensemble. One image appeals to me in particular, a photograph from the mid-nineteenth century, where Burton is sitting cross-legged in a sumptuous Orientalist setting, undoubtedly a London photographer's studio, dressed in Levantine gown and with a small fez on his head, his head cocked at an angle as he looks, fiercely, off to his left (see fig. 1). The photograph was included in Edward Walford's 1867 compendium, *Representative Men in Literature, Science and Art*, and, as noted on the title page, all of the photographs of the men in the book were "portraits from life" taken in the studio of "Ernest Edwards, BA." I am certain that Burton felt he was a man of literature, science, and art, in his fashion, and the photo is certainly the most remarkable in the book. It is an image that refers to his whole life up to that point, bringing together his youth in Lahore, when he was a young soldier in the army of the British East India Company, and his more mature years when he ventured on the haj and published his famous *Personal Account*. The image, especially Burton's pose, is reminiscent of films of the early twentieth century, such as Orientalist street scenes in D. W. Griffith's *Intolerance*, or the opening street scenes in *The Thief of Baghdad*, and Burton himself was a kind of mature "street Arab."

A good deal of literary work is concentrated in this image, which we have read, learned, and interpreted so as to make "meaning" of this photo, taken on that day in the studio. Of course, not a small portion of the meaning we find here was due to Burton's efforts and self-promotion, though even in the early twenty-first century this image is still "knowable" in Raymond Williams's sense of a "knowable community," as the literary/visual references are a part of the greater popular culture of Britain and the United States.

Sheikh Mohamed el Fasi

The second photograph representing the issues addressed in this book is of Robert Cunninghame Graham. The author included this image

Fig. 2. Photograph of Robert Cunninghame Graham. First printed on the frontispiece of *Mogreb-el-Acksa*, 1898.

in early editions of his *Mogreb-el-Acksa* (see fig. 2). What we see here is a photograph of Cunninghame Graham in his "Oriental" guise as Sheikh Mohamed el Fasi (a Turkish doctor with an Arab name), though this image is a bit different. As with Burton's work, this photograph is a feature of a book intended for a popular reading public. In some ways this photograph too is "knowable" as a kind of Orientalist reference, with Cunninghame Graham outfitted in his "native" clothing and posing with a haughty attitude that he has assumed. He is mounted on a horse, a beast only for dignitaries, as he notes in his book. But on the other hand, that he is mounted should also remind us of another literary figure who was important to Cunninghame Graham, Cervante's Don Quixote, the Knight of La Mancha. The latter has a place in Orientalist literature, at least insofar as much of his mad obsession with the literary romance of the knight-errant is intertwined with references to Saracens, various evil Eastern potentates and sorcerers, and the

Prophet of Islam. The reference to Don Quixote—the book and character—is ironic, then, on Cunninghame Graham's part as he attempts to distance himself from the fantasy, even as he falls prey to it in other ways, not the least of which is that his Moroccan escapade has allowed him to see the world, and the British Empire, in a new and apparently more critical light. If Burton used his visual and textual persona to sell his work—and himself—then Cunninghame Graham has used the Knight of the Sad Countenance as a kind of textual prophylactic, sealing off the fantasy of the Orient, extracting him from its clutches, and placing him in the nonaligned, independent, and objective center of a late-nineteenth-century ironist.

Pickthall, a Proper Gentleman

By contrast with the first two examples, the photograph of Marmaduke Mohammed Pickthall depicted here is rather ordinary (see fig. 3). It was printed in February 1922 in the Woking-based journal *The Islamic Review*, though the caption indicates that the photograph was previously published in the *Bombay Chronicle*. Though it was taken well after his 1917 conversion to Islam and his travels and initial years of work abroad, Pickthall appears in the photograph as a rather unassuming middle-aged and middle-class English gentleman, though in some ways this is all he ever was or presumed himself to be. Pickthall is posed at an angle, left shoulder back, as he turns to face the camera; he is groomed in the contemporary British manner with regard to his hairstyle, while his mustache is typical of the early twentieth century. Pickthall is wearing a dress shirt with rounded collar tips, a tie, and a dress coat, though we can only see the upper portion of the latter. The point to take from this photograph is that there is no hint of the "Oriental" in this representation of a man who truly "crossed over" to the East, compared to his predecessors who only assumed a pose or suggested the possibility. Pickthall was not a pretentious man, and this is clear in this photograph, though we can also interpret his "look" and the lack of the (visual) Oriental fetish as of a piece with his religious views. This point works in two respects: Pickthall served as a living example of the modern Muslim in the West in his time;

Fig. 3. Studio photograph of Marmaduke Pickthall. First printed in the *Bombay Chronicle*. Reprinted here from *The Islamic Review* (February 1922) with assistance from the volunteers of the Woking Muslim Mission (www.wokingmuslim.org).

but this synthetic and contemporary point of view is also intertwined with his own interpretation of Islam. Pickthall presents himself as an unassuming, serious, and modern man because his faith requires him to a conduct a jihad for respectability and acceptance in modern democratic society.

Lawrence in Drag?

The last photograph is one of many images that are part of the Lawrence of Arabia legend. Aptly, it was included in Lowell Thomas's first effort as a multimedia impresario, his popular book *With Lawrence in Arabia* (see fig. 4). The photograph is a source of controversy, as some scholars do not believe that this is Lawrence at all.[1] The inclusion of the photograph in early editions of the book and the caption suggest that it was a deliberate choice on Thomas's part, while the representation of Lawrence in disguise as a devout Muslim woman buttresses the myth of his spying prowess. Indeed, it was during a spying foray in such a disguise that he was captured and brutally raped, making such a disguise, if true, with every part of the body covered, all the more

Fig. 4. Photograph of T. E. Lawrence. Printed in the first edition of *With Lawrence in Arabia* by Lowell Thomas. The identity of the person in this photograph is disputed.

poignant and curious. Still, it is odd that Thomas chose this photograph, though as an impresario he surely understood the appeal of such an image to a Western audience.

Compare this image with a subsequent series of well-known images from the Thomas/Chase studio, with Lawrence in his male Arab outfit; or with later images of our hero, posing with his motorcycle; or the particularly sad images of the scrawny, depressed Airman Shaw in his regulation military shorts standing outside of his barracks room. Moreover, looking back at the history of this genre of image, of all the British and Western adventurers to the Orient and their respective Arab disguises and personas, we have to recognize that, as with Pickthall, there is something different here. Lawrence is not playing a game. There is no titillation—"did he or did he not cross over?"—nor is there any pretense, at least not in the same vein as Burton and his ilk. Rather, this photo tells us a good deal about the turn taken in British

Orientalism, as it is intertwined with the new heroic paradigm in modern Britain, as I have outlined in the chapter on Lawrence.

Again, I have offered these four photographs because they condense the arguments and research offered in this book and also complicate it in useful ways. Consider, for example, the connections to popular culture and the commodity form—as text and edible—and the way Empire was understood, and supported, in the period. More than this, however—and in these same images—there are other important themes and ideas that I have alluded to, such as changing conceptions of masculinity and sexuality, the place of religion in modern mass-democratic societies, and modern mass society as a whole. Thus there is more to explore that I can only allude to here or develop in a superficial manner.

Whither the Old Man?

Returning to the first two photographs, of Richard Burton and Robert Cunninghame Graham, and contrasting the other two images, of Marmaduke Pickthall and T. E. Lawrence, we can see how the critique of Orientalism, as an ideology critique, must address gender and sexuality or, simply conflated, masculinity and what this idea means in the context of the 1880–1930 period. I have addressed this point partially in the chapter on Lawrence and the work of the historian Jonathan Rutherford, but it seems apt to extend this critique to all four figures and then to *Reading Arabia* as a whole. Perhaps this book is really about masculinity, for the writing of these first two figures, Burton and Cunninghame Graham, and even their poses in the photographs offered here suggest a conception of masculinity that is very different from that of Pickthall and Lawrence. There are differences of class, at least in the case of Pickthall, which are certainly a factor, but there is more that, I argue, concerns the moment of the Empire and contemporary British social and political life.

With regard to Burton and Cunninghame Graham, we have two subjects who are completely contained and self-sufficient within an ideology, in their prose (both content and style), and in these two images. Burton and Cunninghame Graham presented themselves as outsiders, with the latter suggesting he was a master of irony and the ironic pose.

While the term "outsider" is certainly an overdetermined word/ideology, both Burton and Cunninghame Graham were nonetheless loyal subjects of the crown, as Burton demonstrated by duty as a consul and Cunninghame Graham through national service at various points in his life, especially as a horse procurer for the army during World War I.[2] The confidence of each man to move "outside" his social "place"— so important an idea, as Conrad reminds us in *Heart of Darkness*—to dally with the "other" is not as clear-cut in the work (and images) of Pickthall and Lawrence.

This is obvious in the case of Pickthall, who though an avowed convert to Islam seems to be the same middle-class British gentleman despite his time in India and at the court of the Nizam of Hyderabad, where he was a loyal subject to a non-Western monarch and authority figure. "Gentleman" is the important word here, as Pickthall's masculinity, as limited as it is by the sartorial constraints of class and (cultural) propriety, is evident albeit in a most "normal" sense, though we must wonder how he dressed when in Hyderabad.

By contrast, we have the studio photographs of Thomas and Chase, which link Lawrence back to the Orientalist poses of Burton and Cunninghame Graham, and then the image of Lawrence in disguise as a woman from Thomas's early book. As I have argued, Lawrence's ambivalence about his mass-cultural persona, "Lawrence of Arabia," concerns his ambivalence about mass culture and, by implication, modernity in general—hence his turn to premodern printing techniques and handprinted texts, coupled with his love for custom-built motorcycles. The man of these images, whether (possibly) dressed as a devout Muslim woman or posing as an Arab prince, is interested in posing and the illicit pleasure taken thereof, in a way that differs from the images of Burton. By contrast, Burton commands the image and fully avows it, whereas there is something elusive, if not evasive, in the collection of Lawrence images. Perhaps it is apt that Lawrence covered himself from head to shabby shoe in this image, so that finally it is the most honest image we have of "Lawrence of Arabia" and the man himself.

A useful way to understand the difference between the two pairs of images in these photographs is through Lacan's distinction between the ideal ego and the ego ideal. Again, this is ideology critique that joins the false separation between the personal and the social, between, say, the "real" Lawrence and the studio personality, and what these two images might tell us about Empire and colonial rule. Slavoj Žižek offers a clear distinction between these two Lacanian phrases as follows:

> Here we can clearly discern the function of the Ego-Ideal—that is, of symbolic identification—from its imaginary counterpart: symbolic identification is identification with the ideal ("virtual") point from which the subject looks upon himself when his own actual life appears to him as a vain and repulsive spectacle.[3]

And so, these two phrases mark moments in the trajectory of the development of the subject, and especially the ideal ego, a central idea in Lacan's famous text "The Mirror Stage," his label for the moment when the child identifies with the specular image or, as he puts it, misrecognizes itself in the mirror, bringing form where before there were only disconnected parts. The ego ideal refers to the later stage when the child is socialized within the family and community and so learns about the Law and propriety, a position that marks the child's life with guilt, akin to Gregor Samsa's debt to the family in Kafka's *Metamorphosis*. And so, these images show us how each figure composed himself as a person and as a persona for the gaze of the public and his own critical view.[4] Put another way, these images are about Burton, Cunninghame Graham, Pickthall, and Lawrence, but they are also, in the respective differences they trace, about the changes in the relationship between authority and Empire and how this relationship plays out at an individual level.

In tracing the differences between these images and what this might mean with regard to Empire and authority we should return to the first Lacanian concept, the ego ideal. Žižek explains that the ego ideal is not only about symbolic identification and how this concerns action—in the world or otherwise—but also concerns what he refers to as "interpassivity":

> This "ideal" function of the "big Other" qua ego ideal (as opposed to ideal ego) can also be discerned through the notion of interpassivity,

of transposing onto the Other—not my activity, but my very passive experience.[5]

The example Žižek offers is that of the basketball player who needs to imagine a disabled child who idolizes him in order to play at the highest level. This is, then, a necessary triangulation of the subject, where the third position, that of the voyeur, is critical for the subject to cohere, for the professional basketball player to play well. Žižek adds:

> [I]nterpassivity is not simply a symmetrical reversal of "interactivity" (in the sense, described above, of being active through (our identification with) another): it gives birth to a "reflexive" structure in which the gaze is redoubled, in which I "see myself being seen as likeable."[6]

In the early 1990s, when Žižek was elaborating his interpretation of Lacan's ego ideal, he was also writing and speaking about how Europe and the West viewed and then intervened in the Balkan wars. In so many ways Western foreign policy worked as follows: the republics of the former Yugoslavia were all small baby countries that looked to the West, especially the United States and Great Britain, as a kind of democratic and capitalist ideal. Indeed, this might even have been so with regard to the leadership of some of the republics—but whatever their fantasy was, it did not matter. In fact, the baby republic's gaze was important for the actions materially taken by the West and NATO in bombing campaigns and other forms of intervention. Much of the same ideological scenario has repeatedly played out in the Middle East, most recently during the Arab revolutions and uprisings, and the West has intervened in many ways as the big father country saving the baby proto-democracies of the Arab world from various bloodthirsty sultans, sheiks, and warlords. Of course there is a good deal of truth here, and this should not be overlooked, but the point is that these interventions are about the need of the West to see itself in this mode.

Returning to the photographs with this last point in mind, especially the larger group of Chase photographs of Lawrence, we might now reconsider the instructions he gave for his birching sessions, on direct order from the "Old Man." There is a link between this new conception of the Orient that is intertwined with new forms of subjectivity—specifically sexual subjects of the Empire—and this is very different from that of the earlier generation of Orientalists. At least it is this, that the relationship to power—as an individual relationship now mediated by mass society and political forms—is deeply determined by the revulsion Lawrence feels when he matches himself to the ego ideal. And yet his revulsion, realized with the birchings, is far from being a simple matter of abjection. To take my earlier argument about a charismatic authority figure such as Churchill further, this feeling of revulsion is actually part of a process by which Lawrence recements his place in the symbolic. Lawrence must have a direct relationship with power, albeit violent and abject, and embodied in a single person, the "Old Man." This relationship is characteristic of the appeal of fascism and, again, entails historical determinations such as mass political formations, mass society, and, indeed, mass culture. Yet, Richard Burton never felt this way about authority, and his dalliance as a sexologist was never disavowed and in fact was a permanent feature of his life, both his private life and that of his persona, Captain Richard Burton. Burton is a contained subject in a way that makes Lawrence, his legacy, seem a collection of fragments, a mess of subjectivity.

The Fantasy of the Orient

> I put a spell on you / Because you're mine.
> Screamin' Jay Hawkins, "I Put a Spell on You" (1958)

But how do ideology critique and this book relate to postcolonialism and world literature? This is a fair question, and inadvertently draws out some of the frustrations I have with both areas, as *Reading Arabia* sits squarely in the middle of each area and yet is not properly within either. *Reading Arabia* is about texts that are key to contemporary theories of world literature, such as *The Thousand and One Nights, The Rubaiyat of Omar Khayyam,* and, say, the work of David Damrosch (*What Is World Literature?*). A trenchant theory of world literature would certainly take into account the circumstances and implications of its formation, and I think this is the best part of Pascale Casanova's *The World Republic of Letters*. Though there is a rigorous critique of the place of world literature and the modern market—or market economy—the ideological implications of such a project are untouched. With regard to postcolonialism, what I mean by this is that the roots of any meaningful postcolonial critique of the literature and culture of the modern Middle East and North Africa must engage the colonial roots, not as a matter of what has been banished and transcended but living on in a kind of vampiric half-life. Ann McClintock was an early critic of this failure of postcolonialism back in the early 1990s when so many examples of colonialism persisted in new—or older—forms.

Aijaz Ahmad tied postcolonialism to multiculturalism and—by extension—to identity politics in the West, and given the prevalence of operative notions of absolute identity, he was accurate in his criticism.[7] Others such as Robert J. C. Young and Simon Gikandi have focused on the ways colonial culture persists in everyday practices.[8] As Gikandi comments, postcolonialism is perhaps only useful as a way of "rereading the convergence of structural continuity in the face of temporal disruption, of understanding entrenched memories in the midst of reconfigured desires."[9] Even Edward Said and Gayatri Spivak, though associated with postcolonial theory by many, are skeptical of the movement. Timothy Brennan, a student of Said's and a scholar of the latter's work, argues that for Said Orientalism is the counterpoint to multiculturalism, the new "imperial shibboleth" (Brennan's phrase), and by extension to postcolonialism; while Gayatri Spivak early on wondered aloud in the concluding paragraphs of a well-known essay just why white men must save brown women from brown men.[10]

Where we should take the postcolonial project is back to the metropole, that is, with a rigorous critique of the constitutive function of the fantasy of the Orient in modern Western culture and everyday life, at least to the extent I have outlined here. Indeed, pushing Spivak's point further, we should ask why white men—or Westerners in general—so badly need to save brown women from brown men, and why the ideology of the secular, modern Western state depends on this need as we hear too often in the public justifications of war and other military actions.

It was odd, then, that Stuart Hall, a scholar with significant intellectual and professional ties to the Birmingham school of cultural studies, a movement that would seem to be skeptical toward postcolonialism (as an abandonment of class politics and critique of global capitalism), actually saved postcolonialism from its sharpest critics (Shohat, McClintock, and Dirlik), as well as its proponents in his essay, "When Was 'The Postcolonial'? Thinking at the Limit."[11] This essay is an incisive and dialectical reading of the primary theoretical texts in the field where Hall recognizes the kernel of truth in those who have criticized the analytic accuracy of postcolonialism (Shohat and McClintock), that is, the sense that the colonial period is "over" and past and that we can compare the colonial experiences of, say, Algeria and Australia. Yet Hall also warns against any notion of postcolonialism, or alternately a critique of the field, which proposes a return to a precolonial or originary culture. Instead, and bringing together a polemical point made by Arif Dirlik concerning the absence of political economy in postcolonial theory, and the work of Homi Bhabha on hybridity, postcolonialism is nonetheless useful as it does announce the end of the colonial era and the advent of a new order of global capitalism. Moreover, this new era is not entirely new as ideas and cultural forms from the colonial era either persist or reappear in a new guise and now as global phenomena. Moreover, a revised postcolonial critique is not as invested in regional identifications and labels and is actually quite critical of terms such as the "third world" or "eurocentrism."

In Hall's sense then, the persistence of the fantasy of the Orient, in the West and in the formerly colonized countries of the Middle East and North Africa, and the way the fantasy is intertwined with mass culture—mass publication—and everyday life, further substantiates his reworked use of the term (and the field). And so, Orientalism must be linked to a postcolonial critique that is also a critique of global capitalism.

Yet, the focus here has been on Orientalism as a form of mass culture par excellence, a form that appears at a key moment in the history of commodity culture in Great Britain. Bluntly put, mass culture "interpellates" the public, without regard to class, into the world of commodities and consumption. This seems to be the point of Eugène Atget's multiple photographs of fin de siècle shop windows filled with dolls and mannequins "calling out" like street hustlers to the passersby, "You can buy me and own me for so little."[12] The point is that consumer culture appeals in a different way and brings about different results, as a matter of market and habit (of consumption). Moreover, the appeal deliberately works at the level of the unconscious, which by the twentieth century has become the basis for an ever more refined specialization, that of the advertising agent and his/her craft.

It seems obvious, then, that the best way to understand the way Orientalism and its contemporary legacy functions today is through ideology critique, that is, the terms and method of psychoanalysis, and particularly Slavoj Žižek's blend of Lacan with the Frankfurt School. In the introduction I cited the work of Alain Grosrichard and the commentary on the former's *The Sultan's Court*, and while this book was as groundbreaking as *Orientalism* in its way, and is an important text in the psychoanalysis of Orientalism, I do not think that the way it is argued, through political philosophy and in the context of Enlightenment thought, offers a meaningful way to grasp how Orientalism functions as fantasy in the late modern context of mass culture, a consumer society. To this very point Slavoj Žižek notes that the project is not to gesture toward fantasy but to understand how it mutates in different contexts. After all, the figures who comprise *Reading Arabia* are all productions—as public personae—of mass culture and a new social order in the West and, most important, are all "friends" of the Arab/Muslim world, not latter-day crusaders, anti-Semites, racists, or jingoistic supporters of Western imperial rule.

In the opening chapter of *The Plague of Fantasies*, Žižek lays out the form and function of fantasy as social narrative. First, he argues that fantasy "teaches us how to desire" and adds:

> The role of fantasy is thus in a way analogous to that of the ill-fated pineal gland in Descartes's philosophy, this mediator between the

res cogitans and the *res extensa*: fantasy mediates between the formal symbolic structure and the positivity of the objects we encounter in reality—that is to say, it provides a "schema" according to which certain positive objects in reality can function as objects of desire, filling in the empty places opened up by the formal symbolic structure.[13]

Žižek calls this point the "transcendental schematism" of fantasy and thereby offers us a way of understanding fantasy, especially Orientalist fantasy, in a way that brings together the philosophical discourse about the Enlightenment and attendant (foundational) fears of the lusty and brutal sultan with the personal travelers' accounts and fiction and reportage of, say, Pickthall and Lawrence.

If the Enlightenment is often viewed as the moment of birth of the modern subject and the discourse of subjectivity as we know it in the West (e.g., the citizen, individual, universal rights), then in an everyday sense the subjectivity of consumer society marks an extreme moment in this history, a moment where the values of the Enlightenment are "lived" in a most sentient—and, given that it is Orientalism we are discussing here—sensuous sense. To this end, Žižek points out that fantasy is also "intersubjective," for it not only offers a "schema" by which the subject might function but also and more specifically gives us a place. Fantasy helps the little girl find her place in the world, under the smiles and adoring gaze of her parents, as she voraciously eats strawberry cake—this pleases them and the child as a subject and as the object of parental desire.[14] Later Žižek argues that the emergence of the Law comes with the subject's refusal of *jouissance*—a stain of obscene pleasure associated with drive—which gives place to desire. The loss of *jouissance* is displaced into a scene of fantasy where this source of pleasure takes form as that which was "stolen" from us by the other, that is, the "usual suspects," the "Arab," the "Jew," and other minorities.[15] As Žižek explains—and for our purposes he amplifies Grosrichard's critique of the Enlightenment—the Habermasian notion of a "dialogue" is radically impossible here and rests on idealized contexts, perhaps a smoky Vienna café several hundred years ago, and an idealized set of interactions between the subject as an "a priori" of Enlightenment discourse.[16]

Yet fantasy can never be avowed or taken for reality. Fantasy, as Žižek understands it, is both censorious and a "primordial lie" that is impossible and must always remain "implicit." Indeed, the subject can never identify with the fantasy in the sense that the fantasy has anything to do with the "truth" or the "kernel" of the subject's being.

The mutation in Orientalism from the mid-nineteenth-century explorer accounts (as well as those of the earlier period) to these fantasies of mass culture concerns the relationship between Western subjectivity and the "Orient." In the earlier, pre–mass culture examples the explorers were singular individuals, more akin to the heroes of epic narrative rather than the novel. Their exploits were extraordinary and fully their own and not likely to be repeated or rivaled. This is true of Edward Lane, for example, despite the ordinariness of his account of "modern Egypt," insofar as the detail and expertise of his account entailed an effort hitherto unknown and not to be matched easily. Lane's effort, coupled with his particular sensibility and ethnographic and documentary skill, makes his text unique, as he intended.

There is a bit of this in Burton's work, yet the claim to uniqueness is tempered by its function as a marketing device. Clearly Burton understood at some level that the claim itself—I am the only person to have traveled here and done this—was a way to sell books and to make a popular name, and thus consider the persona of Captain Richard Burton. With Doughty, the particularity of his narrative, the heroism of his abjection if we can think of it this way, is finally a well-known narrative of self-understanding. By the second half of the twentieth century this narrative developed into the kind of existential narrative, wrapped in a journey to North Africa or the Middle East, which is mocked in Paul Bowles's *The Sheltering Sky* and Volker Schlöndorff's film *The Circle of Deceit*.

The point is that Orientalism, under the aegis of the commodity and global capitalism in a time of mass culture and mass consumption, works in accord with a new subject and new processes of political subjectivity. It is more than the historical coincidence I pointed to in the introduction, the Anglo-Egyptian campaign in the Sudan and the burst of consumer culture with an Orientalist character, ranging from football to chocolate bars to cheap literature. It is the political ideology and, more important, the process of interpellation, that is, learning to be a subject and enjoying subjectivity in a new political order.

The key question, beyond historical coincidence, is what makes Orientalist mass culture special in this regard. Again, the narrative of subjectivity—having an existential crisis in Lebanon or Algeria, or "finding" yourself in the Arab world—is one example, while the root of this crisis in the Enlightenment narratives of the sultan bogeyman and his excesses in the harem and torture chamber is another. Though we encounter both of these Orientalist ideas today, as with the characterization of various Arab leaders and the ongoing popularity of films about the journey to North Africa or the Middle East—ranging from the art film *Hideous Kinky* or the Morocco scenes in *Babel* to the popularity of the desert romance in, say, the recent *Sex and the City 2*—there are more interesting examples in the response to the assassination of Osama bin Laden and the Western response to the Arab uprisings.

The fantasy of the Orient, then, plays a constitutive role in the formation and function of Western subjectivity, while its mutation in the late nineteenth and twentieth centuries into a feature of mass culture in the United States and Britain (though I have focused on the latter here) intertwines it with the global economy of our own time. Now, I am not claiming that this fantasy, which is after all a set of ideas that play out in racist actions and even war, is more important than other fantasies and corresponding racist and violent actions and movements. This book is not intended as a form of comparative racist fantasies or a diminishment of concern for anti-Semitism and racism against, say, African Americans in the United States, but rather as an attempt to understand how this one (social) fantasy among others, that of the Orient, has developed into such a central feature of Western society and Western political consciousness (and the political unconscious). Consider again some of the points made from the opening chapters on the translation of *The Thousand and One Nights*. The narratives are entirely about the theft of *jouissance*, whether it is a story about an

African slave cuckolding a king or a hoard of stolen treasure. And of course these stories are framed as a function of desire, by the desire of the king for his young wife, and the fear that someone might "steal" his *jouissance* and cuckold him once again. The connection is an obvious one, then, to so much Western literature about Islam and the character of the Prophet, his wives, and the treatment of Muslim women. Desert romances and their derivation from early modern pornography only substantiate my point.

As to how we should read the archive of British Orientalism, one way is to see the fantasy of the Orient as a symptom that gains exists only in and against a context of global capitalism. This seems obvious when so stated, but a symptomatic reading of the fantasy should not rest on some idea of the fantasy as a passive phenomenon; rather it should be read in a most active or constitutive function, a point I have stressed here. That is, the fantasy comes alive as a feature of mass culture and the related division of labor and modes of production and distribution, first as mass-produced textual culture, and then as the consumer culture of the modern global economy, all of which is simultaneously intertwined with new subjects and new forms of subjectivity in modern Britain.

Yet, if all this is true, then intervention against the fantasy of the Orient is nearly impossible, as we have tracked with regard to our four writers. Žižek comments on such an intervention as follows:

> In short, an authentic act is not simply external with regard to the hegemonic symbolic field disturbed by it: an act is an act only *with regard to some symbolic field, as an intervention into it.*[17]

He explains that this is not an intervention "out of nowhere, but precisely *from the standpoint of this inherent impossibility, stumbling block, which is its hidden, disavowed structuring principle.*"[18] The standpoint for Žižek is class, against its disavowal and obscuration in contemporary life and thought, and I argue that this is so here as well. Yes, the British fantasy of the Orient is foregrounded against a global—imperial and then postimperial—economy, but the critical factor here is class, and a critique of the place of class within a critique of the Oriental fantasy should be the basis for continued research. Of course, the way in which the fantasy of the Orient is not merely so much false consciousness—or just fantasy—serves a complex function that must be deftly untied with formalist and materialist critique is a crucial recognition.

Notes

Bibliography

Index

Notes

Introduction: Britain at the Fin de Siècle and the Orientalist Unconscious

1. I offer this last point with some qualification, for the kind of relative social stability that everyday life requires and then buttresses will only be realized in the middle of the twentieth century in Britain and the United States.

2. I am indebted to many superior examples of such "walking tours," including that of Joad Raymond, whose "walk" through Smith Market in the seventeenth century was particularly influential, and possibly influenced by Dickens's "walk" of Fagin through the same area in *Oliver Twist;* Jonathan Schneer in *London 1900*; and a few New York walking tours, such as E. B. White's *Here Is New York.* It is still a useful critical gimmick that best emphasizes the experience of space in time, and in the first two examples, as a particular textual and political space.

3. Jonathan Schneer, *London 1900: The Imperial Metropolis* (New Haven: Yale University Press, 1999), 17.

4. Eno's Fruit Salts were used for gastrointestinal illnesses and as an antacid.

5. Janice Boddy, "Purity and Conquest in the Anglo-Egyptian Sudan," in *Dirt, Undress, and Difference: Critical Perspectives on the Body's Surface*, ed. Adeline Masquelier (Bloomington: Indiana University Press, 2006),168–189.

6. Schneer, *London 1900: The Imperial Metropolis*, 6.

7. Charles Brown MacDonald, *A Time for Trumpets: The Untold Story of the Battle of the Bulge* (New York: Perennial, 2002), 58.

8. Friedrich A. Kittler, *Gramophone, Film Typewriter*, trans. Geoffrey Winthrop-Young and Michael Wutz (Stanford: Stanford University Press, 1999), 198–200.

9. Ibid., 203.

10. Ibid., 200–214.

11. Ibid., 229.

12. James Joyce, *Ulysses* (Paris: Shakespeare & Co., 1922).

13. Wallace Gray, http://www.mendele.com/WWD/WWDaraby.notes.html #araby (accessed January 1, 2010).

14. James Joyce, "Araby," in *Dubliners* (London: Grant Richards, 1914).

15. Dane Kennedy, *The Highly Civilized Man: Richard Burton and the Victorian World* (Cambridge, MA: Harvard University Press, 2005), 206–247.

16. See, for example, the penny pamphlet *Life and Adventures of the Mahdi: The False Prophet* (London: General, 1885).

17. Edward Ziter, *The Orient on the Victorian Stage* (Cambridge: Cambridge University Press, 2003).

18. Brian Street, *The Savage in Literature* (London: Routledge & Kegan Paul, 1975).

19. Patrick Brantlinger, *Rule of Darkness: British Literature and Imperialism, 1830–1914* (Ithaca, NY: Cornell University Press, 1990).

20. Homi Bhabha, *The Location of Culture* (New York: Routledge, 1994) 66–84.

21. Ibid., 75.

22. Ibid.

23. Ibid., 81.

24. Timothy Mitchell, *Colonizing Egypt*, 2nd ed. (Berkeley: University of California Press, 1991), x.

25. Billie Melman, "The Middle East/Arabia: 'The Cradle of Islam,,'" in *The Cambridge Companion to Travel Writing*, ed. Peter Hulme and Tim Youngs (Cambridge: Cambridge University Press), 105–121.

26. Insofar as this book is about masculinity, and the "love" of the Arabist for the Arab world, in all senses, it is perhaps not surprising that I have not included a chapter on Gertrude Bell. While she was quite influential, and an important Arabist in her own right, her relationship to the ideology, as a very self-identified proper British woman, was limited, which is also to state that she belongs in a different, more focused project about gender and Orientalism, where the first term is contingent, not essential.

27. Manfred Steger, *Globalization: A Very Short Introduction,* 2nd ed. (Oxford: Oxford University Press, 2009), 5–7.

28. Indeed, at the risk of overstating the argument at hand, Said does not account fully for tourism as a crucial factor here, especially for the development of Orientalism, or really for mass culture in general. In the last instance, I argue, modern Orientalism, that of the late nineteenth and twentieth centuries, is firmly rooted in Cook's Tours to North Africa and "the Levant," *Baedeker Guides*, and of course popular accounts of travel and adventure in exotic parts of the British Empire such as Stanley's *In Darkest Africa*, not just in the "high" texts that interested Said, though he focused here for important reasons.

1. The Two Tangents of British Orientalism: Burton and Doughty, Dandy and Prophet in the 1880s

1. Dane Kennedy, *Highly Civilized Man: Richard Burton and the Victorian World* (Cambridge, MA: Harvard University Press, 2005), 254–255.

2. Michael S. Dodson, *Orientalism, Empire, and National Culture: India, 1770–1880* (Cambridge: Cambridge University Press, 2007), 173–183.

3. Ibid., 211–221.

4. This is Robert J. C. Young's argument in chapter 2 of his *Colonial Desire* (Young, *Colonial Desire: Hybridity in Theory, Culture and Race* [New York: Routledge, 1995]. This opposition of culture and civilization bears fruit in the British "native rule" policy—except for Ireland, that is—as theorized by Lugard (ibid., 164).

5. Lisa Sigel, *Governing Pleasures: Pornography and Social Change in England, 1815–1914* (New Brunswick, NJ: Rutgers University Press, 2002), 64–69.

6. Bradlaugh was associated with women's rights causes as well as the Irish Home Rule movement. He was also a close friend of Annie Besant.

7. Sigel rightly contrasts the Cannibals and their privilege of aristocratic power and wealth to others who were persecuted for obscenity and other violations of public morals. She is right to emphasize this point, but there is a touch of moralism in her class analysis that she only undercuts later with her last chapter on pornography for the masses (ibid., 59 and 119–155).

8. I believe this line of argument sharpens the complexity Kennedy brings to Burton's work (Kennedy, *Highly Civilized Man*, 210–211).

9. The Huntington Library collection of Burton-Smithers correspondence bears this point out. The letters from the lawyer to Isabel are polite and even cloying in the first years, and as she repeatedly asks him to return books and refrain from any surreptitious publishing ventures—of Burton-related erotica—his responses grow colder and colder. In fact, over the course of the correspondence the letters move from handwritten and signed letters to brief and, interestingly, typewritten notes (ibid., 255–256; James G. Nelson, *Publisher to the Decadents: Leonard Smithers in the careers of Beardsley, Wilde and Dowson* [University Park: Penn State University Press, 2000]).

10. Richard Burton, *A Plain and Literal Translation of the Arabian Nights' Entertainments, Now Entituled The Book of the Thousand Nights and a Night*, vols. 1 and 10, Printed by the Burton Club for Private Subscribers Only (Denver: Carson Harper, 1900), 93.

11. Robert Irwin, *The Arabian Nights: A Companion* (London: Tauris Parke, 2004), 30.

12. Ibid., 42–62.

13. Ibid., 44.

14. Ibid., 95.

15. Ibid.

16. Irwin, *Arabian Nights: A Companion*, 96.

17. Ibid., 16–17.

18. Peter Caracciolo, *The Arabian Nights in English Literature: Studies in the Reception of The Thousand and One Nights into British Culture* (New York: St. Martin's Press, 1988), 20–27.

19. Ibid., 22.

20. In order to assess the place of the *Nights* in modern (late-nineteenth- and twentieth-century) children's literature, I searched eBay (accessed August 10, 2010) for such books and was surprised to find many examples, including one abridged version of Burton's *Nights* published and distributed by the Sears Roebuck Company. This example alone confirms the status of the *Nights* as a textual commodity.

21. Richard Burton, *Supplemental Nights to the Book of the Thousand and One Nights with Notes Anthropological and Explanatory* (Privately published by the Burton Club, n.d.), 6:360.

22. Caracciolo, *Arabian Nights*, 92.

23. Mary Florence Thwaite, *From Primer to Pleasure in Reading: An Introduction to Children's Books in England from the Invention of Printing to 1914* ((London: Library Association, 1972), 99–100.

24. See Alderson in Caracciolo, *Arabian Nights*, 82–83.

25. Ibid., 84–85.

26. See *Echo*, October 12, 1885; *Edinburgh Review* 335 (July 1886): 1883–1884; *Pall Mall Gazette* 42, no. 6396 (September 14, 1885): 2. All of these sources are mentioned and documented in Dane Kennedy's "Sexologist" chapter in *Highly Civilized Man*. This chapter is about Burton's erotic publications, with some explanation of the historic context. I am indebted to this book and Kennedy's thorough research on Burton, and his always engaging writing.

27. Irwin, *Arabian Nights: A Companion*, 32.

28. Burton, *A Plain and Literal Translation of the Arabian Nights' Entertainments*, 6.

29. Steven Marcus, *The Other Victorians: A Study of Sexuality in the Mid-Nineteenth Century England* (New York: Basic Books, 1966), 44.

30. Lynn Hunt, *The Invention of Pornography: Obscenity and the Origins of Modernity, 1500–1800* (New York: Zone Books, 1996), 11.

31. Irwin, *Arabian Nights: A Companion*, 34. Irwin also argues that the story "How Abu Hasan Brake Wind," another reference to farting, was not original to any manuscript source and was probably "smuggled" in by Burton from a European source, Aubrey's *Lives*.

32. Stephen Tabachnick, ed., *Explorations in Doughty's Arabia Deserta* (Athens: University of Georgia Press, 1987).

33. Ibid., 3–5.

34. Charles M. Doughty, *Travels in Deserta Arabia: With Illustrations Made on the Spot by Edy Legrand* (New York: Heritage Press, 1953), 39.

35. Tabachnick, *Explorations in Doughty's Arabia Deserta*, 5–7.

36. Ibid., 225–253.

37. Ibid., 223.

38. Richard Burton, "Mr. Doughty's Travels in Arabia," *Academy* No. 847, July 28, 1888, 47.

39. Ibid.

40. Ibid.

41. Edward Said, *Orientalism* (New York: Vintage, 1979), 23.

42. Janice Deledalle-Rhodes, "The True Nature of Doughty's Relationship with the Arabs," in Tabachnick, *Explorations in Doughty's Arabia Deserta*, 5–7.

43. Burton, "Mr. Doughty's Travels in Arabia," 48.

44. T. E. Lawrence's introduction first appeared in the 1921 second edition (English). Tabachnick, *Explorations in Doughty's Arabia Deserta*, 226.

45. Tabachnick, *Explorations in Doughty's Arabia Deserta*, 19.

46. Doughty, *Travels in Deserta Arabia*, 19.

47. Ibid., 25.

48. Ibid., 20.

49. Ibid.

50. Ibid.

51. Ibid.

52. Deledalle-Rhodes, "Doughty's Relationship with the Arabs," 111–116.

53. Ibid.

54. Ibid., 126.

55. James Eli Adams, *Dandies and Desert Saints: Styles of Victorian Masculinity* (Ithaca, NY: Cornell University Press), 22.

56. Ibid., 25.

57. Ibid., 31.

58. Ibid., 29

59. Ibid., 41, for Adams's interesting comments on representation and specularity.

60. T. S. Eliot, "Contemporary English Prose," *Vanity Fair* 20 (1923): 51.

61. William N. Rogers, "Arabia Deserta and the Victorians," in Tabachnick, *Explorations in Doughty's Arabia Deserta*, 44–49.

62. This point runs counter to Tabachnick's attempts to explain why *Travels* was not popular and was neglected—its time was specific (ibid., 5–13).

63. Walter Benjamin, *Charles Baudelaire: A Lyric Poet in the Era of High Capitalism* (New York: New Left Books, 1973).

64. Elizabeth Gargano, "'English Sheiks' and Arab Stereotypes: E. M. Hull, T. E. Lawrence and the Imperial Masquerade," *Texas Studies in Literature and Language* 48, no. 2 (Summer 2006): 172.

65. Billie Melman, *Women and the Popular Imagination in the Twenties* (New York: St. Martin's Press, 1988), 90.

66. Susan Blake, "What 'Race' Is the Sheik?: Rereading a Desert Romance," in *Doubled Plots: Romance and History*, ed. Susan Strehle and Mary Panniccia Carden (Jackson: University of Mississippi Press, 2003), 67–85; Emily W. Leider, *Dark Lover: The Life and Death of Rudolph Valentino* (New York: Farrar, Straus & Giroux, 2003), 153.

67. Leider, *Dark Lover*, 152–153.

68. Ibid., 167.

69. Ibid., 169–170.

70. Melman, *Women and the Popular Imagination in the Twenties*, 89; Studlar, *This Mad Masquerade: Stardom and Masculinity in the Jazz Age*, 177–193.

71. See the postcards reproduced in Malek Alloula, *The Colonial Harem* (Minneapolis: University of Minnesota Press, 1986). For more information on Biskra, see Gareth Stanton, "The Oriental City: A North African Itinerary," *Third Text*, nos. 3 and 4: 3–38.

72. E. M. Hull, *The Sheik* (Philadelphia: Pine Street Books, 2001), 4.

73. Ibid., 52.

74. Ibid., 57.

75. Ibid., 60.

76. Ibid., 145.

77. Ibid., 218–219.

78. Sarah Wintle, "*The Sheik*: What Can be Made of a Daydream," *Women: A Cultural Review* 7, no. 3 (1996): 301–302.

79. Hull, *The Sheik*, 246–252.

80. Melman, *Women and the Popular Imagination in the Twenties*.

81. Ibid., 90n2. This comment originally appeared in the *Literary Review*.

82. Ella Shohat, "Gender and the Culture of Empire: Toward a Feminist Ethnography of the Cinema," in *Visions of the East: Orientalism and Film*, ed. Matthew Bernstein and Gaylyn Studlar (New Brunswick, NJ: Rutgers University Press, 1997), 56–57.

83. See Edward Ziter, *The Orient on the Victorian Stage* (Cambridge: Cambridge University Press, 2003), 54–93, for the roots of the "dark lover" and rape/captivity narratives in early-nineteenth-century drama and in the productions of Byron's work.

84. Blake, "What 'Race' Is the Sheik?" 67–85.

85. Gargano, "'English Sheiks' and Arab Stereotypes."

86. Wintle, "The Sheik: What Can be Made of a Daydream."

87. Studlar, *This Mad Masquerade*.

88. See T. J. Clark, *The Painting of Modern Life: Paris in the Art of Manet and His Followers* (Princeton: Princeton University Press, 1984).

89. Wintle, "The Sheik: What Can be Made of a Daydream," 291; Studlar, *This Mad Masquerade*, 177–184.

90. Studlar, *This Mad Masquerade*, 100.

91. Leider, *Dark Lover*, 157.

92. Said, *Orientalism,* 104.

93. The reviewer was especially ad hominem, referring to Caine's forced Shakespearian appearance and the poor quality of his writing.

94. Hall Caine, *The Mahdi, or Love and Race* (London: James Clarke, 1894), 502.

95. Ibid., 604.

96. The pamphlet was originally given as a speech to the Jewish Literary Society of Liverpool. See the copy of "Why I Wrote *The White Prophet*" (London: Private Press and issued by Collier, 1909). Available in the Huntington Library Rare Books Collection, call number 113659.

97. The *New York Times* responded (January 15, 1910) to the pamphlet, tongue in cheek, with a blurb stating some cruel readers might want to ask "why" Caine wrote "Why I Wrote *The White Prophet*" with its "suggestive" title and eloquent tributes to the author's work. The writer concludes that surely the critics of the novel will now feel ashamed.

98. Melman (*Women and the Popular Imagination in the Twenties*, 91–101) outlines and defines the "desert romance," but in a recent article Hsu-Ming Teo updates the list and ties *The Sheik* to recent novels, demonstrating the persistence of the genre (in Ned Curthoys and Debjani Ganguly, *Edward Said: The Legacy of a Public Intellectual* [Melbourne: Melbourne University Press, 2007], 241–262).

99. See the Internet Movie Database (IMDb) site under the film title with either 1927 or 1936. Also, as Wintle ("The Sheik: What Can be Made of a Daydream," 299) notes, Alla Nazimova, a lesbian actress and social figure in the silent film era, starred in another Near Eastern romance, *Eye for Eye,* and was also close to Valentino and both of his wives. Her Hollywood house was, appropriately enough, known as The Garden of Allah, and was a tourist site for many years.

100. Wintle, "The Sheik," 298, notes that while traveling in Egypt Hichens met Oscar Wilde's friend and lover, Lord Alfred Douglas, an encounter which, of course, fed into his most famous and controversial novel. In his autobiography Hichens claims even to have discussed the plan for his novel with Wilde and its similarities to Anatole France's *Thaïs*, as well as a project Wilde mentioned, about an ascetic North African monk who gives up his vows for a voluptuous Egyptian courtesan.

101. Hichens, *The Garden of Allah*, 2:14.

102. Young, *Colonial Desire*, 98.

103. Ibid., 112.

104. Ibid., 181–182. His very last comment concerns the fantasy of postcolonial theorists, "that those in the Western academy at least have managed to free

themselves from this hybrid commerce of colonialism, as from every other aspect of the colonial legacy" (ibid., 182).

105. Young does make an excellent point, and refers to the work of Deleuze and Guattari and their theory of reterritorialization. Colonialism reterritorializes and brings with it an Oedipal ideology with which it conquers and defeats the consciousness of the colonized as effectively as weapons (ibid., 167–173). A good point that does not necessarily exclude a psychoanalytic analysis of the fantasy.

106. Mladen Dolar, "Introduction," in Alain Grosrichard, *The Sultan's Court: European Fantasies of the East* (New York: Verso, 1998), xvi–xvii.

107. Ibid.; Grosrichard, *Sultan's Court,* 100–119.

108. Dolar, "Introduction," xix, xxiii; Grosrichard, *Sultan's Court,* 114–119.

109. Dolar, "Introduction," xxii.

110. Dolar uses Lacanian terms and tells us that this irredeemable lack is only "filled" by that fundamental fetish, the mother's phallus (ibid.).

2. Khartoum Nightmare: Popular Literature of the British Campaign in the Sudan

1. Henry John Newbolt, *Admirals All* (New York: John Lane, 1898)

2. Richard Altick, *The Common Reader: A Social History of the Mass Reading Public, 1800–1900* (Chicago: University of Chicago Press, 1957), 3.

3. See John Carey, *The Intellectuals and the Masses: Pride and Prejudice among the Literary Intelligentsia, 1880–1939* (Chicago: Academy, 2002).

4. An article on the Maxim, the "future" machine gun, appears in *Pall Mall Gazette*, January 24, 1885, 2. This is pre-Kitchener, contrary to Fulton's argument.

5. Edward Ziter, *The Orient on the Victorian Stage* (Cambridge: Cambridge University Press, 2003), chaps. 1 and 5.

6. Janice Boddy, "Purity and Conquest in the Anglo-Egyptian Sudan," in *Dirt, Undress, and Difference: Critical Perspectives on the Body's Surface*, ed. Adeline Masquelier (Bloomington: Indiana University Press, 2006).

7. Martin Green, *Three Empires on the Nile: The Victorian Jihad, 1869–1899* (New York: Basic Books, 1979), chaps. 4–11.

8. The front page of the April 6, 1883 *PMG* reads "Dynamite."

9. For example, see a one-penny pamphlet, Anonymous, *General Gordon, the Hero of China and the Soudan* (London: Ward, Lock, 1885); also, Rudolf C. Slatin, *Fire and Sword in the Sudan: A Personal Narrative of Fighting and Serving the Dervishes: 1879–1895*, trans. Major F. R. Wingate and illustrated by R. T. Kelly with introductory note by J. Ohrwalder (London: E. Arnold, 1896).

10. My source of information on the *Illustrated London News* and the *Pall Mall Gazette* is www.victorianweb.org (accessed October 29, 2013).

11. For example, chap. 15 appears in the February 24, 1883 *ILN*.

12. *Illustrated London News*, January 6, 1883, 20.

13. Ibid. December 1, 4, 24, 1883 and December 15, 1884.

14. www.victorianweb.org.

15. *Pall Mall Gazette*, January 22, 1884, 10.

16. P. M. Holt, *The Mahdist State in Sudan, 1881–1898* (Oxford: Clarendon Press, 1970), 54.

17. Laurel Brake, *Print in Transition, 1850–1910: Studies in Media and Book History* (London: Palgrave, 2001).

18. Russell Miller, *The Adventures of Arthur Conan Doyle* (New York: Thomas Dunne Books, 2008), 211–217.

19. Arthur Conan Doyle, *The Tragedy of the Korosko* (London: Hesperus Press, 2003) 17.

20. Ibid., 18.

21. Edmund Swinglehurst, *Cooks Tours: The Story of Popular Travel* (Worthing, UK: Littlehampton, 1982), chap. 6.

22. Wendy Brown, *States of Injury: Power and Freedom in Late Modernity* (Princeton: Princeton University Press, 1995), chap. 3.

23. Tayeb Salih, *Season of Migration to the North* (Boulder, CO: Lynne Rienner, 1997), 94–95.

24. Benita Parry, "Reflections on the Excess of Empire in Tayeb Salih's *Season of Migration to the North*," *Paragraph* 28, no. 2 (July 2005): 72–90: Saree Makdisi, "The Empire Renarrated: *Season of Migration to the North* and the Reinvention of the Present," *Critical Inquiry* 18 (Summer 1992): 804–820; 72.

25. Sara Blair, "Local Modernity, Global Modernism: Bloomsbury and the Places of the Literary," *English Literary History* 71, no. 3 (Fall 2004): 813–838.

26. Mona Takieddine-Aymuni, ed., *Tayeb Salih's Season of Migration to the North: A Casebook* (Beirut: American University of Beirut Press, 1985).

27. S. Makdisi, "Empire Renarrated," 807.

28. Parry, "Reflections," 72.

29. Ibid., 73.

30. James Joyce, *A Portrait of the Artist as a Young Man* (Oxford: Oxford University Press, 2001), 208.

31. *Parry, 75*

32. Salih, *Season of Migration*, 112–115.

33. S. Makdisi, "Empire Renarrated," 819.

34. Salih, *Season of Migration*, 95.

35. Ibid., 39.

36. Ibid., 95.

37. There is an existentialist-Orientalist literary tradition of the Anglophone and Francophone novel that includes Gide's *L'immoraliste*, Camus' *L'etranger*, and Bowles's *The Sheltering Sky*.

38. In particular I am referring to Bill Ashcroft, Gareth Griffiths, and Helen Tiffin, *The Empire Writes Back: Theory and Practice in Postcolonial Literatures* (New York: Routledge: 2002).

3. A Refusal and a Traversal: Robert Cunninghame Graham's Engagement with Orientalism in *Mogreb-el-Acksa*

1. This chapter was adapted from "A Refusal and Traversal: Robert Cunning-hame Graham's Engagement with Orientalism in *Mogreb-el-Acksa*," *Nineteenth Century Literature* 63, no. 3 (December 2008): 376–410.

2. Nigel Leask, "Byron and the Eastern Mediterranean: Childe Harold II and the 'Polemic of Ottoman Greece,'" in Drummond Bone, ed., *The Cambridge Companion to Byron* (Cambridge: Cambridge University Press, 2004).

3. Moussa Aflalo, *The Truth about Morocco: An Indictment of the Policy of the British Foreign Office with Regard to the Anglo-French Agreement*, preface by R. B. Cunninghame Graham (London: Bodley Head, 1904).

4. Ibid., v. Cunninghame Graham concludes his introduction to Aflalo's book with the following denunciation of travel writing:

> You publish on a royalty of three per cent., arrange for good reviews, send copies to the chief crowned heads of Europe, and get the President of the United States to puff you in true knickerbockers type, are made an X.Y.Z., a member of the league of travelling showmen on the make; then a fond public buys your work by thousands, and declares it is the very book they would themselves have written had they only had the time.

5. Ali Behdad, *Belated Travelers: Orientalism in the Age of Colonial Dissolution* (Durham: Duke University Press, 1994).

6. Cedric Watts and Laurence Davies, eds., *Cunninghame Graham: A Critical Biography* (Cambridge: Cambridge University Press, 1979).

7. Ibid.

8. Robert Cunnninghame Graham, "Sursum Corda," in *Success* (New York: Books for Libraries Press, 1969).

9. Major A. Gybbon-Spilsbury, *The Tourmaline Expedition. With an appendix on South West Barbary as a Field for Colonization [by W. R. Stewart]* (London: J. M. Dent, 1906); Cunninghame Graham, *Mogreb-el-Acksa: A Journey in Morocco* (London: J. M. Dent, 1906), 239. The preamble to the Tourmaline affair, and the background to "At Torfaieh," was the final failure of British merchant Donald McKenzie's North-West Africa Company. For further information see the appendix

article about the company by W. R. Stewart in Gybbon-Spilsbury, *Tourmaline Expedition*.

10. This is what Billie Melman suggests about some of these writers. Melman, "The Middle East/Arabia: The Cradle of Islam," in Peter Hulme and Tim Youngs, eds., *The Cambridge Companion to Travel Writing* (Cambridge: Cambridge University Press, 2002).

11. Christopher GoGwilt, *The Fictions of Geopolitics: Afterimages of Culture: From Wilkie Collins to Alfred Hitchcock* (Stanford: Stanford University Press, 2000).

12. Charles Montagu Doughty, *Travels in Arabia Deserta, "With Illustrations Made on the Spot by Edy Legrand,"* preface by Edward Garnett with an introduction by T. E. Lawrence (New York: Heritage Press, 1953), xiv.

13. Ibid., "Introduction".

14. Robert Cunninghame Graham, *Mogreb-el-Acksa: A Journey in Morocco* (London: William Heinemann, 1898), iii–ix.

15. Ibid., 74.

16. Ibid., 137.

17. Alain Grosrichard, *The Sultan's Court: European Fantasies of the East*, trans. Liz Heron and intro. Mladen Dolar (New York: Verso, 1998).

18. Cunninghame Graham, *Mogreb-el-Acksa*, 244–246.

19. This surname, "Fasi," is possibly related to the Fasi family of Moroccan scholars, who fled Andalusia in the sixteenth century (see Albert Hourani, *A History of the Arab Peoples* [New York: Time Warner Books, 1991], 246).

20. Kaja Silverman, *Male Subjectivity at the Margins* (New York: Routledge, 1992); Joan Copjec, *Read My Desire: Lacan against the Historicists* (Cambridge, MA: MIT Press, 1996).

21. Brian Street notes that this way of dressing was actually impractical and ridiculous in the eyes of the colonized peoples (Brian Street, *The Savage in Literature: Representations of "Primitive" Society in English Fiction 1858–1920* [London: Routledge & Kegan Paul, 1975], 18–48). Also, Conrad's "accountant" comes to mind with his white linen suit and impeccable books in Joseph Conrad, *Heart of Darkness* (New York: Norton, 1998).

22. Cunninghame Graham, *Mogreb-el-Acksa*, 228–229.

23. Street, *Savage in Literature*, 30–37. Kipling's *Kim* is the best example.

24. Cunninghame Graham, *Mogreb-el-Acksa*, 105–111.

25. Ibid., 233.

26. Ibid., 235.

27. Ibid., 244.

28. Ibid., 270.

29. Robert Cunninghame Graham, *The Ipané* (New York: Albert & Charles Boni, 1925), 180–181.

30. Ibid., 182.

31. Edward Said, *Culture and Imperialism* (New York: Vintage, 1994); Achebe, "An Image of Africa: Racism in Conrad's Heart of Darkness," in *Hopes and Impediments: Selected Essays* (New York: Doubleday, 1989).

32. Cunninghame Graham, *The Ipané*, 174.

33. Ibid., 176.

34. Cedric Watts, *Joseph Conrad's Letters to R. B. Cunninghame Graham* (Cambridge: Cambridge University Press, 1969).

35. Stephen Donovan, "Conrad's Unholy Recollection," *Notes and Queries* 49 (March 2002): 82–84.

36. Kelly Boyd, *Manliness and the Boys' Story Paper in Britain: A Cultural History, 1855–1940* (Basingstoke, UK: Palgrave Macmillan, 2003).

37. Conrad's story was accompanied (in the February 1899 number) by reportage pieces ("Jamaica: an Impression," by one Ian Malcolm, M.P.) as well as other creative texts (poetry and fiction) and light journalism.

38. Laurel Brake, *Print in Transition, 1850–1910* (London: Palgrave, 2001), 161–169.

39. Ibid., 145–170. Brake argues that the New Journalism movement was about gender, and also involved now-famous journals such as *Yellow Book* among others.

40. Ibid., 24–25.

41. Ibid., 17.

42. George Orwell, *British Pamphleteers* (London: A. Wingate, 1948), 51.

43. Louis Althusser, "Ideology and Ideological State Apparatuses," in *Lenin and Philosophy and Other Essays*, trans. Ben Brewster (New York: Monthly Review Press, 1971).

44. Cunninghame Graham, *Mogreb-el-Acksa*, x.

45. Again, and by contrast to Cunninghame Graham, Conrad was known for what Leavis dubbed his "adjectival" style, though he too seems infatuated with colloquial speech. See F. R. Leavis, *The Great Tradition: George Eliot, Henry James, Joseph Conrad* (New York: New York University Press, 1963). Also, in *Heart of Darkness* some of the most memorable moments are "spoken" by the natives, as when the "Manager's boy put his insolent black head in the doorway and said in a tone of scathing contempt: 'Mistah Kurtz, he dead.'" It is not just the "insolent black head" that is troubling, though this is enough, but the "black" speech Marlow/Conrad mimics. This moment follows the cannibals' pithy, "Eat 'im" when asked what they would do with captured locals, and then the various words and phrases with which Marlow describes the crew and natives. Again, the fireman is like a dog on his hind legs, while the natives "stamp" on the river bank. Kurtz's African mistress is described in equally odd terms—or with a familiar racist reference to "black"

people's eyes—as she walks away from Marlow's boat: "Once only her eyes gleamed back at us in the dusk of the thickets before she disappeared" (61).

46. Watts, *Joseph Conrad's Letters to R. B. Cunninghame Graham*.

47. Edward Said, *The World, The Text and the Critic* (Cambridge, MA: Harvard University Press, 1983).

48. Ibid., 188.

49. Raymond Williams, *The Politics of Modernism: Against the New Conformists* (New York: Verso, 1993).

50. Said, *World, The Text and the Critic*, 93.

51. Said, *Culture and Imperialism*, 25.

52. Aijaz Ahmad, "Orientalism and After: Ambivalence and Metropolitan Location in the Work of Edward Said," in Patrick Williams, ed., *Edward Said*, vol. 1 (London: Sage, 2001), 1:78–99.

53. Ibid., 86.

54. Said, *Culture and Imperialism*, 80.

55. Michel Foucault, *Language, Counter-Memory, Practice: Selected Essays and Interviews by Michel Foucault*, ed. Donald F. Bouchard and trans Sherry Simon and Donald F. Bouchard (Ithaca, NY: Cornell University Press, 1977), 208.

56. GoGwilt, *Fiction of Geopolitics*.

57. John Carey, *The Intellectuals and the Masses: Pride and Prejudice among the Literary Intelligentsia, 1880–1939* (Chicago: Academy, 2002).

58. Salman Rushdie, *Midnight's Children* (New York: Random House, 2006).

59. Alan Wald, *The New York Intellectuals: The Rise and Decline of the Anti-Stalinist Left from the 1930s to the 1980s* (Chapel Hill: University of North Carolina Press, 1987), 7.

60. Ibid., 368.

61. Ibid.

62. Ibid., 369.

63. Serge Guilbaut, *How New York Stole the Idea of Modern Art: Abstract Expressionism, Freedom, and the Cold War*, trans. Arthur Goldhammer (Chicago: University of Chicago Press, 1983), 169.

64. Ibid.

65. Ibid., 177.

66. *The Guardian*, October 22, 1995.

67. Guilbaut, *How New York Stole the Idea of Modern Art*, 202.

68. Pierre Bourdieu, "The Forms of Capital," in John G. Richardson, ed., *Handbook of Theory and Research for the Sociology of Education* (New York: Greenwood Press, 1986).

69. Said, *Culture and Imperialism*.

4. Orientalism from Within and Without: Marmaduke Pickthall

1. Laurel Brake, *Print in Transition, 1850–1910* (London: Palgrave, 2001), chap. 2.

2. Peter Clark, *Marmaduke Pickthall: British Muslim* (London: Quartet, 1986), 8–12.

3. N. I. Matar, "Turning Turk: Conversion to Islam in English Renaissance Thought," *Durham University Journal* 1 (1994): 33–50.

4. Gordon Brook-Shepherd, *Between Two Flags: The Life of Baron Sir Rudolf von Slatin Pasha, GCVO, KCMG, CB* (London: Weidenfeld, 1972), 68–69.

5. Clark, *Marmaduke Pickthall: British Muslim*, 38.

6. Ibid.

7. Ibid.

8. Ibid., 48–49, 52.

9. There is an Islamic culture and history website with an entry on Pickthall: *dunner99.blogspot.com/2007/09/muhammad.marmaduke.pickthall.html* (accessed January 1, 2010).

10. See Clark, *Marmaduke Pickthall*, 96–107 and 121–124.

11. Marmaduke Pickthall, "The White Prophet," *The Athenaeum*, no. 4270 (August 28, 1909): 233.

12. Anonymous, "Said the Fisherman" [review], *Academy and Literature* (29 August 29, 1903): 190.

13. Marmaduke Pickthall, *Oriental Encounters* (New York: Knopf, 1927), vii.

14. Ibid., viii.

15. Ibid., xii–xiii.

16. Marmaduke Pickthall, *Said the Fisherman* (London: Methuen, 1903), 1.

17. Ibid., 1–2.

18. See this American artist's painting *The Swimming Hole* of 1884–85.

19. There are no photographs in the paperback edition referenced here, though these are a feature of the early hardback editions.

20. Jacob Riis, *How the Other Half Lives* (New York: Hill & Wang, 1968), 148.

21. Sigmund Freud, *Civilization and Its Discontents* (London: Penguin, 2002), chap. 3.

22. Slavoj Žižek, *In Defense of Lost Causes* (New York: Verso, 2008), 107–113.

23. T. E. Lawrence, *Seven Pillars of Wisdom: A Triumph* (New York: Anchor, 1991), 40.

24. Bernard Hourcade, "The Demography of Cities and the Expansion of Urban Space," in *The Urban Social History of the Middle East, 1750 to 1950,* ed. Peter Sluglett (Syracuse: Syracuse University Press, 2008), 180.

25. Ussama Makdisi, *The Culture of Sectarianism: Community, History, and Violence in Nineteenth Century Ottoman Lebanon* (Berkeley: University of California Press, 2000), 145.

26. Pickthall, *Said the Fisherman*, 108.

27. Charles Dickens, *Oliver Twist* (Oxford: Clarendon Press, 1966), 99.

28. Ibid., 162. The passage from the novel is as follows: "Near to the spot on which Snow Hill and Holborn Hill meet, there opens: upon the right as you come out of the city: a narrow and dismal alley leading to Saffron Hill. In its filthy shops are exposed for sale, huge bunches of second hand silk handkerchiefs, of all sizes and patterns; for here reside the traders who purchase them from pickpockets. . . . It is a commercial colony of itself: the emporium of petty larceny: visited at early morning, and setting-in of dusk, by silent merchants, who traffic in dark back parlours; and who go as strangely as they come."

29. Riis, *How the Other Half Lives*.

30. Raymond Williams, *The Country and the City* (New York: Oxford University Press, 1973), 281.

31. Raymond Williams, *Culture and Society* (New York: Columbia University Press, 1983), 298.

32. Pickthall, *Said the Fisherman*, 157–158.

33. Ibid., 301.

34. U. Makdisi, *Culture of Sectarianism*, 2.

35. Ibid.

36. Ibid., 2–3.

37. Ibid., 5.

38. John Carey, *The Intellectuals and the Masses* (Chicago: Academy, 2002), 34–35.

39. On the country and the city Carey makes the following comment, which resonates with my statement about the British colonial preference for Bedouins over Arab city dwellers: "An alternative to promoting the masses to peasanthood is to blame them for not being peasants, or point out how much more attractive they would have been had they remained peasants" (ibid., 37).

40. Brian Street, *The Savage in Literature: Representations of "Primitive" Society in English Fiction 1858–1920* (London: Routledge & Kegan Paul, 1975); Chinua Achebe, "An Image of Africa: Racism in Conrad's Heart of Darkness," in *Hopes and Impediments: Selected Essays* (New York: Doubleday, 1989).

41. *The New Age* was a fin de siècle journal with a Christian socialist editorial position that also featured artwork by (now) major modern artists. Contributors included Arnold Bennett, H. G. Wells, G. K. Chesterton, and Ezra Pound. Also, Pickthall wrote for *Nineteenth Century and After*, the same journal where Cunninghame Graham published his earlier articles on North Africa.

42. Clark, "A Man of Two Cities: Pickthall, Damascus, Hyderabad," 287–288; Clark, *Marmaduke Pickthall: British Muslim*, 31.

43. Pickthall, *With the Turk in Wartime*, 86.

44. Burton and his entourage were involved in a violent and protracted fight with some Greek Christian worshippers while camped out in Jerusalem. He also had several infamous disputes with British missionaries and other non-Muslims during his tenure as consul to Damascus. See Burton's own account in *The Case of Captain Burton: H[er] B[ritish]M[ajesty's] Consul at Damascus* in the Metcalf Collection, The Huntington Library.

45. Clark, *Marmaduke Pickthall: British Muslim*, 33.

46. Marmaduke Pickthall, "The Cause of Massacres," *The New Age*, May 1, 1919, 4–7.

47. Geoffrey P. Nash, *From Empire to Orient: Travellers to the Middle East 1830–1926* (London: I. B. Tauris, 2005), 29.

48. For example, see ibid., 30.

49. Lawrence M. Stratton, "Tory Muslim: The Conversion of Marmaduke Pickthall," *Koinonia* 16 (2004): 94.

50. Marmaduke Pickthall, "Islamic Culture," 1. This essay is the key text—"First Lecture"—in his collection of essays, *The Cultural Side of Islam* (New Delhi: Kitab Bhavan, 1990), 1.

51. Wendy Brown, *States of Injury: Power and Freedom in Late Modernity* (Princeton: Princeton University Press, 1995), 70.

52. See "The Orientalist Express: Thomas Friedman Wraps Up the Middle East," in Edward Said's collection of essays, *The Politics of Dispossession: The Struggle for Palestinian Self-Determination: 1969–1994* (New York: Vintage Books, 1994).

53. Thomas Friedman, "Ballots over Bullets," *New York Times*, June 9, 2009, *http://www.nytimes.com/2009/06/10/opinion/10friedman.html?_r=0* (accessed October 26, 2013).

54. Thomas Friedman, *From Beirut to Jerusalem* (New York: Harper Collins, 2000), 4.

55. James Clifford, *Routes: Travel and Translation in the Late Twentieth Century* (Cambridge, MA: Harvard University Press, 1997), 36.

5. The Arabist as Abject Modern: T. E. Lawrence

1. This chapter was adapted from "The Hidden and the Visible in British Orientalism: The Case of Lawrence of Arabia," *Middle East Critique* 18, no. 1 (Spring 2009): 21–37. Also, see Richard Burton, *A Plain and Literal Translation of the Arabian Nights' Entertainments, Now Entituled The Book of the Thousand Nights and a Night*, vols. 1 and 10, Printed by the Burton Club for Private Subscribers Only (Denver: Carson-Harper, 1900); Richard Burton, trans., *The Kama Sutra of Vatsyayana*

(Cosmopoli: For the Kama Shastra Society of London and Benares, 1883); and *The Perfumed Garden of Cheikh Nefzaou: A Manual of Arabian Erotology* (Cosmopoli: For the Kama Shastra Society of London and Benares, 1886).

2. Michael Warner, *Publics and Counterpublics* (New York: Zone Books, 2002).

3. See James G. Nelson, Publisher to the Decadents: Leonard Smithers in the Careers of Beardsley, Wilde and Dowson (University Park: Penn State University Press, 2000).

4. Dane Kennedy, *The Highly Civilized Man: Richard Burton and the Victorian World* (Cambridge, MA: Harvard University Press, 2005), 206–247.

5. Charles Doughty, *Travels in Deserta Arabia*, "With Illustrations Made on the Spot by Edy Legrand," preface by Edward Garnett with an introduction by T. E. Lawrence (New York: Heritage Press, 1953).

6. J. Meyers, "Revisions of Seven Pillars," *PMLA* 88, no. 5 (October 1973): 1066–1082.

7. T. E. Lawrence, *Seven Pillars of Wisdom* (New York: Anchor, 1991), 24–25.

8. Ibid., 25.

9. Ibid., 431.

10. Ibid., 126.

11. F. D. Crawford and J. Berton, "How Well Did Lowell Thomas Know Lawrence of Arabia?" *English Literature in Transition* 39, no. 3 (1996): 306.

12. See S. C. Rolls, *Steel Chariots in the Desert* (London: Jonathan Cape, 1937).

13. Lawrence, *Seven Pillars of Wisdom*, 563.

14. R. Aldington, *Lawrence of Arabia: A Biographical Enquiry* (London: Collins, 1955).

15. Ibid.

16. Lawrence, *Seven Pillars of Wisdom*, 30.

17. G. Lord, *Andrew Marvell: Complete Poetry* (New York: Random House, 1968), 11–12.

18. H. Orlans, *T. E. Lawrence: Biography of a Broken Hero* (London: McFarland, 2002).

19. Ibid., 61–62, 221–223.

20. Lawrence, *Seven Pillars of Wisdom*, 445.

21. Ibid.; Orlans, *T. E. Lawrence*, 218–229; Kaja Silverman, *Male Subjectivity at the Margins* (New York: Routledge, 1992), 299–238.

22. Edward Said, *Reflections on Exile and Other Essays* (Cambridge, MA: Harvard University Press, 2000), 39.

23. Silverman, *Male Subjectivity*, 299–238.

24. Ibid., 305.

25. Jonathan Rutherford, *Forever England: Reflections on Masculinity and Empire* (London: Wishart, 1997), 70–103.

26. Lisa Sigel, *Governing Pleasures* (New Brunswick, NJ: Rutgers University Press, 2002), 51–80 and 119–155.

27. Ibid., 51.

28. Ibid., 124.

29. See Anne McClintock, *Imperial Leather: Race, Gender and Sexuality in the Colonial Encounter* (New York: Routledge, 1995).

30. Sigel, *Governing Pleasures*, 154–155.

31. Vyvyan Richards, *Portrait of T. E. Lawrence* (New York: Scholastic Book Services, 1967), 11. My copy is a cheap paperback edition of Richards's book, with a luridly colored cover derived from a romantic painting depicting Lawrence riding across the desert horizon on a camel. It seems apt.

32. T. E. Lawrence, trans., *The Odyssey* (London: Walker, Meron & Rogers, 1932).

33. P. M. O'Brien, *T. E. Lawrence and Fine Printing* (Buffalo, NY: Hillside Press, 1980).

34. Nelson, *Publisher to the Decadents*, chaps. 1–4.

35. Warner, *Publics and Counterpublics*, 162.

36. Ibid., 163.

37. Ibid., 165.

38. Ibid., 181.

39. Ibid., 182–183.

40. Ibid., 187–208.

41. Slavoj Žižek, *The Plague of Fantasies* (New York: Verso, 1997), 32–35.

42. David Omissi, *Air Power and Colonial Control: The Royal Air Force 1919–1939* (Manchester, UK: Manchester University Press, 1990), 14 and 21.

43. Ibid., 22 and 25.

44. Ibid., 29–37.

45. See the yearly entries in the T. E. Lawrence Studies website at *http://www.telawrence.net/letters* (accessed October 29, 2013).

46. Julia Kristeva, *Powers of Horror: An Essay on Abjection* (New York: Columbia University Press, 1982), 1.

47. Ibid., 4.

48. Ibid., 9.

49. Ibid., 15–16.

Conclusion: How to Read the Orientalist Archive

1. See postings on the Chase photographs on the *T. E. Lawrence Studies* discussion board for 1/24/99–2/10/99, http://www.telstudies.org/ (accessed October 28, 2013).

2. Burton's anti-Semitism is in evidence here insofar as he was clearly anti-Semitic, demonstrated in statement and deed, and yet he was also a supporter of a

Jewish state in Palestine, which he believed would bring order and modernity to the region. The point is that this split indicates the contrary, not the discourse of someone who was truly outside the dominant discourse, but rather someone who was in fact deeply committed to authority, Queen Victoria.

3. Slavoj Žižek, *For They Know Not What They Do: Enjoyment as a Political Factor* (New York: Verso, 1991), 11.

4. As Fredric Jameson explains this idea (and as cited by Žižek):

> Don Quixote is not really a character at all, but rather an organizational device that permits Cervantes to write a book, serving as a thread that holds a number of different types of anecdotes together in a single form.

See ibid., 18.

5. See Slavoj Žižek, "Class Struggle or Postmodernism? Yes, Please!" in Judith Butler, Ernesto Laclau, and Slavoj Žižek, *Hegemony, Contingency, Universality: Contemporary Dialogues on the Left* (New York: Verso, 2000), 116.

6. Ibid., 117.

7. Aijaz Ahmad, "Postcolonialism: What's in a Name?" in *Late Imperial Culture*, ed. Román De la Campa, E. Ann Kaplan, and Michael Sprinker (New York: Verso, 1995).

8. See Robert J. C. Young, *Postcolonialism: A Very Short Introduction* (New York: Oxford University Press, 2003), chaps. 4 and 6.

9. Simon Gikandi, *Maps of Englishness: Writing Identity in the Culture of Colonialism* (New York: Columbia University Press, 1996), 15.

10. Brennan, "The Illusion of a Future: *Orientalism* as Travelling Theory," in *Edward Said*, ed. Patrick Williams (London: Sage, 2001), 308–332. Also, see Gayatri Spivak, "Can the Subaltern Speak?" in *Colonial Discourse and Post-Colonial Theory: A Reader*, ed. Patrick Williams and Laura Chrisman (New York: Columbia University Press, 1994), 66–111.

11. Stuart Hall, "When Was 'The Postcolonial'? Thinking at the Limit," in *The Post-Colonial Question: Common Skies, Divided Horizons,* ed. Iain Chambers and Linda Curti (New York: Routledge, 1996), 242–260.

12. John Szarkowski and Maria Hambourg, eds., *The Work of Atget,* vol. 4, *Modern Times* (New York: Museum of Modern Art, 1985).

13. Slavoj Žižek, *Plague of Fantasies* (New York: Verso, 1997), 7.

14. Ibid., 9.

15. Ibid., 32–33.

16. Ibid., 10.

17. See Žižek, "Class Struggle or Postmodernism?" 125.

18. Ibid.

Bibliography

Achebe, Chinua. "An Image of Africa: Racism in Conrad's *Heart of Darkness*." In *Hopes and Impediments: Selected Essays*. New York: Doubleday, 1989.

Adams, James Eli. *Dandies and Desert Saints: Styles of Victorian Masculinity*. Ithaca, NY: Cornell University Press, 1995.

Aflalo, Moussa. *The Truth about Morocco: An Indictment of the Policy of the British Foreign Office with Regard to the Anglo-French Agreement*. Preface by R. B. Cunninghame Graham. London: Bodley Head, 1904.

Ahmad, Aijaz. "Orientalism and After: Ambivalence and Metropolitan Location in the Work of Edward Said." In *Edward Said, ed. Patrick Williams*. Vol. 1. Sage Masters in Modern Social Thought. London: Sage, 2001, 78–99.

Aldington, R. *Lawrence of Arabia: A Biographical Enquiry*. London: Collins, 1955.

Allen, Vivien. *Hall Caine: Portrait of a Victorian Romancer*. Sheffield, UK: Sheffield Academic Press, 1997.

Alloula, Malek. *The Colonial Harem*. Translated by Myrna Godzich and Wlad Godzich. Vol. 21, *Theory and History of Literature*. Minneapolis: University of Minnesota Press, 1986.

Althusser, Louis. "Ideology and Ideological State Apparatuses." In *Lenin and Philosophy and Other Essays*. Translated by Ben Brewster. New York: Monthly Review Press, 1971.

Altick, Richard. *The English Common Reader: A Social History of the Mass Reading Public, 1800–1900*. Chicago: University of Chicago Press, 1957.

Anonymous. *General Gordon, the Hero of China and the Soudan*. London: Ward, Lock, 1885.

Anonymous. *Life and Adventures of the Mahdi: The False Prophet*. London: General Publishing, 1885.

Anonymous. *The Lustful Turk*. e-book: Olympia Press, 2005.

Anonymous. Review of "Said the Fisherman." *Academy and Literature* (August 29, 1903): 190.

Appadurai, Arjun, ed. *The Social Life of Things: Commodities in Cultural Perspective*. New York: Cambridge University Press, 1988.

Ashcroft, Bill, Gareth Griffiths, and Helen Tiffin. *The Empire Writes Back: Theory and Practice in Post-Colonial Literatures*. New York: Routledge, 1989.

Barakat, Hoda. *The Stone of Laughter*. Translated by Sophie Bennett. Northampton, MA: Interlink, 2006.

Behdad, Ali. *Belated Travelers: Orientalism in the Age of Colonial Dissolution*. Durham, NC: Duke University Press, 1994.

Bell, Gertrude Lowthian. *The Desert and the Sown: The Syrian Adventures of the Female Lawrence of Arabia*. New York: Cooper Square Press, 2001.

Benjamin, Walter. *Charles Baudelaire: A Lyric Poet in the Era of High Capitalism*. Translated by James Zorn. New York: New Left Books, 1973.

Bettnoti, Julia, and Marie-Francoise Truel. "Lust and Dust: Desert and Fabula in Romances and Media." *Para-doxa* 3, nos. 1–2 (1997): 184–194.

Bhabha, Homi. *The Location of Culture*. New York: Routledge, 1994.

Blair, Sara. "Local Modernity, Global Modernism: Bloomsbury and the Places of the Literary." *ELH* 71, no. 3 (Fall 2004): 813–838.

Blake, Susan. "What "Race" Is the Sheik?: Rereading a Desert Romance." In *Doubled Plots: Romance and History*. Edited by Susan Strehle and Mary Paniccia Carden. Jackson: University of Mississippi Press, 2003.

Blunt, Wilfrid Scawen. *The Future of Islam*. London: Kegan, Paul, Trench, 1882.

———. *Gordon at Khartoum: Being a Personal Narrative of Events in Continuation of "A Secret History."* London: Stephen Swift, 1911.

———. *A Secret History of the British Occupation of Egypt: Being a Personal Narrative of Events*. London: Unwin, 1907.

Boddy, Janice. "Purity and Conquest in the Anglo-Egyptian Sudan." In *Dirt, Undress, and Difference: Critical Perspectives on the Body's Surface*. Edited by Adeline Masquelier. Bloomington: Indiana University Press, 2006, 168–189.

Bourdieu, Pierre. "The Forms of Capital." In *Handbook of Theory and Research for the Sociology of Education*. Edited by John G. Richardson. New York: Greenwood Press, 1986.

Boyd, Kelly. *Manliness and the Boys' Story Paper in Britain: A Cultural History, 1855–1940*. Basingstoke, UK: Palgrave Macmillan, 2003.

Brake, Laurel. *Print in Transition, 1850–1910: Studies in Media and Book History*. London: Palgrave, 2001.

Brantlinger, Patrick. *Rule of Darkness: British Literature and Imperialism, 1830–1914*. Ithaca, NY: Cornell University Press, 1990.

Brennan, Timothy. "The Illusion of a Future: *Orientalism* as Travelling Theory." In *Edward Said*. Edited by Patrick Williams. Vol. 2. Sage Masters in Modern Social Thought. London: Sage, 2001, 308–332.

Bristow, Joseph. *Empire Boys: Adventures in a Man's World*. London: Unwin Hayman, 1991.

Brook-Shepherd, Gordon. *Between Two Flags: The Life of Baron Sir Rudolf von Slatin Pasha, GCVO, KCMG, CB*. London: Weidenfeld & Nicolson, 1972.

Brown, Wendy. *States of Injury: Power and Freedom in Late Modernity*. Princeton: Princeton University Press, 1995.

Burton, Richard Francis. "Mr. Doughty's Travels in Arabia." *Academy* No. 847 (July 28, 1888): 47–48.

———. *Personal Narrative of a Pilgrimage to El-Madinah and Meccah*. New York: Putnam, 1856.

———. *A Plain and Literal Translation of the Arabian Nights' Entertainments, Now Entituled The Book of the Thousand Nights and a Night*. Vols. 1 and 10. Printed by the Burton Club for Private Subscribers Only. Denver: Carson-Harper, 1900.

———. *Supplemental Nights to the Book of the Thousand and One Nights with Notes Anthropological and Explanatory*. Vol. 6. Privately published by the Burton Club, n.d.

Burton, Richard, trans. *The Kama Sutra of Vatsyayana*. Cosmopoli: For the Kama Shastra Society of London and Benares, 1883.

———. *The Perfumed Garden of Cheikh Nefzaou: A Manual of Arabian Erotology*. Cosmopoli: For the Kama Shastra Society of London and Benares, 1886.

Butler, Judith, Ernesto Laclau, and Slavoj Žižek. *Contingency, Hegemony, and Universality: Contemporary Dialogues on the Left*. New York: Verso, 2000.

Caine, Hall. *The Mahdi, or Love and Race: A Drama in Story*. London: James Clarke, 1894.

———. *The White Prophet: A Novel*. New York: Appleton, 1909.

———. "Why I Wrote *The White Prophet*." Self-published pamphlet. London: Collier, 1909.

Caracciolo, Peter L., ed. *The Arabian Nights in English Literature: Studies in the Reception of The Thousand and One Nights into British Culture.* New York: St. Martin's Press, 1988.

Carey, John. *The Intellectuals and the Masses: Pride and Prejudice among the Literary Intelligentsia, 1880–1939.* Chicago: Academy, 2002.

Casanova, Pascale. *The World Republic of Letters.* Translated by M. B. DeBevoise. Cambridge, MA: Harvard University Press, 2004.

Clark, Peter. "A Man of Two Cities: Pickthall, Damascus, Hyderabad." Asian Affairs 25, no. 3 (1994): 281–292.

———. *Marmaduke Pickthall: British Muslim.* London: Quartet, 1986.

Clark, T. J. *The Painting of Modern Life: Paris in the Art of Manet and His Followers.* Princeton: Princeton University Press, 1984.

Clifford, James. "On Orientalism." In *Edward Said.* Edited by Patrick Williams. Vol. 2. Sage Masters in Modern Social Thought. London: Sage, 2001, 20–38.

———. *Routes: Travel and Translation in the Late Twentieth Century.* Cambridge, MA: Harvard University Press, 1997.

Conan Doyle, Arthur. *The Tragedy of the Korosko.* London: Hesperus Press, 2003.

Conrad, Joseph. *Heart of Darkness.* Edited by Robert Kimbrough. 3rd ed. New York: Norton, 1988.

———. "An Outpost of Progress." In *The Portable Conrad.* Edited by Morton Dauwen Zabel. New York: Penguin, 1976.

Copjec, Joan. *Read My Desire: Lacan against the Historicists.* Cambridge, MA: MIT Press, 1996.

Crawford, F. D., and J. Berton. "How Well Did Lowell Thomas Know Lawrence of Arabia?" *English Literature in Transition* 39, no. 3) (1996): 299–318.

Cunninghame Graham, R. B. (Robert Bontine). *The Ipane.* New York: Albert & Charles Boni, 1925.

———. *Mogreb-el-Acksa: A Journey in Morocco.* London: William Heinemann, 1898.

———. *Success and Other Sketches.* Freeport, NY: Books for Libraries, 1969.

Curthoys, Ned, and Debjani Ganguly, eds. *Edward Said: The Legacy of a Public Intellectual.* Melbourne: Melbourne University Press, 2007.

Damrosch, David. *What Is World Literature?* Princeton: Princeton University Press, 2003.

De la Campa, Román, E. Ann Kaplan, and Michael Sprinker, eds. *Late Imperial Culture*. New York: Verso, 1995.

Deledalle-Rhodes, Janice. "The True Nature of Doughty's Relationship with the Arabs." In *Explorations in Doughty's Arabia Deserta*. Edited by Stephen E. Tabachnick. Athens: University of Georgia Press, 1987.

Dickens, Charles. *Oliver Twist*. Edited by Kathleen Tillotson. Oxford: Clarendon Press, 1966.

Djebar, Assia. *Fantasia: An Algerian Cavalcade*. Translated by Dorothy S. Blair. Portsmouth, NH: Heinemann, 1993.

Dodson, Michael S. *Orientalism, Empire, and National Culture: India, 1770–1880*. Cambridge: Cambridge University Press, 2007.

Donovan, Stephen. "Conrad's Unholy Recollection." *Notes and Queries* 49 (March 2002): 82–84.

Doughty, Charles M. *Travels in Deserta Arabia. "With illustrations made on the spot by Edy Legrand."* Preface by Edward Garnett with an introduction by T. E. Lawrence. New York: Heritage Press, 1953.

Edwards, Holly, ed. *Noble Dreams, Wicked Pleasures: Orientalism in America, 1870–1930*. Princeton: Princeton University Press, 2000.

Eliot, T. S. (Thomas Stearns). "Contemporary English Prose." *Vanity Fair* 20 (1923): 51–98.

Foucault, Michel. *Language, Counter-Memory, Practice: Selected Essays and Interviews by Michel Foucault*. Edited by Donald F. Bouchard. Translated by Sherry Simon and Donald F. Bouchard. Ithaca, NY: Cornell University Press, 1977.

Freud, Sigmund. *Civilization and Its Discontents*. London: Penguin, 2002.

Friedman, Thomas. "Ballots over Bullets." *New York Times*, June 9, 2009 http://www.nytimes.com/2009/06/10/opinion/10friedman.html?_r=0. Accessed October 26, 2013.

———. *From Beirut to Jerusalem*. New York: Harper Collins, 2000.

Fulton, Richard. "The Sudan Sensation of 1898." *Victorian Periodicals Review* 42, no. 1 (Spring 2009): 37–63.

Gargano, Elizabeth. "English Sheiks" and Arab Stereotypes: E. M. Hull, T. E. Lawrence and the Imperial Masquerade." *Texas Studies in Literature and Language* 48, no. 2 (Summer 2006): 171–186.

Garnett, Edward. "Books Too Little Known." *Academy and Literature* 64 (January 24, 1903): 86–87.

Gellner, Ernest. "The Mightier Pen: The Double Standards of Inside Out Colonialism." *Times Literary Supplement*, February 19, 1993, 3–4.

Gikandi, Simon. *Maps of Englishness: Writing Identity in the Culture of Colonialism*. New York: Columbia University Press, 1996.

Gilman, Sander. *Difference and Pathology: Stereotypes of Sexuality, Race, and Madness*. Ithaca, NY: Cornell University Press, 1985.

Gilroy, Paul. *Postcolonial Melancholia*. New York: Columbia University Press, 2005.

GoGwilt, Christopher. *The Fiction of Geopolitics: Afterimages of Culture: From Wilkie Collins to Alfred Hitchcock*. Stanford: Stanford University Press, 2000.

Gordon, Charles George. *General Gordon's Khartoum Journals*. Edited by Lord (Godfrey) Elton. New York: Vanguard, 1963.

Graff, Harvey. *The Legacies of Literacy: Continuities and Contradictions in Western Culture and Society*. Bloomington: Indiana University Press, 1991.

Gramsci, Antonio. *Selections from the Prison Notebooks*. Edited and translated by Quintin Hoare and Geoffrey Nowell Smith. New York: International, 1987.

Gray, Wallace. http://www.mendele.com/WWD/WWDaraby.notes.html #araby. Accessed January 1, 2010.

Green, Dominic. *Three Empires on the Nile: The Victorian Jihad, 1869–1899*. New York: Free Press, 2007.

Green, Martin. *Dreams of Adventure, Deeds of Empire*. New York: Basic Books, 1979.

Grosrichard, Alain. *The Sultan's Court: European Fantasies of the East*. Translated by Liz Heron. Introduction by Mladen Dolar. New York: Verso, 1998.

Guilbaut, Serge. *How New York Stole the Idea of Modern Art: Abstract Expressionism, Freedom, and the Cold War*. Translated by Arthur Goldhammer. Chicago: University of Chicago Press, 1983.

Gybbon-Spilsbury, Major A. *The Tourmaline Expedition. With an appendix on South West Barbary as a Field for Colonization [by W. R. Stewart]*. London: J. M. Dent, 1906.

Hall, Stuart. "The Emergence of Cultural Studies and the Crisis of the Humanities." *October* 53 (Summer 1990): 11–23.

———. "When Was 'The Postcolonial'? *Thinking at the Limit.*" *In The Post-Colonial Question: Common Skies, Divided Horizons.* Edited by Iain Chambers and Lidia Curti. New York: Routledge, 1996, 242–260.

Harris, Walter. *Morocco That Was.* London: Eland, 2002.

Henty, G. A. *The Dash for Khartoum: A Tale of the Nile Expedition.* Glasgow: Blackie & Son, 1927.

Hichens, Robert. *The Garden of Allah.* 2 vols. Leipzig: Bernhard Tauchnitz, 1904.

Holt, P. M. *The Mahdist State in Sudan, 1881–1898.* Oxford: Clarendon Press, 1970.

———. *With Kitchener in the Soudan: A Story of Atbara and Omdurman.* New York: Scribners, 1902.

Hourani, Albert. *A History of the Arab Peoples.* New York: Time Warner Books, 1991.

Hourcade, Bernard. "The Demography of Cities and the Expansion of Urban Space." In *The Urban Social History of the Middle East, 1750 to 1950.* Edited by Peter Sluglett. Syracuse: Syracuse University Press, 2008.

Hull, E. M. (Edith Maude Winstanley). *The Sheik.* Philadelphia: Pine Street Books, 2001.

Hunt, Lynn, ed. *The Invention of Pornography: Obscenity and the Origins of Modernity, 1500–1800.* New York: Zone Books, 1996.

Irwin, Robert. *The Arabian Nights: A Companion.* London: Tauris Parke, 2004.

Jones, G. S. *Studies in English Working Class History 1832–1982.* Cambridge: Cambridge University Press, 1996.

Joyce, James. "Araby." *Dubliners.* London: Grant Richards, 1914.

———. *A Portrait of the Artist as a Young Man.* Oxford: Oxford University Press, 2001.

———. *Ulysses.* Paris: Shakespeare & Co., 1922.

Kennedy, Dane. *The Highly Civilized Man: Richard Burton and the Victorian World.* Cambridge, MA: Harvard University Press, 2005.

Khoury, Elias. *Yalo.* Translated by Peter Theroux. New York: Picador, 2009.

Kittler, Friedrich A. *Gramophone, Film Typewriter.* Translated by Geoffrey Winthrop-Young and Michael Wutz. Stanford: Stanford University Press, 1999.

Knightley, P., and C. Simpson. *The Secret Lives of Lawrence of Arabia.* London: Nelson, 1969.

Kristeva, Julia. *The Powers of Horror: An Essay on Abjection*. New York: Columbia University Press, 1982.

Lane, Edward William. *An Account of the Manners and Customs of the Modern Egyptians*. Edited by Edward Stanley Poole. New York: Dover, 1973.

Lane, Edward William, trans. *The Thousand and One Nights, Commonly Called in England The Arabian Nights Entertainments. A New Translation from the Arabic, with Copious Notes*. London: Chatto & Windus, 1889.

Lawrence, A. W. *T. E. Lawrence by His Friends*. London: Jonathan Cape, 1937.

Lawrence, T. E. (Thomas Edward). *Letters: Correspondence with Bernard and Charlotte Shaw 1922–1926*. Vol. 1. Fordingbridge, UK: Castle Hill, 2000.

———. *Revolt in the Desert*. New York: George Doran, 1927.

———. *Seven Pillars of Wisdom: A Triumph*. New York: Anchor, 1991.

———. "With Feisal at Court and Afield." *The World's Work* 42 (July 1921): 277–288.

Lawrence, T. E., trans. *The Odyssey* [Homer]. London: Walker, Meron & Rogers, 1932.

Leask, Nigel. "Byron and the Eastern Mediterranean: Childe Harold II and the 'Polemic of Ottoman Greece.'" In *The Cambridge Companion to Byron*. Edited by Drummond Bone. Cambridge: Cambridge University Press, 2004.

Leavis, F. R. (Francis Raymond). *The Great Tradition: George Eliot, Henry James, Joseph Conrad*. New York: New York University Press, 1963.

Leider, Emily W. *Dark Lover: The Life and Death of Rudolph Valentino*. New York: Farrar, Straus & Giroux, 2003.

Lewis, Bernard. "The Question of Orientalism." *New York Review of Books*, June 24, 1982, 49–56.

Long, Charles Chaille. *The Three Prophets: Chinese Gordon, Mohammed-Ahmed (el Maahdi), Arabi Pasha*. New York: D. Appleton & Co., 1884.

Loomba, Ania. *Colonialism/Postcolonialism*. New York: Routledge, 2001.

Lord, G., ed. *Andrew Marvell: Complete Poetry*. New York: Random House, 1968.

MacDonald, Charles Brown. *A Time for Trumpets: The Untold Story of the Battle of the Bulge*. New York: Perennial, 2002.

MacWilliams, David C. "The Novelistic Melodramas of Hall Caine: Seventy Years On." *English Literature in Transition, 1880–1920* 45, no. 4 (2002): 426–439.

Mahfouz, Naguib. *Midaq Alley*. Translated by Trevor Le Gassick. New York: Random House, 1992.

Makdisi, Saree. "The Empire Renarrated: *Season of Migration to the North* and the Reinvention of the Present." *Critical Inquiry* 18 (Summer 1992): 804–820.

Makdisi, Ussama. *The Culture of Sectarianism: Community, History, and Violence in Nineteenth-Century Ottoman Lebanon*. Berkeley: University of California Press,   2000.

Marcus, Steven. *The Other Victorians: A Study of Sexuality in Mid-Nineteenth Century England*. New York: Basic Books, 1966

Mason, A. E. W. *The Four Feathers*. New York: Penguin, 2001.

McClintock, Anne. "The Angel of Progress: Pitfalls of the Term 'Postcolonialism.'" In *Colonial Discourse and Postcolonial Theory: A Reader*. Edited by Patrick Williams and Laura Chrisman. New York: Columbia University Press, 1994.

———. *Imperial Leather: Race, Gender and Sexuality in the Colonial Encounter*. New York: Routledge, 1995.

Matar, N. I. "Turning Turk: Conversion to Islam in English Renaissance Thought." *Durham University Journal* 1 (1994): 33–50.

Melman, Billie. "The Middle East/Arabia: 'The Cradle of Islam.'" In *The Cambridge Companion to Travel Writing*. Edited by Peter Hulme and Tim Youngs. Cambridge: Cambridge University Press, 2002, 105–21.

———. *Women and the Popular Imagination in the Twenties*. New York: St. Martins, 1988.

———. *Women's Orients: English Women and the Middle East, 1718–1918*. Ann Arbor: Michigan University Press, 1995.

Meyers, J. "The Revisions of Seven Pillars," *PMLA* 88, no. 5 (October 1973): 1066–1082.

Miller, Russell. *The Adventures of Arthur Conan Doyle*. New York: Thomas Dunne, 2008.

Mitchell, Timothy. *Colonizing Egypt*. 2nd ed. Berkeley: University of California Press, 1991.

Nash, Geoffrey P. *From Empire to Orient: Travellers to the Middle East 1830–1926*. London: I. B. Tauris, 2005.

Nelson, James G. *Publisher to the Decadents: Leonard Smithers in the Careers of Beardsley, Wilde and Dowson*. University Park: Penn State University Press, 2000.

Newbolt, Henry John. "Vitai Lampada." In *Admirals All*. New York: John Lane, 1898.

O'Brien, P. M. *T. E. Lawrence and Fine Printing*. Buffalo, NY: Hillside Press, 1980.

Omissi, David. *Air Power and Colonial Control: The Royal Air Force 1919–1939*. Manchester, UK: Manchester University Press, 1990.

Orlans, H. *T. E. Lawrence: Biography of a Broken Hero*. London: McFarland, 2002.

Orwell, George (Eric Blair). *British Pamphleteers*. Vol. 1 London: A. Wingate, 1948–51.

Parry, Benita. "Reflections on the Excess of Empire in Tayeb Salih's *Season of Migration to the North*." *Paragraph* 28, no. 2 (July 2005): 72–90.

Pearman, D. G. *The Imperial Camel Corps with Colonel Lawrence and Lawrence and the Arab Revolt* [catalog of lantern slide show]. London: Newton, 1928.

Pickthall, Marmaduke. "The Armenian Massacres" [letter to the editor]. *The New Age*. December 9, 1915, 141–142.

———. "The Cause of Massacres." *The New Age*. May 1, 1919, 4–7.

———. "Islamic Culture." In *The Cultural Side of Islam*. New Delhi: Kitab. Bhavan, 1990. *Oriental Encounters*. New York: Knopf, 1927.

———. *Said the Fisherman*. London: Methuen, 1903.

———. "Sir Mark Sykes and the Armenians." *The New Age*. May 4, 1916, 6–7.

———. "The White Prophet" [unsigned review of novel by Hall Caine]. *The Athenaeum*, no. 4270. August 28, 1909, 232–233.

———. *With the Turk in Wartime*. London: Dent, 1914.

Raub, Patricia. "Issues of Power and Passion in E. M. Hull's *The Sheik*." *Women's Studies* 21 (1992): 119–128.

Richards, Vyvyan. *Portrait of T. E. Lawrence*. New York: Scholastic, 1967.

Riis, Jacob A. *How the Other Half Lives: Studies among the Tenements of New York City*. New York: Hill & Wang, 1968.

Robbins, Bruce. "The East Is a Career: Edward Said." In *Edward Said*. Edited by Patrick Williams. Vol. 1. Sage Masters in Modern Social Thought. London: Sage, 2001, 173–197.

Rogers, William N., II. "Arabia Deserta and the Victorians." In *Explorations in Doughty's Arabia Deserta*. Edited by Stephen E. Tabachnick. Athens: University of Georgia Press, 1987.

Rolls, S. C. *Steel Chariots in the Desert*. London: Jonathan Cape, 1937.

Rutherford, J. *Forever England: Reflections on Masculinity and Empire*. London: Wishart, 1997.

Said, Edward W. *Culture and Imperialism*. New York: Vintage, 1994.

———. *Orientalism*. New York: Vintage, 1979.

———. *The Politics of Dispossession: The Struggle for Palestinian Self-Determination: 1969–1994*, New York: Vintage Books, 1994.

———. *Reflections on Exile and Other Essays*. Cambridge, MA: Harvard University Press, 2000.

———. *The World, The Text and the Critic*. Cambridge, MA: Harvard University Press, 1983.

Salih, Tayeb. *Season of Migration to the North*. Boulder, CO: Lynne Rienner, 1997.

Schneer, Jonathan. *London 1900: The Imperial Metropolis*. New Haven, CT: Yale University Press, 1999.

Shohat, Ella. "Gender and the Culture of Empire: Toward a Feminist Ethnography of the Cinema." In *Visions of the East: Orientalism in Film*. Edited by Matthew Bernstein and Gaylyn Studlar. New Brunswick, NJ: Rutgers University Press, 1997.

———. "Notes on the 'Postcolonial.'" *Social Text* 31/32 (1992): 99–113.

Sigel, Lisa Z. *Governing Pleasures: Pornography and Social Change in England, 1815–1914*. New Brunswick, NJ: Rutgers University Press, 2002.

Silverman, Kaja. *Male Subjectivity at the Margins*. New York: Routledge, 1992.

Slatin, Rudolf C. *Fire and Sword in the Sudan: A Personal Narrative of Fighting and Serving the Dervishes: 1879–1895*. Translated by Major F. R. Wingate. Illustrated by R. T. Kelly with introductory note by J. Ohrwalder. London: E. Arnold, 1896.

Sluglett, Peter, ed. *The Urban Social History of the Middle East, 1750–1950*. Syracuse: Syracuse University Press, 2008.

Soueif, Ahdaf. *The Map of Love*. New York: Anchor, 2000.

Stanton, Gareth. "The Oriental City: A North African Itinerary." *Third Text* 2, nos. 3 and 4 (1988): 3–38.

Steger, Manfred. *Globalization: A Very Short Introduction*. 2nd ed. Oxford: Oxford University Press, 2009.

Stoler, Ann Laura. *Carnal Knowledge and Imperial Power: Race and the Intimate in Colonial Rule*. Berkeley: University of California Press, 2002.

Strachey, Lytton. *Eminent Victorians.* New York: Modern Library, 1999.

Stratton, Lawrence M. "Tory Muslim: The Conversion of Marmaduke Pickthall." *Koinonia* 16 (2004): 78–100.

Street, Brian V. *The Savage in Literature: Representations of "Primitive" Society in English Fiction 1858–1920.* London: Routledge & Kegan Paul, 1975.

Studlar, Gaylyn. *This Mad Masquerade: Stardom and Masculinity in the Jazz Age.* New York: Columbia University Press, 1996.

Swinglehurst, Edmund. *Cooks Tours: The Story of Popular Travel.* Worthing: Littlehampton, 1982.

Szarkowski, John, and Maria Hambourg, eds. *The Work of Atget.* Vol. 4, *Modern Times.* New York: Museum of Modern Art, 1985.

Tabachnick, Stephen E. "Art and Science in *Travels in Arabia Deserta.*" In *Explorations in Doughty's Arabia Deserta.* Edited by Stephen E. Tabachnick. Athens: University of Georgia Press, 1987.

Takieddine-Amyuni, Mona, ed. *Tayeb Salih's Season of Migration to the North: A Casebook.* Beirut: American University of Beirut Press, 1985.

Thomas, L. *Boys' Life of Colonel Lawrence.* New York: Century, 1927.

———. "Lawrence of Arabia as a Train Wrecker." *World's Work* 53 (March 1927): 511–533.

———. "Thomas Lawrence Prince of Mecca." *Asia: Journal of the American Asiatic Association* (September 1919): 819–828.

———. *With Lawrence in Arabia.* New York: Star Books, 1925.

Thwaite, Mary Florence. *From Primer to Pleasure in Reading: An Introduction to Children's Books in England from the Invention of Printing to 1914.* London: Library Association, 1972.

Wald, Alan M. *The New York Intellectuals: The Rise and Decline of the Anti-Stalinist Left from the 1930s to the 1980s.* Chapel Hill: University of North Carolina Press, 1987.

Walford, Edward. *Representative Men in Literature, Science and Art.* London: A. W. Bennett, 1867.

Warner, Michael. *Publics and Counterpublics.* New York: Zone Books, 2002.

Watts, Cedric. *R. B. Cunninghame Graham.* Boston: Twayne, 1983.

Watts, Cedric, ed. *Joseph Conrad's Letters to R. B. Cunninghame Graham.* Cambridge: Cambridge University Press, 1969

Watts, Cedric, and Laurence Davies. *Cunninghame Graham: A Critical biography.* Cambridge: Cambridge University Press, 1979.

Williams, Patrick. "Nothing in the Post?—Said and the Problem of Postcolonial Intellectuals." In *Edward Said*. Edited by Patrick Williams. Vol. 2. Sage Masters in Modern Social Thought. London: Sage, 2001, 314–334.

Williams, Patrick, and Laura Chrisman, eds. *Colonial Discourse and Post-Colonial Theory: A Reader*. New York: Columbia University Press, 1994.

Williams, Raymond. *The Country and the City*. New York: Oxford University Press, 1973.

———. *Culture and Society: 1780–1950*. New York: Columbia University Press, 1983.

———. *The Politics of Modernism: Against the New Conformists*. New York: Verso, 1993.

Wintle, Sarah. "The Sheik: What Can be Made of a Daydream." *Women: A Cultural Review* 7, no. 3 (1996): 291–302.

Young, Robert J. C. *Colonial Desire: Hybridity in Theory, Culture and Race*. New York: Routledge, 1995.

———. *Postcolonialism: A Very Short Introduction*. New York: Oxford University Press, 2003.

Ziter, Edward. *The Orient on the Victorian Stage*. Cambridge: Cambridge University Press, 2003.

Žižek, Slavoj. *For They Know Not What They Do: Enjoyment as a Political Factor*. New York: Verso, 1991.

———. *In Defense of Lost Causes*. New York: Verso, 2008.

———. *The Plague of Fantasies*. New York: Verso, 1997.

Index